Pursuing an Elusive Unity

A History of the Church of Central Africa Presbyterian as a Federative Denomination (1924–2018)

Rhodian Munyenyembe

ACADEMIC

© 2019 Rhodian Munyenyembe

Published 2019 by Langham Academic (Previously Langham Monographs)
An imprint of Langham Publishing
www.langhampublishing.org

Langham Publishing and its imprints are a ministry of Langham Partnership

Langham Partnership
PO Box 296, Carlisle, Cumbria, CA3 9WZ, UK
www.langham.org

ISBNs:
978-1-78368-644-5 Print
978-1-78367-727-5 ePub
978-1-78368-729-9 PDF

Rhodian Munyenyembe has asserted his right under the Copyright, Designs and Patents Act, 1988 to be identified as the Author of this work.

All rights reserved. No part of this publication may be reproduced, stored in a retrieval system or transmitted, in any form or by any means, electronic, mechanical, photocopying, recording or otherwise, without the prior written permission of the publisher or the Copyright Licensing Agency.

Requests to reuse content from Langham Publishing are processed through PLSclear. Please visit www.plsclear.com to complete your request.

Scripture quotations marked (ESV) are from The Holy Bible, English Standard Version® (ESV®), copyright © 2001 by Crossway, a publishing ministry of Good News Publishers. Used by permission. All rights reserved.

Scripture quotations marked (NIV) are taken from the Holy Bible, New International Version®, NIV®. Copyright © 1973, 1978, 1984, 2011 by Biblica, Inc.™ Used by permission of Zondervan.

British Library Cataloguing-in-Publication Data
A catalogue record for this book is available from the British Library

ISBN: 978-1-78367-644-5

Cover & Book Design: projectluz.com

Langham Partnership actively supports theological dialogue and an author's right to publish but does not necessarily endorse the views and opinions set forth here or in works referenced within this publication, nor can we guarantee technical and grammatical correctness. Langham Partnership does not accept any responsibility or liability to persons or property as a consequence of the reading, use or interpretation of its published content.

Contents

List of Figures xi
Foreword xiii
Acknowledgements xvii
Introduction 1
List of Abbreviations 3
Chapter 1 5
The Origins of the CCAP: Theological and Revival Roots
    Introduction 5
        Calvin's Theology...5
        Calvin's Church Polity: The Presbyterian System........................8
    Reformed Soteriology 10
    Presbyterianism in Scotland 12
    The Dutch Reformed Church in the Netherlands 17
    The Dutch Reformed Church in South Africa...........................19
    The Difference between Reformed and Presbyterian..................19
    Revivals and the Birth of the CCAP...21
        A Brief History of Revivals..22
        Revival History and Malawian Church History 23
        The CCAP as a "Child" of Revivals.......................................24
        The Influence of Revivals on Dr David Livingstone,
            the Missionary Explorer 31
        Conclusion 44

Chapter 2 47
The CCAP Tributaries
    Introduction 47
    Early Cooperation between Livingstonia and Blantyre Missions........47
    The Livingstonia Mission 48
        The Move to Bandawe and Ministry among the Tonga and
            the Ngoni 52
        William Koyi and Other Xhosa Missionaries 54
        Indigenous Malawians' Contribution to Early Cooperation 56
        The Move to Khondowe 58
        The Overtoun Institution 58

  Emerging African Leadership in Livingstonia Mission 59
 The Blantyre Mission 62
  The First Phase of Blantyre Mission History 62
  Blantyre Mission "Re-founded" 67
 The Dutch Reformed Church Mission..71
  DRCM Stations Established 74
  Separation from Livingstonia Mission...................................76
  Challenges Unique to the DRCM...77
  The MMU Hands over Responsibility to the General
   Mission Committee of the Cape DRC Synod 77
 The Formation of the CCAP...78
 Related Developments to the Formation of the CCAP................82
 The Concept of Comity and Its Application in Malawi...............84
 Harare Synod...86
 Synod of Zambia 88
 Conclusion 89

Chapter 3 91
The CCAP: One Denomination, Several Independent Synods
 Introduction 91
 Constitutional Matters...92
 Liturgy...94
 Theological Training 98
 Education in the CCAP Synods...102
 Women's Ministry..104
  Women's Guilds...104
  Women as Ordained Ministers 106
 Non-ordained Men's Ministry..108
 Youth Ministry...109
 Church and State Relations among the Synods 112
  The Colonial Period...112
  The Single Party Era 115
  The Transition Period from Single-Party to
   Multiparty Politics 116
  The Era of Multiparty Democracy 117
 Conclusion 122

Chapter 4... 125
Pangs of Unity in Diversity among the Synods
 Introduction 125
 Early Tensions in the Unity of the CCAP..................................125

Differences in Practice 128
Border Disputes in the CCAP 131
    The Livingstonia – Nkhoma Border Dispute 132
    Legal, Political and Theological Implications of the
        Border Disputes 147
Conclusion 153

Chapter 5 155
Challenges Rocking the CCAP General Assembly

Introduction 155
Constitutional Direction of the CCAP General Assembly 156
    Change of Name from General Synod to
        General Assembly 156
    Changes in Some of the Names of the General Assembly's
        Leadership Positions 157
    The Office of the General Assembly Moderator 159
    The Meetings of the General Assembly 160
    Commissioners of the General Assembly 161
    Attempts at Empowering the General Assembly 162
The Efficiency of the General Assembly versus the Autonomy of
    the Synods 166
    Lack of Adequate Funding for the General Assembly 167
    Lack of Adequate Infrastructure 168
    Lack of Adequate Personnel 170
    Inability to Implement Decisions 170
    Lack of Knowledge Concerning the General Assembly
        among Ordinary CCAP Members 171
Inter-Synodical Wrangles and the Stability of the
    General Assembly 173
Partner Churches and the Stability of the General Assembly 177
Political Machinations and the Stability of the
    General Assembly 179
Private Initiatives at Reconciling the Synods and Strengthening
    the General Assembly 181
Current Trends in the General Assembly 184
Conclusion 185

Chapter 6 189
Foreign Relations and Current Developments in the CCAP

Introduction 189
The Genesis of Foreign Relations 189

The Development of Foreign Relations 190
The Synod of Livingstonia and Its Foreign Partners....................... 191
    The Church of Scotland.. 191
    The Presbyterian Church in Ireland 194
    Focus on Malawi... 195
    The Raven Trust... 196
    The Presbyterian Church in Canada 197
    The Presbyterian Church of the USA.. 198
    The GZB (Gereformeerde Zendingsbond) 200
    Conclusion 200
Blantyre Synod and Its Foreign Partners... 200
    The Church of Scotland.. 200
    The Presbyterian Church of Victoria (Australia)..................... 201
    Presbyterian Church of the USA.. 202
    Presbyterian Church in Canada 204
    Scotland Malawi Partnership 206
    The GZB (Gereformeerde Zendingsbond) 206
    Conclusion 207
Nkhoma Synod and Its Foreign Partners.. 207
    Dutch Reformed Churches in South Africa 208
    The Church of Scotland.. 212
    The Presbyterian Church in Taiwan (PCT) 212
    The Reformed Church in America... 213
    Word and Deed Ministries... 213
    The GZB (Gereformeerde Zendingsbond) 214
    First Presbyterian Church of Quincy, Massachusetts 214
Harare Synod and Its Foreign Partners... 214
    Madison Avenue Presbyterian Church (MAPC)..................... 214
    Presbyterian Church of Australia... 215
The Synod of Zambia and Its Foreign Partners............................... 216
    The Presbyterian Church of the USA (PCUSA) 216
    The Presbyterian Church of Australia....................................... 216
    The Presbyterian Church in Ireland 216
    The Romans 1:11 Trust... 217
    Conclusion 218
Foreign Relations and the Unity of the CCAP Synods 218
An Evaluation of the CCAP Synods' Foreign Relations................. 218
    Mutuality and Equality... 219
    Criticism against Partnerships.. 220

  The Position of a Missionary in a Resource-Poor
    Partner Church 223
  Who Controls Whom? 225
  Conclusion 226

Chapter 7 229
Unity beyond Border Disputes
  Introduction 229
  Oneness of the Synods without Borders 229
  Consolidating Synodical Independence 231
  Foreign Expansion 232
  Loose Cooperation and Synodical Sisterhood 237
  The Synods as Different Denominations 238
  More Unity of the Synods Reconsidered 240
    The First Option: More Independence of the Synods with
      No Boundaries 243
    The Second Option: A Stronger General Assembly and
      Presbyteries with No Synods 245
    An Ecclesiological Evaluation of the Two Options 246
  Conclusion 247

Chapter 8 249
Concluding Thoughts

Bibliography 253

Index of Subjects 281

Index of Names 293

List of Figures

Figure 1: Map of South Rukuru and Dwangwa Rivers Watershed, showing the post Commission of Inquiry proposed boundary between Livingstonia and Nkhomasynods of the CCAP. 146

Figure 2: A sample of newspaper cartoons depicting a caricature of the Border Dispute between the synods of Livingstonia and Nkhoma. 154

Figure 3: The first CCAP General Assembly leadership after the change from General Synod. 186

Foreword

It is indeed a great privilege for me to write the foreword to this publication. I believe the author of this book in many ways is already carrying, and even more so in the years ahead, will carry, one of the major flags of high academic standards for future Malawian theology.

Dr Munyenyembe is not only part and parcel of the Malawian context and history, but he also has a great commitment for this fascinating, beautiful but complex country with all its socio-economical and other challenges. And because of so many ties with not only Central-East Africa but also Southern Africa, what happens in Malawi will also have some reverberations in the broader area.

The Langham Monographs, which this study is part of, analyzes different contemporary issues, among others of a historical, missiological, social and moral nature. Langham Partnership presents works of evangelical scholars from the developing world, and this institution is therefore playing a major role in the building of and the development of theological and ecclesiastical academic work in the Majority World. With this contribution to the global church, they can only be encouraged on and be commended for.

Rhodian Munyenyembe is currently based at the Department of Theology and Religious Studies at the Mzuzu University in the Northern Region of Malawi. He holds a BA and an MA degree from the University of Malawi, an MEd from the Concordia University of Portland (Oregon, USA) and a PhD from the University of the Free State (South Africa). Some of his prime interests would be religion and contemporary issues, church and state relationship, religion and African values, and religious freedom and education. I have no doubt in my mind about the academic standards that Rhodian wishes to attain but also strives for in his work. He is definitely capable of critical thought. In this study his meta-theoretical presuppositions are clearly stated and his methods are scientifically sound. He is also well equipped to do proper historical research and was well trained in different contexts, inter alia, by one of his great Malawian mentors Professor Klaus Fiedler. In this study, Munyenyembe covered the field of primary and secondary sources with great commitment and accuracy. He also takes a great interest in socio-political matters related to the Malawian society, and therefore his interest in the CCAP's need for unity, also for the sake of a common voice and witness, is well understood.

The story of the Church of Central Africa Presbyterian (CCAP) comes a long way with many fascinating positive and sometimes less positive sides to it. It is not my task to go into any detail except for stating the fact that it developed because of various theological and ecclesiastical reasons into five separate Synods, and this is a long-standing reality. The fact that they have a lot in common, but also various aspects that are dividing them, cannot be ignored. In the course of its history the need for greater cooperation developed positively but sadly at stages also negatively.

This book contains a church historical study with a combined denominational-ecumenical perspective, and a church polity study with a presbyterial-synodical approach. Next in focus are the issues related to diversity and unity and how this church is at pains to realize some form of unity in spite of different challenges. The reality of local and sometimes parochial issues overshadowing a more united front also come into play. In his research on the growth of the CCAP from 1924 to 2018 he clearly points out the problematic process of development in the church with the conception of a General Assembly. The focus is therefore strongly on the CCAP as a federative denomination. Munyenyembe's research hypothesis that the CCAP has, by means of its General Assembly, become a loose umbrella body of five different denominations, has been largely validated.

In the future of the CCAP many issues, but especially two, are at play. First, the lack of greater unity in the CCAP as the second largest established church in Malawi and from reformed evangelical background, has serious implications for the church's prophetic witness, for its social care and for all forms of education in Malawi. Second, though the General Assembly as the over-arching umbrella was meant to foster a closer unity of the three constituent synods, it still remains an unstable entity. This future is likely not to be a vibrant one as long as the constituting synods do not surrender a major part of their autonomy to a body which is at least administratively above them. Most of the church's power is still vested in these five separate synods. Therefore the loftiness of the General Assembly with its poorly maintained structures and minimal personnel, will last for some time, while it has little powers. But this also reflects the value that the five Synods ascribe to the General Assembly.

All in all this book on the history but also the future potential of a very important aspect of the life of the church and of theology (i.e. the unity of the body of Christ) is a major contribution to this discourse, also in the African context. Together with its pains and challenges we should never have doubt about the need for, but also the tremendous witness of, a united church, whichever form it takes. I hope this book will not only provide many satisfying moments of interesting reading, but that it will also serve as an important guideline for future leaders in the CCAP of Central, South and East Africa.

Prof J. W. (Hoffie) Hofmeyr, ThD
Emeritus, University of Pretoria, South Africa
Evangelical Theological Faculty, Leuven, Belgium
Vice Chancellor and Rector, Nkhoma University, Malawi

Acknowledgements

Many people have contributed to the success of this work in many and varied ways and I will always remain indebted to them. Since it is not possible to mention everyone according to his or her contribution, below are just some of the many people whom God has used to bless me in the course of this work.

Many thanks are due to Professor J. W. (Hoffie) Hofmeyr, whose guidance and encouragement has made it possible for this work to see the light of day. Words cannot fully express my gratitude to him.

I acknowledge the generosity of the Langham Partnership for awarding me a scholarship that funded a good part of the research expenses for this study. I also thank Langham Partnership for incorporating me into the worldwide family of Langham Scholars through the award of their prestigious evangelical theological scholarship. Special thanks also go to the following Langham Partnership personnel: Dr Ian Shaw, the Rev Dr Bill Houston, Dr Joel Carpenter, Dr Fred Gale, Mrs Gaynor Harvey, Mrs Ruth Slater, Mrs Stefanii Ferenczi, Elizabeth Hitchcock, and Vivian Doub of Langham Publishing.

Associate Professor J. S. Nkhoma and all colleagues in the Department of Theology and Religious Studies at Mzuzu University deserve a special mention for their support and understanding during the time I was busy with this work. I say thank you to Mr Mervin Khoromana (officemate), Professor Klaus Fiedler, Mr T. A. Chafera, Dr Rachel Fiedler, Dr Qeko Jere, Dr Winston R. Kawale, Mr Francis Kudzula, Mrs Grace Banda-Saguga, Ms Ruby Kondowe, Mrs Doreen Mikwanda and Ms Gertrude Nyirenda. In the same vein, I thank the Management of Mzuzu University for the administrative support rendered to me during the entire period of researching and writing this book.

In a very special way, I thank the Rt Rev Bishop Fanuel Magangani of the Anglican Church's Diocese of Northern Malawi for his generosity and fatherly love to me during the entire period of writing this book.

I also thank Dr Richard Gadama, fellow Malawian UFS PhD student, for his assistance and encouragement in our academic journey.

I am very grateful to the three synods of the CCAP in Malawi – Livingstonia, Blantyre and Nkhoma – for sharing with me the information I needed from them. From Livingstonia, I especially thank the Rev Dr L. N. Nyondo (General Secretary), Rt Rev Dr T. P. K. Nyasulu (Education Secretary and General Assembly Moderator), Rev Douglass Chipofya (Moderator), Rev K. R. M. Nyirenda (former General Assembly Deputy Secretary General 1), Dennis Nyirenda (Stone House Librarian and Archivist); from Blantyre Synod special thanks go to Rev Dr Felix Chingota (former General Assembly Moderator), Rev Colin M'bawa (General Assembly Secretary General), Rev M. L. Mbolembole (St Michael's and All Angels Church), Rev Innocent Chikopa and Mr Hanock Chakhaza; from Nkhoma Synod, I thank Rev Dr K. J. Mgawi, Rev M. Likhoozi, Mr Nathaniel Kawale and Mr Greshan Kamnyamata.

The following people deserve a special thank you for working behind the scenes to make sure that I was assisted in every way during my research writing: Mrs Ingrid Mostert (UFS) and Mrs Marlene Schoeman (Stellenbosch Archives).

I also thank Dr Mwenda Ntarangwi of the Theological Book Network in Grand Rapids, Michigan, for his meticulous evaluation of this book in the process of its evolution to this stage.

My father and mother deserve special mention for their love, prayers and support, as do my brothers and sisters: Paul (Dr), McSard, Martha, Molly, Addison and their families.

Finally, I express my heartfelt gratitude to my family for the most needed moral support and even for just being there for me all the time: many thanks to my wife Faith, son Victor, daughter Louisa, niece Elina and nephew Dhumisani.

May the Lord Jesus Christ richly bless you all!

Introduction

Can a church organization be one and five denominations at the same time? Is it possible for a church denomination to be in competition for membership growth against none other than itself? These questions may sound absurd, but they represent the inner life of the Church of Central Africa Presbyterian (CCAP).

This study traces the history of the CCAP, which currently exists as a General Assembly with five synods by the names of Livingstonia, Blantyre, Nkhoma, Harare and Zambia. The first three synods are in Malawi while the last two are in Zimbabwe and Zambia, respectively. All five synods of the CCAP share theological, historical and revival roots in such a way that it would constitute a single fully-fledged denomination. However, the synods currently work so independently of one another that they technically function as different denominations.

This book presents a comprehensive history of the CCAP as a federative denomination and explores the lack of its true unity despite efforts to make the denomination one in the course of its long history. Some researchers on the CCAP have concentrated on the history of only one synod or one issue in a single synod, leaving out some important information regarding this denomination's unique composition.

Three missionary traditions merged in the years 1924 and 1926 to form the CCAP. The denomination came out of three missions: the Church of Scotland's Blantyre Mission, the United Free Church of Scotland's Livingstonia Mission and the Dutch Reformed Church in South Africa's Nkhoma Mission. The former missions became presbyteries prior to the formation of the CCAP and eventually rose to the status of synods in their evolutionary history. Initially, the synods had an agreement known in studies of missions as comity, where missions that accept one another's theology and

Christian witness as valid agree to work cooperatively while respecting each other's territorial boundaries. Of late, some CCAP synods have irreparably violated this agreement. Consequently, one now sees Syond of Livingstonia congregations mushrooming in the Central Region of Malawi, which used to be Nkhoma Synod's territory, and Nkhoma Synod is also establishing congregations in the Northern Region of Malawi, which used to be the exclusive territory of the Synod of Livingstonia. Besides, the three Malawian synods have congregations side by side in South Africa, where they are perpetuating their synodical differences at the expense of the unity of the denomination.

The behaviour of the CCAP synods makes them de facto denominations even though they are under the General Assembly, which ought to be understood as the legal denominational organization with synods operating under it. Many observers cannot understand why these synods behave in this manner, though they consider monetary, ethnic and linguistic factors as some of the reasons for this state of affairs. I argue, in view of this observation, that the CCAP is not one denomination but five distinct denominations that maintain a meta-denominational association in their General Assembly – hence the problems dogging its unity.

This book explores some suggested options as possible directions the CCAP may take after scrutinizing the current situation in consideration of its future configuration.

After reading this book, you will have a better understanding of the CCAP General Assembly and its synods, from both past and contemporary developments, which will increase your knowledge of church history in Malawi and in some of its neighbouring countries such as Zambia, Zimbabwe, South Africa and even Tanzania.

List of Abbreviations

ACEM	Association of Christian Educators in Malawi
AIDS	Acquired Immune Deficiency Syndrome
BMO	Board of Mission Overseas
CBFM	Consultative Board of Federated Missions
CCAP	Church of Central Africa Presbyterian
CCAPSO	Church of Central Africa Presbyterian Student Organisation
CCAPYUFS	Church of Central Africa Presbyterian Youth Fellowships
CCAPYUM	Church of Central Africa Presbyterian Youth Urban Ministry
CHAM	Christian Health Association of Malawi
CLAIM	Christian Literature Action in Malawi
DPP	Democratic Progressive Party
DRC	Dutch Reformed Church
DRCM	Dutch Reformed Church Mission
DRCSA	Dutch Reformed Church in South Africa
FCU	Forum for CCAP Unity
FMC	Foreign Mission Committee
GAC	General Administrative Committee
GK	Gereformeerde Kerk
GZB	Gereformeerde Zendingsbond
HIV	Human Immunodeficiency Virus
LDC	Leadership Development Committee
LISAP	Livingstonia Synod AIDS Programme

LMS	London Missionary Society
LUANAR	Lilongwe University of Agriculture and Natural Resources
LWBCA	*Life and Work in British Central Africa*
MAPC	Madison Avenue Presbyterian Church
MCP	Malawi Congress Party
MMU	Ministers' Mission Union
NGK	Nederduitse Gereformeerde Kerk
NHK	Nederduitsch Hervormde Kerk
NIV	New International Version
PAC	Public Affairs Committee
PCI	Presbyterian Church in Ireland
PCM	Presbyterian Church of Malawi
PCT	Presbyterian Church in Taiwan
PCUSA	Presbyterian Church of the USA
PresAid	Presbyterian Aid
PWS&D	Presbyterian World Service and Development
RCA	Reformed Church in America
SADC	Southern African Development Community
SCOM	Student Christian Organisation of Malawi
SSPCK	Scottish Society for the Propagation of Christian Knowledge
TEEM	Theological Education by Extension in Malawi
UDF	United Democratic Front
UFC	United Free Church of Scotland
UK	United Kingdom
UMCA	Universities Mission to Central Africa
UP	United Presbyterian Church of Scotland
UPC	United Presbyterian Church
URCSA	Uniting Reformed Church in Southern Africa

CHAPTER 1

The Origins of the CCAP: Theological and Revival Roots

Introduction

The history of the Church of Central Africa Presbyterian is tied to its Reformed roots as shaped by the teachings of John Calvin. The origins of the churches that gave birth to the CCAP with its Presbyterian system of church government and Reformed Theology trace their history to the figure of John Calvin and other reformers in the sixteenth century.[1]

Calvin's Theology

Calvin's theology was so influential that it did not remain in Geneva alone. The theological system known as Calvinism found its way into such countries as France, Germany, Poland, Holland, Scotland and Switzerland itself. However, for the sake of this book we are only interested in the development of this theological tradition as it planted itself in Scotland and Holland (and eventually South Africa), those being the countries that nurtured the growth of this brand of Christianity before it came to Malawi in the latter half of the nineteenth century, eventually leading to the formation of the CCAP in the first half of the twentieth century.

The theology known as Reformed or Calvinist Theology is distinguished from other theological systems mostly on the basis of church government and the doctrines of grace. There is a general consensus that the theology of Calvin centred on the doctrine of the sovereignty of God, as it perceived God

---

1. Barry, "John Calvin."

to be the one behind all that happens in the universe and taught that it is his predetermined purposes that succeed. It is, however, argued that Calvin is not the sole originator of Reformed Theology despite the prominence accorded to him when discussing this system of theology.[2] There can be no doubt, though, that Calvin was the greatest contributor to what is now known as Reformed Theology despite the contributions of other reformers and later divides in the course of the history of Reformed churches.

It is, therefore, important at this juncture to appreciate a general understanding of Calvin's theology. As earlier alluded to, Calvin's theology starts with the idea of the sovereignty of God. For Calvin, "God is providentially in control of all things that come to pass, including evil things, but this does not make him the author of evil."[3] Having settled the question of God, Calvin went on to expound the Doctrine of Man.[4] According to Calvin's view, which is the position of Reformed Theology, humanity was created in the image of God and was pure before the fall. Due to the fall, humans lost their original purity and became depraved. This depravity is so thorough that all the faculties of humankind have been affected. It is, therefore, not possible for humans to seek God unaided because even their wills have been tainted so much that they cannot, on their own, seek God. Humans, therefore, become saved, in the Christian sense of the term, when God takes the initiative on their behalf.

The initiative God takes in his plan of saving humankind finds full expression in the person of Jesus Christ, the God-man, who bridges the gap between the righteous God and sinful humanity. With regard to the nature of Christ after the incarnation, Calvin closely follows the orthodox patristic view of the two natures in one person. It is on record that Calvin was the first theologian to describe the work of Christ in terms of the threefold office of prophet, priest and king:

---

2. "Calvin is sometimes made to be the exemplar of Reformed theology (and perhaps rightly so), but Reformed theology is, by no means, limited to him. So, rather than tracing Reformed theology to Calvin as the sole source, Reformed theology is better imagined as a river into which many sources flow and from which many streams originate." Robert Johnson, "What Is Reformed Theology?"

3. Theopedia, "John Calvin," www.theopedia.com/John_Calvin, accessed 11 Mar 2013.

4. I am using the word "man" here to mean humanity in general. This is so in view of lack of a better way of expressing these ideas in a language that would be perceived to be more inclusive.

As prophet, Christ's teachings are proclaimed by the apostles for the purpose of our salvation. As priest, Christ's sacrifice of himself and his mediation before the Father secures the salvation of men. As king, Christ rules the Church spiritually in the hearts of its members.[5]

With regard to the person and work of Christ, it can be argued that Calvin's theology was not unique in its formulation, except perhaps in its emphases. His description of the three-fold office of Christ has nowadays become very popular and is accepted by all theological traditions. Besides, its scriptural backing is not hard to comprehend.

On the part of the Holy Spirit, Calvin taught that it is him who unites humans to Christ when Christ is received and believed in by faith through the testimony of the scriptures. The work of the Holy Spirit is so important that without its manifestation, it is not possible for any person to have a saving faith in Jesus Christ.[6] In line with the rest of the reformers, Calvin also stressed the doctrine of justification by faith, which is understood in Reformed Theology as the result of the mercy of God and not the merits of human beings.[7]

With regard to the teaching on sacraments, Calvin restricted himself to the only two dominical sacraments: Baptism and the Lord's Supper. In contradistinction to sacramentalists, who are of the view that sacraments are a means of justifying grace, Calvin taught that they are the marks of Christian profession, testifying to God's grace.[8] Calvin believed that infants were proper objects of baptism. He, therefore, did not object to infant baptism. His view, however, differed from that of the Roman Catholic Church and Martin Luther in that he taught that baptism did not regenerate infants who were baptized. For Calvin, infant baptism symbolized entrance into the New Covenant just as circumcision did for the Old Covenant.[9]

Calvin's theological acumen was again manifested in the way he came to understand the sacrament of the Lord's Supper, especially in regard to

---

5. Theopedia, "John Calvin."
6. Niesel, *Theology of Calvin*, 24.
7. Calvin, *Institutes of the Christian Religion*, 3.17.8.
8. Calvin, 4:1–53.
9. Calvin, 4:23.

the presence of Christ within it. Calvin took a middle position over and against Martin Luther and the Roman Catholic Church, on one hand, who believed that the body of Christ was literally present in the sacraments and that of Ulrich Zwingli, on the other, who taught that the Lord's Supper was a mere memorial.[10] Specifically, Calvin's position was against the doctrines of transubstantiation and consubstantiation as believed and taught by Roman Catholics and Lutherans, respectively. It has been argued that the elements, as a symbol, could not be the thing they signified, whereas Zwingli's position of memorialism divorced the symbol from the substance. The Calvinist position is that when one receives the bread and wine, which are literal food and drink, in a spiritual sense, he receives the spiritual food and drink of the Christian; Christ being spiritually present when the Eucharist is received by faith.[11]

Calvin's Church Polity: The Presbyterian System

Perhaps the most notable thing about Calvin as one of the fathers of the Reformation was his formulation of the Presbyterian system of church government. As with all other things in history, the Presbyterian system of church government has somewhat evolved from the time of John Calvin to the present day. The system has also taken on the flavour of the localities wherein it has been established. Nevertheless, the foundation and structure of the Presbyterian system of church government started with John Calvin in Geneva. This means that it is right and proper to refer to John Calvin as the father of the Presbyterian system of church government.

In regard to church government, Calvin came up with his new ordinance in the year 1541. He considered the medieval church to have deviated from the New Testament pattern, and so, in his thinking, he was trying to go back to the apostolic model of church government. He, therefore, started by abolishing the office of bishop, making all ministers equal. They had to preach and teach the word, administer the sacraments and look after the spiritual welfare of the people. They were also responsible for the moral discipline of the people, helped by the elders, who were from among the lay people. According to the arrangement of the time in Geneva, these elders

---

10. Theopedia, "John Calvin."
11. Theopedia, "John Calvin."

were elected by the city council. Though eventually the mandate of electing church elders and deacons became exclusively that of the church, the element of democracy with regard to ecclesiastical offices had been introduced in the Presbyterian system of church government. From that time onwards, the church would have different courts of the clergy (teaching elders) and the lay elders (ruling elders) from the session all the way to the synod.[12]

Calvin's system consisted, at the lowest level, of a local council of pastors responsible for teaching and shepherding the church. Above the council was the consistory, which was a larger council comprising pastors and lay elders elected according to district. This body was responsible for maintaining church discipline and watching over the moral lives of the church members. Above the consistory was the presbytery, which was a regional body and above it was a provincial synod and a national synod.[13]

This pattern has been followed over the centuries in all the churches that belong to the Presbyterian tradition.[14] In the Central African setting, following the developments in Scotland, Holland and South Africa, the lowest court in the CCAP is called the session. This is the body responsible for the running of the affairs of the church at congregational level. It is a body comprising the pastor, who is the teaching elder (known as the moderator), and elected lay elders and deacons. The name congregation in this context is a bit tricky in that it is more than a congregation would mean in other churches. The church where the pastor is resident may have several small congregations which are referred to as prayer houses. These smaller congregations or prayer houses send their representatives to the mother congregation, which houses the session, as it were, and the prayer houses are members of that session where decisions are made for them. In some synods, for example the Synod of Livingstonia, it is vestries that form the session, which means the vestries are responsible for the administration of prayer houses.

---

12. Paas, *Ministers and Elders*, 54–56.
13. Theopedia, "John Calvin."
14. See Uprichard, *What Presbyterians Believe*, 79–87.

Reformed Soteriology

The churches referred to as Presbyterian and Reformed follow a certain understanding of the Christian teaching on soteriology, or the salvation of mankind. Due to historical circumstances the teachings of Calvin on soteriology have been summarized into five points.[15] It is interesting to note that these teachings in their crystallized form of five points were not formulated by John Calvin himself. However, many scholars are of the view that all the points in this system point to the teachings of John Calvin, thereby validating the nomenclature "Calvinism."[16]

Historically, though, the five points were not hammered out by Calvinists in their leisure time while appreciating the theological depth of their founder. They were actually a response to the followers of James Arminius, who came up with the five ways of refuting Calvinism in 1610.[17] Eventually the five points of Calvinism under the acrostic TULIP were formulated at the Synod of Dort in the Netherlands in the year 1618. Ever since, these points have been part and parcel of Calvinistic theology for better or for worse. The "T" in the acronym refers to "Total Depravity" (or total inability). This means that the fall of humanity affected all the departments of human life without leaving any area untouched. There is always an explanation from the sympathizers of this view that this does not mean that mankind is as evil as evil can be, but only that all the parts of humanity, such as mind and body, have been marred by the presence of sin. Since humans are affected in totality by sin, it is not possible that they can do anything to redeem themselves – hence the concept of total inability.[18] The Arminians were of the view that depravity was partial in that humans still had the potential to respond to the gospel and be saved without being aided in a special way despite the fall.

The "U" in the acronym stands for "Unconditional Election." This follows logically from the above position. If humans are totally depraved and unable to save themselves, then only God can save them. Since all humans are sinful it follows that those that are saved are not saved because of their ability

---

15. See Seaton, *Five Points of Calvinism*.
16. Warfield, *Calvin and Calvinism*.
17. Seaton, *Five Points of Calvinism*, 7.
18. Seaton, 8.

but because God chose to redeem them unconditionally, without anything from them compelling God to save them. This point was emphasized by Calvinists at the Synod of Dort in contradistinction to the Arminian position which argued that God elected some people unto salvation because in his foreknowledge he had seen that they would respond to the Gospel. His choice, according to Arminianism, was therefore based on the condition that the people were able to respond to the divine message.

The third letter in the acronym stands for "Limited Atonement," meaning that the number of people who are to be saved is exactly as God has intended in electing some people unto salvation. This means that even though the blood of Jesus is enough to atone for all humanity, in practical terms only the elect are atoned for, therefore, the availability of Christ's atonement is "limited" to the number of the elect.[19] This position was emphasized against the Arminian view that Christ's atonement is potentially available for all without any reference to the elect.

The "I" in the acronym stands for "Irresistible Grace," meaning that those who have been atoned for, following their unconditional election, cannot resist the grace of God to have them saved. This means that humans are compelled to be saved and they cannot do otherwise but eventually respond to the gospel call no matter their initial resistance or hardness of heart.

Finally, the "P" stands for "Perseverance of the Saints." This means that the saints who have thus been drawn to God are in no danger of falling away from their effectual calling as their security is guaranteed. They may in the course of their journey face "many dangers, toils and snares,"[20] but in the long run the will of God for their salvation and glorification shall prevail.[21]

The Calvinist understanding of the doctrines of grace as elucidated here is highly cherished by those that know them and believe in them. On the other hand, those that know them but do not believe in them have nothing but contempt for them. Some even make suggestions that these teachings are against the Scriptures, making their source less holy. As a matter of fact,

---

19. Whether the people to be saved will be more than the damned, Reformed Soteriology does not explain, though the Bible talks of multitudes from every nation, tribe, people and language (Rev 7:9).

20. Quoted from John Newton's hymn, "Amazing Grace."

21. Seaton, *Five Points of Calvinism*, 20–22.

many CCAP Christians do not know about these teachings. The reason for the ignorance of many Christians on such teachings is largely the absence of such teachings from the pulpit. In any case, this is the teaching of the CCAP as endorsed in the various books of doctrine that explain the faith as understood from a Presbyterian and Reformed perspective. A good example of the literature that forms the theology of the CCAP apart from the writings of John Calvin and his successors is the *Westminster Confession of Faith*. This doctrinal document is in most cases accompanied by *The Shorter Catechism* and *The Larger Catechism* that also teach about the same things.[22]

Presbyterianism in Scotland

After the reformer, John Calvin, had established the Presbyterian system of church government in Geneva, he went further and established the Geneva Academy, which eventually had a profound effect on the spread of the Calvinist understanding of the Christian faith in the rest of Europe.[23] It was through the influence of this school that John Knox, the harbinger of the Presbyterian system into Scotland, became acquainted with the teachings and manner of John Calvin.[24] An often repeated quote of John Knox concerning the Genevan Academy is that it was "the most perfect school of Christ since the time of the apostles."[25]

John Knox is the credited leader of the Reformation in Scotland though it is on record that he alienated many by his rigid and censorious attitude.[26] It has to be remembered, however, that these were times of both political and religious upheavals. Consequently, the reformers could not afford to be responsible only for spiritual matters, for the success of spiritual matters largely depended on favourable political conditions. In 1559, John Knox returned to Scotland from continental Europe and became a vocal proponent of Reformed Theology and the concept of Presbyterian leadership in the

---

22. From a Malawian point of view, Handwell Hara's work makes a nice introduction to the relationship between Reformed Soteriology and the Malawian context. See Hara, *Reformed Soteriology and the Malawian Context*.

23. Dowley, *History of Christianity*, 390.

24. Ridley, *John Knox*.

25. Dowley, *History of Christianity*, 390.

26. Dowley, 390.

church. A number of Scottish lords had already been agitating for religious reformation in the Scottish church, and they enthusiastically embraced John Knox's teaching. Under Knox's leadership, these "Lords of the Congregation" wrote the *Scottish Confession of Faith* in 1560, which ended papal jurisdiction in Scotland and outlawed the Mass. The *Scottish Confession* remained the primary doctrinal guide for the Church of Scotland until the publication of the *Westminster Confession* in 1647.[27]

When the reformation started taking place in the Church of Scotland, there were three factors that impacted it and eventually determined the route that the Scottish Reformation was going to take. The first factor was the continental reformation, especially as led by John Calvin in Geneva. The second factor was the reality of a national Episcopal church that needed to be reformed and lastly the struggle between church and state for the authority of the church.[28] This means that the reformation in the Scottish church was to a large extent the result of another instance of the practicability of John Calvin's ideas with regard to church polity. It was what Calvin had taught, starting in France and finally in Geneva, that the church in Scotland considered worth adopting in its reforming exercise. However, some scholars have observed that the development of Presbyterianism in Scotland did not absolutely follow the pattern laid down by John Calvin.[29] This was so because of the unique situation in Scotland which differed significantly from the contexts in which John Calvin's ideas were first practiced and adopted. Nevertheless, the nucleus idea was the same.

With regard to the second factor, the reformation in Scotland was not supposed to develop alongside Roman Catholicism. There was a desire to have the whole national church, which was Episcopalian, change according to the dictates of Reformed ideas of church polity. There was, therefore, some kind of compromise for the sake of facilitating a national reformation between those that wanted the church to be thoroughly reformed by giving absolute powers to the church as a whole and the sympathizers of

---

27. Dowley, 390.
28. Van Wyk, *Historical Development of the Offices*, 22.
29. See Jack C. Whytock, "The Scottish Reformers: Calvin and Knox," *Presbyterian Record* 33, no 4 (April 2009): 33–34. Also Aaron Denlinger, "How the Scots Changed the World," https://www.ligonier.org/learn/articles/how-scots-changed-the-world, accessed 30 May 2019.

the Episcopalian system who, politically, wanted the state to have a say in the running of the church through the office of the bishop. As it happened, the pure Presbyterian way of doing things, as proposed by John Calvin, was altered by elevating the courts (or assemblies) which eventually had the same authority as the bishop in a diocese – except that, in the case of the presbytery, it was a group of people instead of an individual. It is because of such observations that Jurgens Johannes van Wyk argues that the offices of the church according to the Presbyterian system are yet to be developed.[30] According to Van Wyk, "It was this ambivalent tradition that was brought to Central Africa by the various Scottish missionaries, embraced by Dutch Reformed Church missionaries with their Scottish background, and accepted and maintained by the African Church."[31]

Due to the difficulties that the Church of Scotland faced with regard to the issue of ecclesiastical control, there was a "time bomb" that was not diffused in the early decades of the Scottish Reformation which would eventually explode in the nineteenth century in the event known as the Disruption of 1843. The Disruption was a schism that took place in the established Church of Scotland, where 450 ministers of the church broke away over the issue of the church's relationship with the state to form the Free Church of Scotland. The events leading to the Disruption can be traced with accuracy to the event that took place in the year 1712 when the Patronage Act was passed, giving local lairds legal powers to choose ministers for their congregations. In effect this meant that congregations had no say in who preached the word of God to them.[32] This ruling often caused deep unhappiness, as local church members felt they had a right to say who should preside over their worship. Gradually, ministers began to leave the church, starting with the resignation of the Stirling minister, Ebenezer Erskine, whose secession is sometimes referred to as the Original Secession.[33] This was followed by

---

30. Van Wyk, *Historical Development of the Offices*, 128.

31. Van Wyk, 13.

32. Travel Scotland, "The Great Disruption of 1843," http://www.scotland.org.uk/scotland-in-the-nineteenth-century/disruption?highlight=WyJncmVhdCIsIidncmVhdCIsIidncmVhdCcuIiwiZGlzcnVwdGlvbiIsImdyZWF0IGRpc3J1cHRpb24iXQ==, accessed 29 May 2013.

33. Travel Scotland, "Great Disruption of 1843."

the second secession of Thomas Gillespie in 1761, who then founded the Relief Church.[34]

The last straw in the build-up to the Disruption was the Reform Act of 1832 and the establishment of a group of evangelicals within the church, who, among other things, wanted the church to be serious about missionary work. These evangelicals found themselves in tension with the Moderates who easily aligned themselves with the lairds. As the power of the opposing group grew, they insisted that the church should allow congregations to have their own ministers and that ties with the government be relaxed. In 1834, the Church of Scotland's General Assembly passed the "Veto Act," which allowed prominent members within a congregation to reject a patron's choice of minister for the congregants. This landmark act would have gone a long way in ensuring that the church was back in the hands of ordinary Christians if it were not for the legal battle started by one John Hope, who was at the time one of Scotland's leading legal figures. John Hope challenged the "Veto Act" in court, making the church endure a protracted legal battle which ended in the House of Lords ruling that the General Assembly did not have the legal right to amend the law that gave patrons the power to appoint ministers for congregations.[35]

These developments had greatly affected the relationship between the church and the government by the year 1842.[36] The General Assembly tried to assert its ecclesiastical powers by drawing up a Claim of Right, barring the state from interfering in ecclesiastical matters. This Claim of Right elevated Christ, and not the government, as the head of the church.[37]

By 1843 some ministers wanted to convince the government that they were not deliberately trying to cause trouble. However, among their ranks there were some who wanted to part ways with the established church because they were convinced that the established church had surrendered its ecclesiastical powers to the state and that the state had weakened the church's spiritual power. It happened, therefore, that during the meeting of the General Assembly in May of 1843 some ministers walked out of the

---

34. Rankin, *Handbook of the Church of Scotland*, 57.
35. Travel Scotland, "Great Disruption of 1843."
36. Burleigh, *Church History of Scotland*, 334–335.
37. Travel Scotland, "Great Disruption of 1843."

meeting into the nearby Tanfield Hall where they elected Thomas Chalmers as their first moderator of the newly established Free Church of Scotland. Following this development, a total of 474 ministers left the established Church of Scotland.[38]

As time went by the issues that had caused the Disruption were abandoned by the established Church of Scotland, and government control of the church was stopped altogether. With the issues that had caused the division no longer there, it became possible for the two sides to re-unite. In the year 1900 the Free Church of Scotland joined the United Presbyterian Church of Scotland (UP) to form the United Free Church of Scotland.[39] It was this United Free Church of Scotland that re-united with the Church of Scotland in 1929.

The above historical developments in Scotland had a bearing in Malawi, which was the mission field for both the Free Church of Scotland and the Church of Scotland before the reunion. The Free Church of Scotland was responsible for the establishment of Livingstonia Mission in Malawi in 1875, which eventually became the CCAP Synod of Livingstonia, and from there the CCAP Synod of Zambia was also born. On the other hand, the Church of Scotland was responsible for the establishment of Blantyre Mission in Malawi in 1876, which eventually became the Blantyre Synod of the CCAP. This clearly shows that the history of these two synods is a history of churches whose "mother" church knows unity, division and re-union.

Another significant thing to note is that Robert Laws, one of the most popular Scottish missionaries in Malawi, was, back home in Scotland, a member of neither the Church of Scotland nor the Free Church of Scotland but of the United Presbyterian Church of Scotland. Due to the cooperation between the Free Church of Scotland and the United Presbyterian Church of Scotland it was possible to have Robert Laws in the Free Church's missionary party, being the only ordained minister in the group when it set out for Malawi. The merger of the Free Church of Scotland and the United Presbyterian Church of Scotland that took place in 1900 did not unsettle Robert Laws at all since he was already working for both churches

---

38. Burleigh, *Church History of Scotland*, 334.

39. The United Presbyterian Church of Scotland was a merger of the Relief Church and the United Secession Church established in the year 1847.

as a missionary. Robert Laws's cooperation with the missionary party of Blantyre Mission also found fruition in the re-union of the Free Church of Scotland and the Church of Scotland through the merger of the Church of Scotland with the United Free Church of Scotland in 1929. Though this happened after he had retired as a missionary, he was still alive and might have rejoiced at the event.

This section, therefore, clearly shows how the Presbyterian system of church government and the theological tradition known as Reformed Theology found their way from John Calvin in Geneva in the sixteenth century to Malawi in the nineteenth century via Scotland. This connection caters to the establishment of the Synod of Livingstonia and Blantyre Synod of the CCAP in Malawi. Therefore, there is need to also trace the history which lead to the coming of the Dutch Reformed Church missionaries to Malawi from South Africa – missionaries credited with establishing the Nkhoma Synod of the CCAP, which later gave birth to the Harare Synod.

The Dutch Reformed Church in the Netherlands

The Nkhoma Synod of the CCAP is a child of the Dutch Reformed Church in South Africa, which had come from the Netherlands in the seventeenth century. Interestingly, the South African church has retained its name while the mother church in the Netherlands changed its name in the nineteenth century, and it has experienced such a metamorphosis through its many amalgamations that it is no longer the original Dutch Reformed Church that was born out of the sixteenth-century Reformation.

The original Dutch Reformed Church was born in the sixteenth century as a result of the desire for freedom from both political and religious oppression among the people of the Netherlands. In the sixteenth century, the Netherlands were under the Spanish monarchy, which was against its subjects being drawn towards Protestantism because of its support for Roman Catholicism. As a result, King Charles V of Spain even established the inquisition in the Netherlands in 1522 in order to deal with those that were agitating for reforms in the church.[40] Through influential leaders such as

---

40. Matt Stefon, "Netherlands Reformed Church," *Encyclopaedia Britannica*, http://www.britannica.com/EBchecked/topic/410259/Netherlands-Reformed, accessed 28 May 2013.

William the Silent, the Dutch shook the Spanish yoke off their necks and became an independent nation. As an independent nation, they decided to adopt Protestantism as their religion and it so happened that the brand of Protestantism that was most popular with them was that of Calvinism. The first general synod of the Dutch Reformed Church took place in the year 1571 and thereafter other general synods followed. Having fallen for Calvinistic theology, it was not surprising to see the Dutch Reformed Church following the Presbyterian system of church government. The *Belgic Confession* of 1561 and the *Heidelberg Catechism* of 1563 were accepted as standards of doctrine in the Dutch Reformed Church which became the national church of the Netherlands.[41]

In the year 1798, the Dutch Reformed Church was dis-established as the national church of Holland, though the government still retained some influence over it. In 1816 the Dutch Reformed Church was renamed the Netherlands Reformed Church after it had undergone some reorganization by King William I. Due to theological disputes, the church was not spared from breakaways. In 1834 the Reformed Churches in the Netherlands broke away from the Netherlands Reformed Church. However, the Netherlands Reformed Church remained the most influential Protestant church in the Netherlands, though it did not become the largest church until the twentieth century.

More developments were to take place within this church. In May 2004, the Netherlands Reformed Church (formerly Dutch Reformed Church) and the Reformed Churches in the Netherlands joined with the Evangelical Lutheran Church to form the Protestant Church in the Netherlands. This church has become the largest Protestant denomination in the Netherlands with over 2.5 million members currently.[42]

Our interest though is mostly with the group that left Holland in the seventeenth century for the Cape of Good Hope in South Africa. This group carried the Dutch Reformed Church to South Africa where the name has remained until now, even though the original church changed its name in the nineteenth century.

---

41. Stefon, "Netherlands Reformed Church."
42. Stefon, "Netherlands Reformed Church."

The Dutch Reformed Church in South Africa

The Dutch Reformed Church in South Africa is a denominational family of three sister denominations that trace their history back to the Dutch Reformed Church of the Netherlands which was born out of the Reformation in the Netherlands.[43] This church came to South Africa in 1652 when Jan van Riebeeck and the first Dutch colony established it at the Cape as a church of their homeland. From the Cape the church spread into many parts of South Africa and neighbouring countries.

It is this church that became the mother church of the Nkhoma Synod of the CCAP, owing to the fact that the first missionaries who came to plant this brand of Christianity in Malawi came from South Africa after the church had been there for over two centuries. As shall be seen in subsequent sections, the coming of Dutch Reformed Church missionaries to Malawi was well received by the Scottish Presbyterian missionaries who were in the missions of Livingstonia and Blantyre. These had been in the country for over a decade and were quite familiar with the mission field, so they could provide a base for their South African Dutch colleagues who, like them, were Reformed in their theology and Presbyterian in their church polity.

It is interesting to note that despite the differences in nationality and theological emphases, all three missions could trace their history back to the ministry of John Calvin in Geneva in the sixteenth century. It can therefore be argued that with regard to their historical origins, these three synods have always been one church together with the synods of Harare and Zambia which are mature and independent daughters of the synods of Nkhoma and Livingstonia, respectively.

The Difference between Reformed and Presbyterian

In the history of Reformed and Presbyterian churches, sometimes a question is asked with regard to the difference between the two: Are all Reformed churches Presbyterian? And are all Presbyterian churches Reformed? It has

---

43. These sister churches are Nederduitse Gereformeerde Kerk (NGK), Nederduitsch Hervormde Kerk (NHK) and Gereformeerde Kerke (GK). Sourced from Wikipedia, "Dutch Reformed Church in South Africa," https://en.wikipedia.org/wiki/Dutch_Reformed_Church_in_South_Africa, accessed 8 Apr 2013.

to be pointed out that it is not easy to untangle the two because their histories are so intricately woven together. For instance, Reformed Theology is sometimes referred to as Calvinism even though it is well known historically that Calvin was not the sole developer of Reformed thinking. He, however, ended up eclipsing all those who came before and after him in the thinking that has come to be known as Reformed Theology.

A simple explanation of the difference between the two is that first and foremost the term Presbyterian specifically refers to a form of church government led by elders (presbyters) in opposition to government by bishops (Episcopal system, prelacy) or by congregations (congregationalism, independency) – though it may also refer to a system of scriptural doctrine.[44] The Presbyterian system falls between the Episcopalian and Congregational systems.[45]

The Presbyterian system of church government provides ruling courts – comprised of teaching and ruling elders – for the churches at various levels. The teaching elders are ordained clergy whereas the ruling elders are lay members of the church, though some of them may have undergone theological training.

On the other hand, Reformed Theology specifically refers to the Reformation teaching that slightly differed from the position of Martin Luther. This teaching in itself is quite diverse and expresses a kind of plurality which is found in the various catechisms and confessions of the Reformed churches such as *The French Confession* of 1559, *The Scots Confession* of 1560, *The Belgic Confession* of 1561, *The Heidelberg Catechism* of 1563, *The Second Helvetic Confession* of 1566, *The Thirty-Nine Articles of the Church of England* of 1562 and 1571, *The Canons of the Synod of Dort* of 1619, the *Westminster Confession of Faith* and catechisms of 1647 and the *Formula Consensus Helveticus* of 1675.[46]

Apart from the above works, included in the Reformed Theology corpus are all the various works of leading representative theologians of the churches referred to as Reformed churches, such as Ulrich Zwingli and Heinrich Bullinger of Zurich, Martin Bucer of Strasburg and Cambridge, John Calvin

---

44. Clowney, "Presbyterianism," 539–531.
45. McHugh, "Presbyterianism."
46. Letham, "Reformed Theology," 569.

and Theodore Beza of Geneva, Peter Martyr Vermigli of Strasburg, Oxford and Zurich, and other recognized writers in the tradition such as Karl Barth and G. C. Berkouwer.[47]

All the churches with the name Presbyterian are also Reformed or Calvinistic in their theology. However, not all churches that are Reformed are also Presbyterian.[48] This means that Reformed Theology is bigger than Presbyterianism. Some congregational and Baptist churches also belong to the Reformed family, though in terms of church government they are not Presbyterian.[49] With regard to the synods under focus in this book, it is interesting to note that it is only the synods with a Scottish mother church (i.e. Livingstonia, Blantyre and Zambia) that are coming from a background where the name Presbyterian was used. On the other hand, the Dutch Reformed Church in South Africa and its parent, the original Dutch Reformed Church of the Netherlands, never used the word Presbyterian in their names though they were Presbyterian in terms of church government. This means that whatever differences there may be between Reformed and Presbyterian, in the Central African context the two are combined within the CCAP via their Scottish and Dutch roots all the way back to John Calvin in the sixteenth century.

Revivals and the Birth of the CCAP

This section aims to give an overview of revival history as it affects Malawian church history, with special reference to the CCAP denomination in order to underscore the importance of revivals in mission formation and the spread of the Christian faith. The goal is to show how missions, which in most (if not all) cases are born in revivals, influence the church's theology and history. It will eventually be shown that if it were not for revivals, the Protestant brand of Christianity, of which the CCAP is part, would not have come to this part of Africa.[50]

---

47. Letham, "Reformed Theology," 569; Hara, *Reformed Soteriology and the Malawian Context*, 42–113.
48. Uprichard, *What Presbyterians Believe*, 79–80.
49. See Uprichard, 80.
50. Cf. Fiedler, *Missions as the Theology of the Church*, 25.

In this book the word revival refers to those moments in the history of the church when there is an extraordinary outpouring of the Holy Spirit on the believers. It is "God's quickening visitation of his people, touching their hearts and deepening his work of grace in their lives."[51] This greatly affects the believers who, consequently, become empowered to preach, teach, counsel, pray and do other extraordinary things with great zeal and fervour. It is during revivals that many non-Christian people and nominal Christians become converted since revivals are renewal moments in the life of the church.

A Brief History of Revivals

Before the sixteenth-century Reformation there were many activities within Christianity which can be referred to as revivals.[52] However, for the sake of modern church history, scholars like to start counting revivals from the Reformation period (1517). Following this pattern of counting revivals, the second revival is that of Puritanism in Britain and Pietism in continental Europe, starting around 1572. On the third position we have the Great Awakening from the year 1734. The fourth one is the Holiness Revival which some scholars call the Second Evangelical Awakening (1859). The Pentecostal Revival of the 1900s would be the fifth revival and the Charismatic Revival of the 1960s the sixth and the last major revival so far.[53]

It has to be noted, though, that there have been many revivals in different places even after the Reformation which cannot all be mentioned here. These revivals are in most cases not mentioned because they are considered to have occurred in localized places and at a smaller scale. However, the influences of even such revivals have been immense in the history of the church when considering their impact with the advantage of hindsight.[54]

---

51. Packer, "Theology of Revival," 588.
52. See Allen, *History of Revivals of Religion*.
53. There is no name for subsequent revivals after the Charismatic Revival. Many scholars like to talk about waves within the charismatic movement. This means that there are several waves within the same charismatic movement – e.g. first wave, second wave and third wave – but no distinct name for any other revival yet.
54. An example of such revivals would be the 1860 Cape Revival which is treated at length in this chapter's subsequent sections, especially in relation to the establishment of Nkhoma Mission in Malawi.

Revival History and Malawian Church History

The year 1861 marks the beginning of the Church in Malawi. This is so because this is the year when the first mission station in the country, the Universities Mission to Central Africa (UMCA), was initially established.[55]

As a result of the Great Awakening, there emerged many missionary societies in Europe and America which eventually evangelized Africa and other parts of the world in the years that followed. The missions from this revival have been termed classical missions.[56] It was the classical missions that first established the church in Malawi, beginning with the UMCA in 1861, the Livingstonia Mission in 1875 and the Blantyre Mission in 1876. The last two eventually formed the CCAP together with Nkhoma Mission, which came into the country a little over a decade later via the Dutch Reformed Church in South Africa.

After the classical missions, Malawian church history was influenced by the coming of post-classical missions rooted in the Holiness Revival. These included Joseph Booth, through whose influence missions like Zambezi Industrial Mission (now Zambezi Evangelical Church), Nyasa Industrial Mission (now Evangelical Church of Malawi) and others were established in the country.[57]

The Pentecostal Revival has affected Malawian church history through the arrival of such churches as the Assemblies of God, Apostolic Faith Mission, Four Square Gospel and the various Zionist churches which, though distinct from the rest of the Pentecostal churches, have roots in the Pentecostal Revival which is responsible for their birth.[58]

Lastly, the Charismatic Revival which has its roots in the mainline churches came to Malawi in the 1970s and 1980s. The Charismatic Revival was introduced in Malawian Christianity through para-church organizations like Scripture Union, Life Ministry and the Student Christian Organisation

---

55. See Tengatenga, *The UMCA in Malawi*. The UMCA was the first mission to be established in the country as a direct result of the appeal of David Livingstone. Livingstone had been in the country some years before, but he only passed through as an explorer without establishing any mission station himself.

56. See Fiedler, *Story of Faith Missions*, 20–22.

57. Langworthy, "Africa for the African"; Fielder, *Making of a Maverick Missionary*.

58. Fiedler, "Process of Religious Diversification in Malawi." For the history of the Zionist churches in Malawi see Strohbehn, "Zionist Churches in Malawi."

of Malawi (SCOM).⁵⁹ This revival continues to express itself in the formation of new charismatic churches and to influence mainline churches where innovative groups sometimes remain contained within the confines of their mother denominations. Church splits occur when these innovative groups cannot be contained.⁶⁰

The history of revivals clearly shows that the church in Malawi is made up of different denominations which have their roots in different revivals from the past as well as the present. This means, for purposes of church typology in Malawi (and the world as a whole), it is important to take note of the churches' links with the history of revivals as the waves of revivals continue with the ever-unfolding history of the church militant.

The CCAP as a "Child" of Revivals

Andrew Walls argues that it was actually voluntary associations that spread the Christian faith in the mission fields rather than the established churches themselves.⁶¹ In some cases the established churches were even suspicious of missionary organisations, fearing that they had revolutionary aims under their cloak of civil and religious liberty.⁶² Andrew Walls observes that "the Church as then organized, whether Episcopal, or Presbyterian, or Congregational could not effectively operate missions overseas. Christianity had accordingly to 'use means' to do so."⁶³

The voluntary associations that committed themselves to the spread of the Christian faith had, in most cases, people who had been touched by the transforming power of revivals. These people were ready to serve in faraway mission fields, sacrificing their comfort back home for the sake of the gospel. It was such individuals who came together to form the missionary societies that became responsible for missionary work in overseas countries including Malawi. It was such endeavours that led to the establishment of

---

59. Kawamba, *Blantyre Spiritual Awakening*.

60. See Fiedler, "Charismatic and Pentecostal Movements"; and Munyenyembe, *Christianity and Socio-Cultural Issues*, 37–38. It is interesting to note that some scholars refer to the charismatic denominations as "neo-charismatics" because for them the charismatics proper have not left their churches to form new denominations. For example, see Nyika, "Apostolic Office amongst Malawian Neo-Charismatic Churches."

61. Walls, "Missionary Societies," 141–155.

62. Walls, 3.

63. Walls, 5. Cf. Carey, *Enquiry into the Obligations of Christians*.

the Presbyterian missions in Malawi starting in the 1870s and culminating into the formation of the CCAP in the twentieth century.

However, it has to be noted that the missionary spirit was not easily awakened among the Scots and the Dutch in order for them to start engaging in cross-cultural missions. It is, therefore, important to trace the history of missions within the Church of Scotland and the Dutch Reformed Church in order to situate the time and context in which the missions that came to Malawi were born. We shall also evaluate the revival influence on the formation of these missions within the wider context of the debate on the influence of revivals on missionary work. For the sake of chronological order, it is appropriate to begin by looking at the Scottish church, which produced the two Presbyterian missions of Livingstonia and Blantyre, and afterwards to look at the Dutch Reformed Church which was responsible for the establishment of Nkhoma Mission.

Revivals and Missionary Endeavours in the Church of Scotland

The Church of Scotland never seriously engaged in mission work between the years 1560 and 1824.[64] The former is the year when the Reformation in Scotland was launched while the latter is the year when the General Assembly of the Church of Scotland formally launched into the area of missions. Prior to 1824, some Scottish churchmen who wanted to serve as missionaries in foreign lands did so not through the Church of Scotland but through other avenues.[65] Such was the case with Robert Moffat of Kuruman who left for Africa in 1816 under the auspices of the London Missionary Society because his own church, the Church of Scotland, had no foreign mission organization then to direct and support the zeal of such an intrepid church man.[66]

The explanation for the lack of any missionary endeavours overseas in the Church of Scotland prior to 1824 can be traced back to the sixth century when Columbanus monks evangelized most of the remaining "pagans" of Scotland. The early church lost its missionary zeal when hordes of barbarians

---

64. Ritchie, *Scottish Church and Foreign Mission*, 1.

65. Ritchie, 1.

66. The London Missionary Society was not Presbyterian but Congregational in its church government, but it was open enough to people from diverse backgrounds who wanted to serve as missionaries. This is a clear instance of how free and accommodating missionary organizations born in revival can be.

and other people joined the church en masse after the end of the persecution in the fourth century AD. In the same way, many Scottish people became nominal Christians after the sixth century's evangelizing efforts, thereby killing the church's missionary zeal.[67] Things did not improve even during the Reformation when there was a lot of evangelization among the Protestants, but this was confined to only Europe without extending to other peoples across the seas.[68]

As part of the Protestant family, the Reformed churches also suffered from merely fighting for survival after the Reformation, and this fighting to a large extent was among themselves.[69] Besides, there was a perception among many Christians in the West that the evangelical task of the church had already been accomplished by the creation of European Christendom.[70] This explains why there was a tendency in the Reformed Tradition to hold that the office of "evangelist" was no longer applicable.[71] This is gathered from the fact that the Presbyterial form of church government contains a very revealing section on the offices of the church in connection with the term evangelist, where the office of the evangelist together with that of the apostle are understood to have ceased in the Apostolic church.[72] Thus we see that in the sixteenth century, the Church of Scotland did not really find the impetus for foreign mission work to the unreached peoples of the world even though some documents of Reformed thinking mention the issue of reaching the unreached and the gospel being preached to all peoples of the world before Christ's return.[73]

In the seventeenth century, the Church of Scotland was greatly affected by internal conflicts. It was during this period, however, that some of the most important works of Presbyterianism were written. These include *The*

---

67. Ritchie, *Scottish Church and Foreign Mission*, 1. See also Tucker, *From Jerusalem to Irian Jaya*, 28, and Mackichan, *Missionary Ideal in the Scottish Churches*, 51.

68. The Roman Catholic Church was during this time far ahead of all Protestant churches in evangelizing the peoples of foreign lands. See Fuller, *Going to the Nations*, 46–47.

69. Ritchie, *Scottish Church and Foreign Mission*, 1; Tucker, *From Jerusalem to Irian Jaya*, 24.

70. Cf. Paul, "Reformed Churches and Evangelism," 354.

71. Ritchie, *Scottish Church and Foreign Mission*, 1–2, fn. 7.

72. Ritchie, 4.

73. Cf. Calvin, *Harmony of the Gospels*.

Westminster Confession of Faith, The Larger Catechism, The Shorter Catechism, The Form of the Presbyterial Church Government and *The Directory for Public Worship*. In all these documents the issue of missions is very silent and where it is apparently mentioned, like in *The Larger Catechism*, it is only mentioned with regard to the exposition of the Lord's Prayer, with no sense of urgency in it.[74]

According to Andrew Walls, the Westminster documents' mention of the non-European peoples' embrace of the gospel is viewed as an action of God eschatologically rather than as a responsibility of the church in the present time.[75] Even though the Westminster documents mention the conversion of the Jews and the gathering in of the fullness of the Gentiles, the practice of the Westminster tradition is contrary to this thinking.[76] Ritchie argues that this was the case because of the Covenant Theology prominent in the Church of Scotland and the Puritan emphasis on the coming of the kingdom of God inwardly to the individual rather than outwardly to the world.[77]

It has sometimes been suggested that the cause of lack of missionary zeal in the Scottish church was the Reformed doctrine of double predestination which is clearly stated in the Westminster documents.[78] Though this view is debatable, some scholars echo it unreservedly as does L. K. Fuller:

> Theologically, many Protestants believed so strongly in predestination that they thought evangelism was useless because God had already decided who would be saved and who would be lost, and nothing could change this. They believed that if the heathen were lost, God was punishing them for their sins by purposely blinding their eyes, and nobody should interfere.

---

74. Ritchie, *Scottish Church and Foreign Mission*, 3–4.
75. Walls, "Missions."
76. Ritchie, *Scottish Church and Foreign Mission*, 4.
77. Ritchie, 4.
78. *The Westminster Confession of Faith* states the doctrine thus: "By the decree of God, for the manifestation of His glory, some men and angels are predestinated unto everlasting life, and others foreordained to everlasting death. These angels and men, thus predestinated and foreordained, are particularly and unchangeably designed, and their number is so certain and definite, that it cannot be either increased or diminished." See 3.3–4. Alexander McPherson, ed, *Westminster Confession of Faith* (Glasgow: Free Presbyterian Publication, 1994).

They believed the Great Commission was a command only to the original twelve apostles.[79]

Bruce Ritchie, whose view is representative of the scholars who are hesitant to conclude that double predestinarian theology or philosophy automatically translates into passivity with regard to missionary endeavours, argues, in the first place, that very few theological systems are totally consistent:

> Philosophically the Westminster doctrine of election might nurture passivity, but on the other hand there was the clear biblical command of Jesus to take the Gospel into the whole world. Theological systems which seek, however imperfectly, to base their conclusions on Scripture, are always open to powerful biblical imperatives which have the ability [to] break through the 'system' itself. The piety nurtured both by Calvinism and Westminster was a piety which placed great importance on obedience, whether God's will was fully understood or not. As such, an 'inconsistency' between a theological system and biblical imperative was not to be questioned. Obedience to the imperative could over-ride everything else. It is doubtful if any Church, or even any theological movement, has ever followed the logical implications of its philosophy to full conclusion.[80]

The churches which come from the school of Westminster Calvinism became very much involved in mission work in later generations though it can be argued that they were following the lead of other churches.[81] In any case, their Reformed Theology's emphasis on double predestination did not deter them from evangelizing the peoples of the world once they became aware of their mandate in meeting the needs of the unevangelized. However, it cannot be denied that the literature that guided Presbyterian thinking in the seventeenth century has little to say on the mandate of the church to carry out mission work in foreign lands.

The next phase in considering the history of the Church of Scotland's position vis-a-vis foreign missions is the eighteenth century. Many things

---

79. Fuller, *Going to the Nations*, 46.
80. Ritchie, *Scottish Church and Foreign Mission*, 5.
81. Ritchie, 5.

happened during this century, the details of which are beyond the scope of the present study. Suffice it to say that this was the century in which the Church of Scotland experienced peace from political upheavals. Be that as it may, the church settled down to a routine kind of spirituality and became inward looking. In the words of Bruce Ritchie, "Eighteenth-century Scotland regarded itself as a Christian nation, but not as a Missionary nation."[82] It is significant to note, however, that during this century, Scotland saw the establishment of some independent missionary societies that became channels for those that wanted to spread the gospel but could not do so under the auspices of the established church. The independent missionary societies were the Scottish Society for the Propagation of Christian Knowledge (SSPCK), established in 1707, and the Propagation of the Gospel at Home, established in 1798. These independent mission organizations were founded amidst a general apathy towards foreign mission work and even though they tried all they could, their work was not generally successful. The SSPCK, for example, had tried to do mission work in New England and met with little success. It was later, through the work of David Brainerd, that there was some success in the work of the SSPCK, though Brainerd himself did not come from Scotland but worked on behalf of the Scottish organization.[83]

Towards the end of the eighteenth century, many in Scotland were beginning to realize the importance of foreign missions, and there was a lot of support from the Church of Scotland to the SSPCK in the area of personnel and finances. This shows that the Church of Scotland was now willing to support independent missionary societies for the propagation of the gospel abroad but was not ready to be directly involved in the exercise. This position of the Church of Scotland reached its peak in the 1796 General Assembly where the church rejected proposals by its own synods of Fife and Moray to be fully and directly involved in foreign mission. The first reason cited for the Church of Scotland's lack of enthusiasm for foreign mission work was that the heathen were not refined enough in their manners to embrace the teachings of the gospel. Second, some people felt there was great need for the gospel within Scotland itself, so much so that it was not prudent to spend

---

82. Ritchie, 6.
83. Grigg, *Lives of David Brainerd*.

energies on a faraway people when one could equally serve his or her own people. Third, it was argued that the poor in Scotland were suffering through want and scarcity, and it was not acceptable to be making huge collections of money for the mission field when there were poor people just next door.[84]

Thus, from 1796 to 1824 the Church of Scotland lived in a period in which it had definitely said "no" to direct involvement in mission work. However, this was also the period when there was a lot of agitation for missionary work because of the influence of the Great Awakening. This means that people who could not get involved in the work of missions through the Church of Scotland found ways of doing so through other means. It was through the influence of one Dr James Bryce, who had worked as a chaplain in India, that the Church of Scotland reconsidered its stance on foreign missions. The issue was tabled at the 1824 General Assembly of the Church of Scotland.[85] This time around it was possible for the church to unanimously accept the responsibility of the church in foreign missions. The position taken by the Church of Scotland at this stage did not in any way alter the theology or spirituality of the church. As Ritchie remarks:

> Traditional Calvinism had always had an emphasis on the importance of the mind, as well as the heart, as the place where God's Spirit has its effectiveness within the individual. This tradition meant that this very Presbyterian missionary enterprise of the Church of Scotland was not simply "pietist" but had an emphasis on evangelism through education. The Evangelical's emphasis on "piety" and "feeling" became combined with the Moderates' emphasis on "mind" and "intellect." These emphases would become a hallmark of all missions carried out under the aegis of the Church of Scotland.[86]

It is important, at this juncture, to ask why the Church of Scotland now became supportive of being directly involved in missionary work when initially it was against the move. The answer can be found in the observation

---

84. Ritchie, *Scottish Church and Foreign Mission*, 5.

85. Hunter, *History of the Free Church*, 8–9; Chambers, "Church of Scotland's Nineteenth Century Foreign Missions Scheme," 115–138.

86. Ritchie, *Scottish Church and Foreign Mission*, 23.

that most of the people who were agitating for mission work at this time were touched in one way or another by the power of revival through the Great Awakening. It can, therefore, be argued that through the influence of revival, the Church of Scotland was now ready to start sending its sons and daughters to foreign mission fields in fulfilment of the Great Commission, which had not previously been the case.

The apathy of the Church of Scotland toward mission work was not an isolated case. Many Protestant churches in Europe were apathetic to the work of missions for many centuries until after the Great Awakening and the pioneering works of people such as William Carey who were obviously influenced by Jonathan Edwards and the spirituality of the Great Awakening and the Evangelical Awakening, in America and Europe respectively.

It can now be safely asserted that the coming of the gospel to Malawi, especially through the work of the Scottish missions, was as a direct result of the influence of revival on mission work. This validates the observation that missions are children of revivals. The succeeding sections are therefore an attempt at showing how revivals brought the church to Malawi through the means of missions.

The Influence of Revivals on Dr David Livingstone, the Missionary Explorer

It is interesting to note that even Dr David Livingstone, the missionary explorer who opened up Malawi and neighbouring countries for missionary work, was himself greatly influenced by revivals. Peter Hammond comments:

> Books and tracts from the Revival movement sweeping America reached Scotland and created much excitement and deepening of spiritual life and vision. David Livingstone received a pamphlet written by Karl Gützlaff, of the Netherlands Missionary Society. In it Gützlaff appealed for medical missionaries to go to China. David was inspired at how a medical missionary could be much more effective in converting the lost.[87]

As is well known with the advantage of hindsight, the door for David Livingstone's missionary work did not open in China but in Africa, where,

---

87. Hammond, "Family, Faith and Upbringing of David Livingstone."

through the influence of Robert Moffat of the London Missionary Society, he led his own mission stations in present day Botswana before abandoning the stationed missionary ministry for that of a missionary explorer. He thus reminisced:

> I had fondly hoped to have gained access to that then closed empire by means of the healing art; but there being no prospect of an early peace with the Chinese, and as another inviting field was opening out through the labours of Mr. Moffat, I was induced to turn my thoughts to Africa; and after a more extended course of theological training in England than I had enjoyed in Glasgow, I embarked for Africa in 1840, and, after a voyage of three months, reached Cape Town.[88]

The views of David Livingstone with regard to the work of Christian missionaries were greatly influenced by the theology of revivals. Any discussion of David Livingstone with regard to his goals for the missionary enterprise in Africa includes the following: Christianity, commerce and civilization. And yet these ideas did not originate with David Livingstone but were given much more prominence by him at a time when most European powers were interested in nothing but imperialism. While trying to defend Livingstone against anti-colonial critics, Fidelis Nkomazana argues that the missionary explorer has been wrongly identified as the harbinger of colonialism, which only benefited the western powers and not the indigenous peoples.[89] To the contrary, Livingstone was in agreement with the rest of the Christian thinkers and missionaries of the time whose spirituality was greatly influenced by revivals. What Livingstone was championing for with regard to Christianity had already proven to be a successful approach towards alleviating human misery as observed in the initiatives of Thomas Chalmers, who multiplied the churches and schools in order to bring Christian witness and education closer to the people of impoverished Scotland after he himself had embraced an evangelical spirituality born out of revival.[90] The same ideas had also been

---

88. Livingstone, *Missionary Travels and Researches in Africa*, 8.
89. Nkomazana, "Livingstone's Ideas of Christianity, Commerce and Civilization."
90. Nkomazana, 46.

embraced earlier on by William Carey (considered by many to be the father of modern missions), who had actually gone to practice them in India.[91]

While Livingstone initially came to Africa as a stationed missionary, he is generally known in history as a missionary explorer who believed that the interior of Africa was supposed to be opened up for the spread of the Christian faith and legitimate commerce.[92] Realizing that someone needed to go deeper into the interior of Africa in order to explore the land and give an accurate picture of what used to be perceived as the "Dark Continent" by most Westerners, Livingstone came to the conclusion that he was the man to do that kind of job. Consequently, he resigned from the role of a stationed missionary in order to concentrate on the work of exploration, which he considered crucial if there was going to be any success in the work of evangelizing Africa.

Owing to his conviction, Livingstone made three epic journeys into the interior of Africa, making important geographical observations for the people outside Africa. During his second journey he came to the land adjacent to Lake Malawi, where he felt a mission station could be successfully established. Though Livingstone's methods were not without criticism among his contemporaries, his labours eventually vindicated him as Christian missions and trade later flourished in the same areas where he had envisioned their success.[93]

It is interesting to observe that even before any mission station was established in the country, the person who had to "clear the ground" was himself a product of the spirit of revival, thereby underscoring the fact that missionary endeavours are indeed influenced by revivals.

Revivals and the Formation of the Livingstonia Mission

The Livingstonia Mission, originally established in 1875, started as a mission of the Free Church of Scotland (1843–1900). It has to be noted that among the issues that separated the Free Church of Scotland from the established Church of Scotland was the issue of evangelicalism. Thomas Chalmers, who was one of the leaders of the Church of Scotland before the Disruption,

---

91. Nkomazana, 47.
92. Livingstone, *Missionary Travels and Researches in Africa*, 28.
93. See Moir, *After Livingstone*, 1–6; and Jack, *Daybreak in Livingstonia*, 350.

did not have evangelical convictions prior to 1810. However, after 1810 his convictions tilted towards evangelicalism.[94] This can only mean that he was eventually influenced by the evangelical spirit of revival. This was to have far-reaching consequences because, when the Disruption took place in 1843, Chalmers led the split which took the name Free Church of Scotland.[95] This means that right from the beginning the Free Church was a church of evangelical convictions and revival spirituality as led by Thomas Chalmers and other leaders following in his footsteps.[96]

The Livingstonia Mission is in the category of classical missions, which refers to those missions that emerged as a result of the Great Awakening.[97] These are missions of the period referred to as the "Great Century" by Kenneth Scott Latourette.[98] It may not be possible to trace the spirituality of each and every individual that enlisted with Livingstonia Mission during the early decades of the mission but suffice it to say that the zeal of most of these missionaries was a result of the revival fire which had touched them back home in Scotland. Some, as we shall see later, actually tried to replicate in the mission field the same revival tendencies of the Scottish church which they had experienced while still in their own country.[99]

It is a well-known fact that the establishment of the Livingstonia Mission was the brainchild of Dr James Stewart of Lovedale, who, in response to Dr David Livingstone's appeal and influence during his missionary travels, wanted to establish a mission station in one of the places Dr David Livingstone had explored.[100] Though James Stewart was himself not to lead

---

94. Roxborough, "Legacy of Thomas Chalmers," 173–176.//
95. Wright and Badcock, *Disruption to Diversity*.//
96. Roxborough, *Thomas Chalmers*.//
97. It has to be noted, though, that individual missionaries were also influenced by subsequent revivals both at the national and international levels.//
98. See Fiedler, *Story of Faith Missions*, 13; and Latourette, *History of the Expansion of Christianity*, 281.//
99. A case in point here is Donald Fraser who, when he was sent to minister among the Ngoni of Mzimba, encouraged huge sacramental conventions which were modelled after nineteenth-century Scottish Highland gatherings, though in the Malawian case they included both baptism and communion. See Thompson, "Fraser, Donald," 224; Thompson, *Christianity in Northern Malawi*; and Thompson, *Ngoni, Xhosa and Scot*, 75–93. It has to be pointed out that Donald Fraser was influenced by the Holiness Revival (otherwise known as the Second Evangelical Awakening). See Paas, *Faith Moves South*, 192.//
100. Jack, *Daybreak in Livingstonia*, 19.

the mission station, the role he played in the formative years of the mission cannot be overemphasized. Noteworthy is the fact that he was himself a child of revival as he was greatly influenced by evangelical revivalism in Scotland. The same can be said concerning his colleague Robert Laws, who carried on with the mission work from where James Stewart left off. Robert Laws was eventually to become the chief architect of the mission in its first fifty years of existence.[101]

Thus it can be argued that the impetus for missionary work, in as far as the Scottish initiative to establish the Livingstonia Mission is concerned, was directly or indirectly a result of the spirit of revival prevailing in Scotland at the time. It has to be pointed out again that, when the Disruption took place in the Scottish church in 1843, most of the leaders that left the Church of Scotland for the revivalist Free Church of Scotland were those that had been influenced by the revivals, whereas the remaining clergy in the Church of Scotland were those of the "party" of the Moderates.[102] It is interesting also to note that all missionaries joined the Free Church of Scotland after the Disruption because they could not place themselves under the Moderates.[103] This observation will prove quite useful in making comparisons between the enthusiasm that was in the Livingstonia Mission during its formative years and a lack of the same in the Blantyre Mission which was founded by the Church of Scotland, which continued to be led by the Moderates.

Revivals and the Formation of the Blantyre Mission

The history of the formative years of Blantyre Mission is full of contradictions when one considers the general background to the work of missions, especially in relation to the influence of revival and the legacy of the great missionary explorer Dr David Livingstone. The story that due to David Livingstone's labours and emotional funeral, many a Scot were stirred to follow in the footsteps of the great missionary explorer, lacks the "sound and fury" that one generally expects from a story so widely retold and believed.

Many missiologists agree that missions are children of revival(s). Within this kind of understanding it has to be stated that it is, therefore, safer to

---

101. McCracken, *Politics and Christianity in Malawi*, 281.
102. McIntosh, "The Disruption," accessed 26 Jun 2019.
103. Travel Scotland, "The Great Disruption of 1843."

intone that even the Blantyre Mission of the Church of Scotland was established as a result of revival(s). However, it has to be noted that this mission was a child of the church that had remained with the Moderates after the Disruption. To what extent that spirit of moderation was responsible for the lackadaisical attitude of many to respond to the appeals for mission work in the case of Blantyre Mission is not easy to establish. What is known, though, is that despite the grandeur of naming Blantyre Mission after the birth town of the famous missionary explorer, there was no enthusiasm for the mission and it was not easy for the organizers of the mission to find pioneer volunteers for the work.[104]

Was there a revival in Scotland at that time which could accelerate the work of missions by producing enthusiasts that were ready and willing to go forth into Africa, full of confidence in the Saviour's cross? The testimony of the time shows that there was indeed a revival even during this time in Scotland. The revival most referred to during this time is that triggered off by the Moody and Sankey mission to Scotland. It is claimed that this mission greatly influenced Scottish churches, so much so that the Christian life of many was deepened in many denominations.[105] Somehow it cannot be explained why there were no volunteers for missionary work when in fact the churches had actually been stirred by a revival. The explanation, however, must be found in the fact that it was not from established church structures that most of the missionaries came forward. Even the Livingstonia Mission, which was a child of the Free Church of Scotland, did not receive its backing from the church directly but from a committee of Glasgow businessmen.[106] This observation is very much in line with the observation made by Andrew Walls that missionary societies were a fortunate subversion of the church in that direct appeals from the churches yielded little, if anything, whereas the missionary societies were the ones that succeeded in planting the church in distant lands.[107]

I argue that Blantyre Mission faced difficulties in getting started because of reliance on volunteers who were expected to come from a church that was

---

104. Ross, *Blantyre Mission*, 18.
105. Ross, 18.
106. Ross, 18.
107. Walls, "Missionary Societies and the Fortunate Subversion of the Church."

unashamedly lukewarm in its approach due to being led by the Moderates. This church was aiding and abetting those with moderate views in the church over and against those that were clearly enthusiastic, who had been influenced by the spiritual fervour of revival and evangelicalism.[108] This partly explains why it was not easy for the organizers of the Blantyre Mission to find even a single ordained pastor who could accompany the first missionary party when the time came for the party to depart for the mission field – as we shall see later in this study.

Even though missions are children of revival, it was not always that Christians were stirred in the context of revival to go for mission work abroad. It is also necessary to conclude that the apparent enthusiasm of the Scottish people to send missionaries to Africa, and Malawi in particular, as a result of Dr David Livingstone's influence, was not as simple and as straightforward as it is often thought. There were hurdles to overcome, regardless of the general feeling that there was need for something to be done for the sake of the work that Dr David Livingstone had begun in Africa.

So far we have seen how, directly or indirectly, the two Scottish missions were influenced by revivals and the missionary zeal of Dr David Livingstone. Though there is reason to doubt the direct impact of the two in the case of Blantyre Mission, it still stands that missions to Malawi from Scotland were precipitated by revivals, as is the case with missions generally, and also the romance of Dr David Livingstone's life, regardless of the lack of dramatic enthusiasm. We now turn to the influence of the Dutch Reformed Church on the formation of the Nkhoma Mission.

Revivals, the Dutch Reformed Church and the Formation of Nkhoma Mission

The argument that missions are born in revival rings true for the Nkhoma Mission as well. This mission was started by the Dutch Reformed Church in South Africa (or by an organization of pastors of that church), but we

---

108. Even though it was Livingstonia Mission that was first to come to Malawi, the initiatives to start a Scottish mission in the country had actually started with the Church of Scotland representatives. It was Dr John Macrae who first contacted Lt E. D. Young to lead a missionary party to Malawi, but Young later responded to James Stewart's request and joined the Livingstonia party because Dr Macrae had not yet succeeded in appointing staff nor received any firm offers of service. See Ross, *Blantyre Mission*, 18.

cannot appreciate the history behind it without first of all trying to see the history of revival within the Dutch Reformed Church itself, in Holland and then in South Africa.

The Dutch Reformed Church (DRC) in Holland, which merged with other churches in 2004, is the indisputable mother of the Dutch Reformed Churches in South Africa, where the name has been retained. From this church originated missions which can only be described as having been born in revival, one of which is responsible for the establishment of Nkhoma Mission in Malawi in the late 1880s.

The Nadere Reformatie in Holland

The sixteenth-century Protestant Reformation itself is taken to be a revival in that the life of the church was greatly influenced by it and many Christian nations were renewed. However, immediately after the Reformation there followed a period of spiritual dryness, commonly referred to as Reformation Orthodoxy, which emphasized the intellect and neglected the emotions to the extent that the vibrancy of church life reached a low point. It was during this time that the Nadere Reformatie started in Holland. This was a movement, roughly starting in 1600 and ending in 1750, that emphasized applying Reformation principles at the individual level in the Dutch Reformed Church. The term *Nadere Reformatie* can be understood in the English language as the "Dutch Second Reformation," "Further Reformation" or "Continuing Reformation."[109]

This movement was characterized by a desire to live out the doctrines of the Reformation in the lives of individuals, in the home and in the church.[110] It can therefore be rightly said that the Nadere Reformatie was the first revival in the history of the Dutch Reformed Church, and parallels have been drawn between it and Puritanism in England and Pietism in Germany. It is actually even argued that English Pietism had a profound effect on the Nadere Reformatie due to the presence of some English Puritans and Scottish Covenanters in Holland as refugees in the seventeenth century.[111] It was more or less this kind of spirituality that found its way into South Africa in

---

109. Beeke, *Dutch Second Reformation*.
110. Beeke.
111. Beeke.

the decades after 1652 when a number of Dutch settlers began to settle at the Cape following the lead of Jan van Riebeeck and the pioneer settlers.

The 1860 Revival at the Cape

There have been negative descriptions of the life of the Dutch vis-a-vis the indigenous peoples at the Cape and elsewhere in the years following their settlement. It cannot be denied that some of these descriptions are exaggerations, but it is generally true that the spirituality that accompanied the Dutch from Holland under the influence of the Nadere Reformatie had to eventually wear out as is always the case between periods of revival. Thuo Mburu observes:

> [T]he Church has tended to slide to a state of lethargy and compromise in the periods between successive revivals. Such dark phases have been characterized by apathy to the plight of the suffering/problems in society, loss of the prophetic voice and decline in missionary zeal. Preoccupation with institutional expansion and the maintenance of ecclesiastical order has always tended to mask the divine component of the nature and function of the Church.[112]

It was therefore in correction to the life that the Dutch Reformed Church members were living that a distinct revival came upon them in 1860. Prior to this revival the Cape Colony has been described as nothing but a spiritual wilderness.[113] The reasons for describing the Cape Colony as a spiritual wilderness arise from the low level of Christian life and witness to which the Dutch Reformed Church had sunk in the years before the revival. It was the Dutch East India Company that was in control of the appointments of pastors and the establishment of congregations of the DRC. It is observed that for a period of over 150 years that the Dutch Reformed Church was in existence at the Cape, it only managed to establish five congregations within a 130 km radius of its influence. This is a clear indication of the members' lack of zeal in spreading their faith to the surrounding peoples. The testimony of Rev Nicolaas Hofmeyr is that he despaired at the unresponsiveness of his

---

112. Mburu, "Revival and Mission Movements."
113. Hammond, "Andrew Murray and the 1860 Revival."

congregation in Calvinia where, for six years, people did not respond to his pleas for prayer meetings in any way.[114] His congregation even opposed his initiatives to evangelize the coloured peoples in the vicinity of their parish. Even the attempt by Gottlieb van der Lingen to establish Christian schools did not stir the people into affirmative response.[115]

The coming of revival within the Dutch Reformed Church in South Africa in 1860 presents a sharp contrast to the facts highlighted above. In the first place, it is recorded that, whereas it was originally very difficult to find people who were willing to train as pastors – with the result that the church greatly suffered from lack of adequate pastors – young men were now offering themselves freely to train for the pastoral ministry.[116]

In January 1862, Revs Andrew Murray Jr. and Servaas Hofmeyr launched a Bible-based newspaper titled *Die Volksvriend*, which contributed to the blowing of a new breeze of life on the church with the result that all the previous resistance to mission work that was there before the revival evaporated.[117] From now onwards missions were launched with an understanding that it was the responsibility of the church to continue spreading the gospel. The first DRC missionaries, by the names of Alexander McKidd and Henri Gonin, were sent to Transvaal. Women also became zealously involved in missionary work, establishing the Women Missionary Union(Die Vrouwen Zendingsbond) with Emma Murray serving as its founding president.[118]

The missionary vision of the Dutch Reformed Church exploded, with mission stations being established in many lands beyond South Africa. It was this initiative that eventually led to the missionary venture that sent missionaries to Malawi, which eventually became responsible for the founding of the Nkhoma Mission. The missionaries who were entrusted with the task of establishing a mission station in Malawi were A. C. Murray and T. C. B. Vlok. Details of their labour will be highlighted later in this book. Suffice it to say at present that this connection underscores the fact that it

---

114. Hammond.
115. Hammond.
116. Hammond.
117. Hammond.
118. Hammond, "Andrew Murray and the 1860 Revival." Andrew Murray Jr. was a leading figure in the Holiness Revival or the Second Evangelical Awakening, as it is sometimes known. See Fiedler, *Story of Faith Missions*, 218–219. See also Paas, *Faith Moves South*, 91–95.

is revival that gives birth to missions, and, in the case of Nkhoma Mission, the connection is very clear, as J. L. Pretorius testifies:

> The DRC Mission to Nyasaland is the direct result of a religious revival in South Africa during the nineteenth century. There was an urge among many members of the church to do more for the spread of the Gospel than they were doing, at the time, among the coloured people in their midst.[119]

The establishment of the Nkhoma Mission also presents another instance of the observation of Andrew Walls concerning missionary societies and the fortunate subversion of the church, for in this case also it was a missionary organization that brought the Dutch Reformed Church to Malawi, with the church taking over only at a later stage. The mission was founded through the initiative of a hundred members of the Ministers' Missionary Union of the DRC, but it came under the direct control of the Cape DRC Synod in 1903 after a period of fifteen years of the missionary society's control.[120]

Scottish Connections of the 1860 Cape Revival

It is really interesting to see how intertwined the histories of the three Malawian synods of the CCAP are, especially concerning their revivalist and theological roots. While it is generally understood that the mainline churches in Malawi are products of the missionary endeavours of the Great Awakening, otherwise known as classical missions, it has to be noted that the individual missionaries that came to the mission field were influenced by different subsequent revivals. It is in the course of following this chase that we see that the Nkhoma Mission was a product of the Cape Revival of 1860 in South Africa with regard to direct missionary initiatives. Also of vital significance in this regard is the Scottish connection to this revival, which, in a way, links the Nkhoma Mission, via revival to the other two missions of Livingstonia and Blantyre which eventually formed the CCAP in the mid-1920s.

The Scottish connection to the 1860 Cape Revival concentrates on one family. This is the family of the Murrays: Andrew Murray Sr., Andrew

---

119. Pretorius, "Story of the Dutch Reformed Church," 12.
120. See McCracken, *Politics and Christianity in Malawi*, 216, fn. 76. Also Phiri, *Women, Presbyterianism and Patriarchy*, 44, fn. 59.

Murray Jr. and John Murray. However, it has to be noted that Andrew Murray Sr. did not come alone from Scotland, but led an eleven man team of pastors which eventually had the effect of revitalizing the spirituality of the Dutch Reformed Church in South Africa some decades before the revival. These pastors came as a result of the British policy of Anglicization which championed the suppression of the Dutch language in schools and government. This policy indirectly made the British prefer having Presbyterian pastors from Scotland serving the Dutch Reformed Church in South Africa instead of pastors from the Netherlands.[121]

Coming back to the Murrays, the sons of Andrew Murray Sr, Andrew Murray Jr. and John Murray, went to Scotland to live with their uncle, the Rev John Murray, in order to receive a British education. After graduating with MA degrees from the University of Aberdeen, the two boys went to Holland for further studies in theology and the Dutch language at the University of Utrecht. It was here that Andrew and John Murray became pastors and were ordained by the Hague Committee of the Dutch Reformed Church on 9 May 1848.[122] While their stay in Holland exposed the boys to liberal theological thinking which was popular at the time, it can be argued that they had already been toughened against such influences through their stay in Scotland. This is so because in Scotland they had been brought into contact with some of the most powerful Reformed preachers of the day, including Dr Thomas Chalmers and William Burns.[123]

Andrew Murray Jr. was destined to play a major role in the Cape Revival as well as in the whole life of the Dutch Reformed Church in South Africa in the period after the revival and its subsequent orientation into mission work. One testimony points to a prayer by Andrew Murray Jr. during a conference in Worcester as being the actual moment of the start of the 1860 revival:

---

121. Hammond, "Andrew Murray and the 1860 Revival."

122. Hammond.

123. Hammond. The two brothers became members of Het Réveil, a religious revival movement opposed to the rationalism which was in vogue during their stay in the Netherlands. However, their opposition to theological liberalism cannot necessarily be explained by their joining this movement because it can also be argued that they found this movement attractive because of the anti-liberal stand which they might have developed while in Scotland. In any case, their spirituality was moulded before coming to the Netherlands. Their anti-liberal stand proved quite useful in fighting against liberalism in the South African Church after their return.

Ds. Murray (Jnr.)'s participation during the first part of the conference was limited to one prayer, but it was a prayer so full of power and emotion that people came under deep conviction of sin. You can safely say that the Revival dates from that moment.[124]

While it is generally understood that the revival started in the Cape, the fire soon spread to surrounding places and beyond, so much so that eventually the revival became referred to as the South African Revival of 1860. Andrew Murray Jr. continued to lead the church in several capacities. After serving in Bloemfontein, he served as pastor of Worcester from 1860 to 1864, served in Cape Town between 1864 and 1871 and then moved to Wellington where he worked until his retirement in 1906. During his ministry as a pastor in the DRC, Andrew Murray Jr. was elected moderator of the Nederduitse Gereformeerde Kerk (NGK) Synod in 1862, 1876, 1883, 1890 and 1894.[125]

Andrew Murray Jr.'s brother John was also significant in the work of the church. He is credited, together with Nicolaas Hofmeyr and Johan Neethling, for establishing the Stellenbosch Kweekschool, which was initially launched for the purpose of training pastors due to the church's despair in obtaining suitable pastors from Holland at the time.[126]

Thus we see that the revival in the Dutch Reformed Church in South Africa was not an isolated event in the history of the church in general but had connections with happenings in other parts of the world.

Of significance in this section has been the endeavour to show the Scottish connections to this revival in order to demonstrate how the Nkhoma Synod of the CCAP, which is one of the many results of the 1860 Cape Revival, shares not only its theological roots but also revival roots with its sister synods of Livingstonia and Blantyre in Malawi.

---

124. C. Rabie, quoted in Hammond, "Andrew Murray and the 1860 Revival." Rabie was a teenager during this conference and later became a pastor of the Dutch Reformed Church in South Africa.

125. Smith, "Murray, Andrew, Jr."

126. Hammond, "Andrew Murray and the 1860 Revival."

Conclusion

In this chapter I have discussed the genesis of the churches that eventually influenced the formation of the CCAP in Malawi, tracing their origins from the time of the Reformation. The path of Reformed Theology and Presbyterianism has been traced from Geneva in Switzerland to Scotland, Holland and South Africa. There has also been a discussion in this chapter on the difference between the terms Presbyterian and Reformed, even though they are in most cases wrongly taken to mean one thing. The overall presentation of the material in this chapter shows the common roots of the missions that gave birth to the CCAP and argues that the amalgamation was a natural consequence of these seemingly estranged siblings.

This chapter also looked at how the three mission stations that evolved into the CCAP were influenced by revivals. Special reference has been given to their cooperation right from the beginning so that their oneness is emphasized prior to the amalgamation – albeit not without problems – that eventually took place in the first half of the twentieth century.

In agreement with mainstream missiological thinking, it has also been seen, though only in passing, that missions are mostly done not by the established churches or denominations but by missionary organizations which may be totally independent of established denominations or somehow affiliated to them. In the end, though, when missions get established, the churches in the mission fields eventually come under the jurisdiction of the established churches with which the missionaries are affiliated.

In the case of Blantyre Mission, which was the mission of the established Church of Scotland, we saw that there was not much enthusiasm on the part of would-be missionaries to volunteer for the work of mission, especially at the beginning. This observation apparently appears to contradict the observation concerning the eagerness of many people to join the work of missions when touched by the fire of revival. Besides which, it also seems to throw some doubt on whether the Scots were really stirred by the example of the life and death of the great explorer, Dr David Livingstone (who was their own man), as most legendary stories of the time purport.[127] I argue, in spite of this observation, that the general context in which the Presbyterian

---

127. Cf. Ross, *Blantyre Mission*, 18–23.

missions were launched for the evangelization of Malawi was that of revival, especially the impact of the Great Awakening/Evangelical Awakening on the Presbyterian churches in general and the Holiness Revival(1859) on some individual missionaries. In the case of the Scottish missions, the influence of David Livingstone adds flavour to the general context, though, as with any situation where generalizations are employed, there are always individual cases that seem to act against the rule. These become exceptions. However, exceptions to the rules do not change the rules. This would be the case in the current discussion concerning the initial lackadaisical attitude of the Church of Scotland during the formative years of Blantyre Mission.

Notwithstanding the above observation, it can still be safely concluded that the Church of Central Africa Presbyterian (CCAP) is a child of revivals, just like all other churches. It has also been shown that the three original synods of the CCAP share not only their theological roots but their revival roots as well, as seen in regard to the movements of the people of Scotland and Holland via South Africa to Malawi. The next chapter will logically discuss the establishment of the three missions in Malawi in order to provide the background to the formation of the CCAP in 1924.

CHAPTER 2

The CCAP Tributaries

Introduction

In this chapter, I first present a brief history of the three original missions that formed the CCAP, from their establishment to the formation of the CCAP amidst the clamour of ecumenism in the third decade of the twentieth century. Special attention has been paid to the ever-cooperative spirit of these missions' early missionaries and the eventual establishment of the CCAP as an appropriate response to the historical context and a result of progressive and cumulative missionary strategy. Here, the relationship to related developments in other African countries has also been tackled. The concept of comity is also discussed in this chapter in order to show how it was practically applied in the case of Malawi. Afterwards, I also present brief histories of the synods of Harare and Zambia, being the synods that were born later, after the establishment of the CCAP, as daughters of the synods of Nkhoma and Livingstonia, respectively.

Early Cooperation between Livingstonia and Blantyre Missions

The three missions of Livingstonia, Blantyre and Nkhoma are the tributaries that eventually poured into the CCAP in the years 1924 and 1926. However, it will be appreciated that cooperation among the three missions started long before they were actually established in the country. In the case of the two Scottish missions, it is interesting to note that the Blantyre Mission party would have been the first to set out for Africa if the process of recruiting its volunteers had been swift. However, due to the delays in the process of acquiring recruits, especially the reluctance of people to volunteer for missionary work, the organizers of the Livingstonia Mission managed to overtake their Blantyre counterparts. Nevertheless, when the Livingstonia party set out, there were some Blantyre personnel travelling with them in order to scout for a place where Blantyre Mission could be established.[1] This is a clear indication that the coming of the Livingstonia and Blantyre missions to Africa was characterized by cooperation rather than competition.[2]

The Livingstonia Mission

The irony of history is that there seems to have been initially no direct connection between David Livingstone, in whose memory the Livingstonia Mission was named, and the leadership of the Free Church of Scotland which gave birth to the memorial mission. As observed by McCracken:

> Not only was the Free Church's decision to found a mission in East Africa unconnected with Livingstone's appeals, its authorities were ignorant of the area he had selected for Evangelization. Only the fortuitous appearance of [James] Stewart and his suggestion of a title and location for the new mission connected Livingstone with its foundation at all.[3]

This observation underscores the fact that David Livingstone's influence in the establishment of mission stations in the southern interior of Africa went beyond direct connections with him. His legacy was such that a suggestion of connection with him, whether direct or indirect, would still carry the day. It is, therefore, not surprising to find that while the Livingstonia Mission took his name, its counterpart, the Blantyre Mission, took the name

---

1. See Ross, *Blantyre Mission*, 41.
2. See Ross, 18–21. Andrew Chirnside, however, was of the view that the Church of Scotland decided to send its mission to this area because it did not want to be seen to be lagging behind the Free Church of Scotland: "Now, with every desire to be just, it is impossible not to feel that jealousy of the Free Church was the chief cause which made the Church of Scotland's Foreign Mission Committee decide to plant a rival mission not far from the projected Livingstonia Mission on Lake Nyassa." See Chirnside, *Blantyre Missionaries*, 8.
3. McCracken, *Politics and Christianity in Malawi*, 58.

of the missionary explorer's birth town back in Scotland, thereby popularizing both his name and his birth place in the mission field.

It has to be noted, however, that the founding of the mission that would be Livingstonia encountered many a problem, and the idea was even abandoned at first, while David Livingstone was still alive. This was so because of changes in the circumstances of the place that the explorer had identified for a mission prior to James Stewart's visit to the area. James Stewart visited the place when it was greatly ravaged by the evils of the slave trade, which David Livingstone had not witnessed in his earlier journey. Consequently, James Stewart advised against establishing a mission station in the area despite his earlier enthusiasm following Livingstone's appeal.[4]

In the meantime, Stewart was sent to South Africa where he worked for over five years, heading the Lovedale Mission and having, to all appearances, forgotten about establishing a mission station – according to David Livingstone's wishes – in the area around Lake Malawi. Whether Stewart had indeed forgotten about the Lake Malawi mission idea is debated among historians. What is not debatable, though, is that when the opportunity came for him to consider the issue again, he was enthusiastically ready to embrace it. This was during the time of David Livingstone's funeral in England, an event which stirred the hearts of many people with regard to the convictions of the great explorer. Even those who had been Livingstone's critics during his life now became admirers and champions of his cause. It was this circumstance that, in a way, encouraged James Stewart to persuade the leadership of the Free Church of Scotland to consider establishing a mission station in the area near Lake Malawi. To do so, he had to argue against the Free Church's idea of establishing a mission in Somalia through Indian connections and prevail over contrary voices.[5]

It was eventually accepted that a mission station should be established for the propagation of the gospel in the area around Lake Malawi, and the task of organizing the recruitment of personnel fell on the shoulders of James Stewart, aided by Rev Dr Alexander Duff, Mr James Stevenson, Mr James White of Overtoun, Dr James Young of Kelly, Sir William McKinnon, Sir

---

4. McCracken, 54.
5. McCracken, 57–58.

John Cowan, Mr John Stephen, Rev Robert Howie of Govan, Dr John Moir of Edinburgh, Rev Dr William Henry Goold and other well-wishers.[6]

One of the most remarkable things about the establishment of the Livingstonia Mission is the ecumenical cooperation that was experienced during the formative period of the mission in Scotland. People of different social and denominational backgrounds joined hands in supporting the mission irrespective of the differences they had with the Free Church of Scotland, which was unmistakably the owner (denominationally speaking) of the mission. Dr John Macrae, who was appointed by the Church of Scotland to chair an African Mission Committee, went as far as addressing an official note to the Free Church's Committee, stating that he was anxious for some form of co-operation with them in this business of African missions.[7] James William Jack reports that on receipt of this note the Foreign Missions Committee of the Free Church of Scotland, under the influence of Dr Alexander Duff, would have gone in for full cooperation or even union, but things did not work out like that because the initiative was only regarded as an extension of the work at Lovedale which was a purely Free Church of Scotland institution.[8] In any case, this incident underscores the fact that even in their embryonic phase the missions of Livingstonia and Blantyre were intertwined and had a common future in the offing.

The Livingstonia Mission as an organization can be taken to have been publicly founded on 8 January 1875 following a meeting that took place in Glasgow in Scotland. The goal of this mission was to spread the Christian faith in the land adjacent to Lake Malawi and to provide some kind of influence for the industrial and commercial development of the area.[9] To that end, the pioneer mission party had to be composed of people of various skills besides their Christian convictions. The following was the team that Dr James Stewart managed to find for the task ahead: Mr George Johnston (carpenter); Mr Allan Simpson (blacksmith); Mr John MacFadyen

---

6. Jack, *Daybreak in Livingstonia*, 30.
7. Jack, 36.
8. Jack, 36.
9. To evangelization and industrial training were added the emphasis on education and medical work. Practically, all three missions that formed the CCAP had these four components in their missionary work even when not emphasized by some. See Laws, *Reminiscences of Livingstonia*, 6; and Elmslie, *Among the Wild Ngoni*, 9.

(engineer); Mr Alexander Riddell (agriculturist) and Mr William Baker (a sailor).[10] In addition to these five, there was Lieutenant Edward Young of the Royal Navy, the leader of the party; Rev Dr Robert Laws of the United Presbyterian Church, the only ordained clergy in the team; and Mr Henry Henderson, the missionary appointed by the established Church of Scotland to scout for what would eventually become Blantyre Mission.[11]

This group of pioneer missionaries left London on 21 May 1875 for South Africa, where they were supposed to rest for some time before embarking on their journey for the interior.[12] They arrived in Cape Town on 17 June 1875 and, after spending a week and a few days in Cape Town, they left on 26 June 1875.[13] It is important to note that the arrival of the missionary party bound for Lake Nyasa attracted a gathering of some eminent men in South Africa. This can partly be explained by the fact that Dr James Stewart had left London ahead of the party in order to arrange for their arrival and departure in South Africa, but also because of the adventure and sensationalism surrounding the purpose of their journey. Of special importance among the people who attended to the missionary party in South Africa was the Rev Dr Robertson of the Dutch Reformed Church, whose own missionaries would in later decades be received by the Blantyre and Livingstonia Mission staff in the field in order to pave way for the establishment of the DRCM in Malawi, which eventually became Nkhoma Synod of the CCAP.[14]

With much difficulty, the missionary party kept on pressing northwards until it reached the southern tip of Lake Malawi in October 1875 and established the first Presbyterian station in the country at Cape Maclear. The CCAP's Synod of Livingstonia is currently associated with the northern region of Malawi, yet the first mission station was in the southern part of the country. From Cape Maclear, circumstances kept on pushing the headquarters of the Livingstonia Mission northwards as we shall see in the succeeding sections of this work. The initial headquarters of the Livingstonia Mission was to be advantageous to the establishment of the Blantyre Mission

---

10. Jack, *Daybreak in Livingstonia*, 37.
11. Jack, 37.
12. Jack, 41.
13. Jack, 41.
14. Jack, 41.

which would greatly need the assistance of some Livingstonia missionaries during a period of crisis. Back in Scotland, when the missions were being formed, the founding fathers had hinted at possible cooperation and even assistance in times of trouble:

> [They] agreed that each Church should have its own distinct settlement at Lake Nyasa [Lake Malawi], with its own stores and supplies, and should send out its own staff of missionaries, under its own Committee; but that the two settlements should not be so far distant from each other as to forbid easy intercourse and possible assistance in time of danger.[15]

What the founders of the missions had feared indeed came to pass between the years 1876 and 1878, as Blantyre Mission found itself in such a crisis that it was inevitable for some Livingstonia senior personnel to go to Blantyre and assist in calming down the situation before the arrival of an able leader for the mission. This happened after Henry Henderson had asked for some assistance from the Livingstonia personnel at a time when Blantyre Mission came to a "standstill and [was] in danger of utter collapse."[16]

The Move to Bandawe and Ministry among the Tonga and the Ngoni

Using Cape Maclear as a base, the missionaries, with the aid of the Ilala (their steam ship named after the district in which David Livingstone had died in Zambia), started exploring the northern and upper parts of the lake. It had become obvious to them that Cape Maclear was not the right place for a mission station even though the place was well suited for a harbour. Eventually, a station that had been founded at Bandawe among the Tonga in 1878 became the new headquarters in 1881.[17] The movement of the mission from Cape Maclear to Bandawe was necessitated by the problem of malaria and the fact that the mission was separated from the surrounding villages. Besides, the activities of those involved in the slave trade made the area not conducive for a mission station at the time.

---

15. Jack, 36.

16. James Stewart of Lovedale to Alexander Duff, 20 December 1876, NLS 7876, quoted in McCracken, *Politics and Christianity in Malawi*, 84.

17. Thompson, *Ngoni, Xhosa and Scot*, 95.

From Bandawe the Livingstonia Mission's influence continued spreading northwards and eventually opened up sub-stations in Njuyu (1882), Ekwendeni (1889), Khondowe (1894) and Loudon (1902).[18] Khondowe was to become the new headquarters of the mission in 1894 after transferring it from Bandawe. In any case, Bandawe was understood to be a temporary headquarters while searching for a more permanent and better place conducive to European settlement.[19]

It was during its settlement at Bandawe that the Livingstonia Mission proved to have come into the country to stay as the fruits of its labour began to manifest. This was mostly due to the fact that the Tonga people readily accepted the presence of the mission in their midst and enthusiastically embraced the schools which the missionaries were establishing. It has to be noted, however, that the Tonga's embracement of the mission was not only because of the Christian message which the missionaries brought but the protection their presence promised in the midst of the upheaval caused by the Ngoni raids in their vicinity. Though not necessarily the policy of the mission, some white people signed agreements with some Tonga chiefs promising them help in the event that they were attacked by the Ngoni or any other enemy. On their part, the Ngoni caused quite a consternation in the eyes of the missionaries, and for a long time they made the missionaries' stay in the country quite precarious because of their warlike culture.[20]

Besides other factors that might have contributed to the pacifying of the Ngoni, the presence of the Livingstonia Mission and all the tactics that the missionaries used played a significant role in making sure that this ethnic group changed its behaviour towards other groups.[21] It has to be noted that right from Cape Maclear after its establishment in the country, the Livingstonia Mission wanted to have an influence among the Ngoni people. To that effect Dr Robert Laws visited the Ngoni Chief Chikuse in a bid to explore the possibility of opening a mission station in his area. However, this did not immediately materialize, and, due to the influence of James Stevenson, who wanted to develop a transport corridor in the north going

---

18. McCracken, *Politics and Christianity in Malawi*, 125, 130, 156, 163.
19. Thompson, *Ngoni, Xhosa and Scot*, 95.
20. See Elmslie, *Among the Wild Ngoni*.
21. Fraser, *Winning a Primitive People*.

all the way to Tanganyika, the influence of the Livingstonia Mission kept on pushing northwards.[22] The result was that the Mission was to eventually have influence on the M'mbelwa Ngoni of northern Malawi rather than on the Chikuse Ngoni of central Malawi.[23]

William Koyi and Other Xhosa Missionaries

In the entire Mission's encounter with the Ngoni, the role played by William Koyi cannot be overemphasized. Koyi was a Lovedale graduate of Xhosa origins who joined the Livingstonia Mission in 1876, together with three fellow Lovedale graduates who had responded to the call to volunteer for missionary work in Malawi after the Scottish missionaries had seen that the work of fellow Africans would be of much help among the inhabitants of Malawi.[24] It was upon the request of those that were in Malawi that Dr James Stewart of Lovedale challenged the young Lovedale gentlemen to enlist for missionary work in Malawi, working alongside their Scottish counterparts.[25] Four young men volunteered for the missionary work in Malawi. These were William Koyi, Mapassa Ntintili, Isaac Williams Wauchope and Shadrack Mngunana. Of the four, it was William Koyi whose contribution to the history of the Synod of Livingstonia in its early years was to have the greatest significance, though during the first months it was mostly Shadrach Mngunana and Mapassa Ntintili whom the Scottish missionaries used to praise for their contributions. It is significant to note that even before reaching their destination, Koyi was already being looked upon as a kind of leader among fellow Xhosa evangelists as can be deduced from Isaac Williams Wauchope's correspondence aboard the *Ansgarius*:

> We are all well yet and hope to be spared to the end. We love one another very much and there are no quarrels among us. We are still looking forward without any doubts and expect to

---

22. Thompson, *From Nyassa to Tanganyika*.
23. The Chikuse Ngoni of Central Malawi were eventually evangelized by the DRC Mission.
24. See Thompson, *Touching the Heart*; and Thompson, *Ngoni, Xhosa and Scot*.
25. Thompson, *Touching the Heart*, 15–24.

face all difficulties like men. William Koyi is *like a father to us and we are like sons to him.*[26]

This description of Koyi by a fellow Xhosa evangelist en route to Malawi was partly because of Koyi's age, which was a bit advanced compared to his friends, but also because of his agreeable and generous spirit which made his presence a blessing to the others.[27]

Besides their work with the Livingstonia Mission, two of the Xhosa missionaries, William Koyi and Mapassa Ntintili, were to contribute significantly to the work of the Blantyre Mission during its early days when the mission almost came to a standstill. Following the plea for help that came from Henry Henderson, Dr Robert Laws and the two James Stewarts (Dr James Stewart of Lovedale and Mr James Stewart, Civil Engineer) heeded the plea and went to provide leadership at Blantyre Mission following the confusion and depression that the Blantyre party experienced from the time when the six founding missionaries joined Henry Henderson who had been sent to scout for a place.

Mapassa Ntintili was the first of the Xhosa missionaries to arrive at Blantyre Mission during the period referred to as "the rescue operation."[28] Due to his carpentry skills, it was felt that Ntintili would be of great help in the work of building Blantyre Mission. Apart from his carpentry contributions, Mapassa Ntintili also contributed in the area of education and was able to produce a good number of schooled young men from his teaching endeavours. One of the most important persons to have been taught by Mapassa Ntintili during his stay at Blantyre Mission, which lasted eighteen months, was Kagaso Sazuze, whom he taught for almost a year. Afterwards, Kagaso Sazuze was able to continue with his education at Lovedale, where he greatly excelled and returned to Malawi in 1883. After returning to Malawi, he was posted to Zomba, where Blantyre Mission had opened an outstation.

---

26. Isaac Williams to Mr Bennie, in *Lovedale News*, 25 October 1876, quoted in Thompson, *Touching the Heart*, 33 (emphasis added).

27. Koyi's personality was responsible for attracting Joseph Bismark to the missionary party as a young man who wanted to go back to his area of birth from Quelimane, where he had found himself after being enslaved as a boy. He was eventually to become a significant figure in Blantyre Mission in his later years, thanks to Koyi who helped him in re-directing the course of his life. See Thompson, *Touching the Heart*, 32–33.

28. Thompson, 64.

He worked in Zomba as a teacher while training as a medical orderly before dying prematurely in 1888.[29]

On the other hand, William Koyi's arrival at Blantyre was a little later in January 1878. He worked side by side with Ntintili in the work of evangelization, and together they experienced the adventures of the early years of Blantyre Mission, especially in the issue of safeguarding the mission from thieves and other ill-intentioned people.[30] The significance of their relations with the Church of Scotland's Blantyre Mission in the late 1870s, as argued by T. Jack Thompson, was that both Ntintili and Koyi played a significant role in ensuring the survival of Blantyre Mission at a time when it was in danger of collapse.[31]

All this shows the intricate interconnectedness of the two missions during their formative years. One cannot help but marvel at the cooperation of the brains behind the establishment of the two missions back in Scotland, the cooperation during the initial voyages of the missionary parties from Scotland to Malawi via South Africa and the cooperation in the mission field, not only in the contribution of the Scottish missionaries but also of the Xhosa missionaries and native Malawians as shown in the succeeding section.

Indigenous Malawians' Contribution to Early Cooperation

It has to be noted that indigenous Malawians also played a significant role in the cooperation that was there during the formative years of the missions that evolved into the CCAP. The first DRC missionaries could not have survived without the assistance of their Scottish colleagues, but more so their work could not have started so successfully if it were not for the help of Malawian Livingstonia "boys." Among these were Tomani and Albert Namalambe and many others from Bandawe Mission who accompanied the DRC missionaries to their new settlement.[32]

When the DRC missionaries A. C. Murray and T. C. B. Vlok established their first school at Mvera, they recruited Tomani, who had come from Cape

---

29. Thompson, 64–68.
30. See Ross, *Blantyre Mission*, 53–54.
31. Thompson, *Touching the Heart*, 73.
32. See Pauw, "Mission and Church in Malawi," 65.

Maclear, as their first teacher.³³ Tomani had been taught by Rev J. H. Bain of the Livingstonia Mission, and he proved to be one of the best pioneer teachers in the DRCM schools.³⁴

Albert Namalambe, the first convert of Livingstonia Mission at Cape Maclear, was a former servant of one of the sons of a Makololo chief named Ramakukani. These sons had joined the mission school but they were not to stay long enough.³⁵ When the royal boys left the mission, Albert remained and eventually distinguished himself as a hardworking boy during the early years of the mission. On 25 March 1881, he was baptized while at Bandawe station after expressing his own wish to do so and with full approval by Dr Robert Laws, who was convinced without doubt of his genuine conversion and zeal for the gospel.³⁶ He later became a teacher and an evangelist. The establishment of Livulezi Mission in 1886 is credited to his successful visit and negotiations with Chief Chikuse in 1885.³⁷ When the Livingstonia Mission moved its headquarters to Bandawe, he was put in charge of the Cape Maclear Mission settlement as an outstation.³⁸ In 1890 he visited Mvera Mission station with two teachers who proved to be of much help in consolidating teaching in the DRCM.³⁹ Some of the early scholars of this initiative include Amoni Phiri Ndiwo who was ordained a minister in 1929.⁴⁰ Albert Namalambe later had a glorious ministry as a teacher and an evangelist in the DRCM after the Livingstonia Mission had transferred him to the former, together with Livulezi and Cape Maclear stations. He is also recognized with Louis Murray as a founder of Malembo Mission station of the DRCM in 1904.⁴¹

---

33. Pauw, 67.
34. Pauw, 67.
35. Livingstone, *Life of Robert Laws of Livingstonia*, 180.
36. Livingstone, 181. A little later Namalambe's wife was also baptized at Bandawe. See Livingstone, 218.
37. See Pauw, "Mission and Church in Malawi," 72; and Jack, *Daybreak in Livingstonia*, 180–181.
38. Jack, *Daybreak in Livingstonia*, 141.
39. Pauw, "Mission and Church in Malawi," 69.
40. Pauw, 69, fn. 83.
41. "List of Founders of Various Mission Stations" (poster at the Nkhoma Museum).

The Move to Khondowe

Having moved the headquarters from Cape Maclear to Bandawe, the Livingstonia missionaries continued to search for a more appropriate place to permanently settle as it was understood that Bandawe – as it was also on the lake – was not very different from Cape Maclear as far as the problems of malaria and hot temperatures were concerned. The next move of the mission headquarters was to go further north and further upwards.

In 1894 the mission headquarters came to Khondowe among the Phoka-Tumbuka people of the hills.[42] The mission headquarters was to remain at Khondowe until the twentieth century when further considerations moved it southwards to Mzuzu City, no longer as the Livingstonia Mission headquarters but as the headquarters of the Synod of Livingstonia of the Church of Central Africa Presbyterian.[43] Khondowe was praised at the time for being a much safer place in terms of malarial attacks and also for having the cool temperature characteristic of a high altitude.[44] One of the significant developments at the new headquarters of Khondowe was the establishment of the Overtoun Institution, an academic institution of the highest quality in the whole of Central Africa during the colonial period.[45]

The Overtoun Institution

The establishment of the Overtoun Institution was one of the most ambitious projects ever attempted by the Scottish missionaries in Malawi during the colonial era. While the institution could not have been there without the imagination and ambition of the Scottish missionaries, much credit is given to Messrs. Overtoun and Stevenson, without whose financial muscle the project would have remained a mere dream with no hope of fulfilment. On the part of indigenous Malawians, it was their receptivity of the Christian message and their desire to have the missionaries settle in their midst that made sure this project succeeded.[46]

---

42. Livingstone, *Laws of Livingstonia*, 276–279.
43. For this move to Mzuzu see Mwangomba, "Life and Work of the Rev Wedson Paul Chibambo and Lucy Chibambo."
44. Morrison, *Forty Years in Darkest Africa*, 10.
45. McCracken, *Politics and Christianity in Malawi*, 171–196.
46. McCracken, 171.

Of especial importance is the fact that despite the many praises that have been showered on Dr Robert Laws and other Scottish missionaries for this singular achievement, the irony is that the project remained controversial throughout the career of Robert Laws from the time he conceived the idea to the time when he retired in 1927.[47] In 1894 for example, Kerr Cross accused Laws of acting as if he were the pope, when trying to highlight Laws's perceived weakness in not consulting others on many issues including his ideas concerning the Overtoun Institution, which according to Cross was a good idea but ill-timed.[48]

Whether one wants to side with Laws at this stage or not, the issue is that despite the criticisms levelled against the institution, it was nevertheless to become very famous in the subsequent years, training many young men (and a smaller number of young women) in this part of the world who could not have had their potential developed if it were not for the presence of this institution in the vicinity of their birth place.[49] It was these very Overtoun Institution graduates that became quite handy for the colonial administration, business people and planters who came to settle in the country after the arrival of the missionaries and the establishment of Christianity and schools. The impact of this institution was felt throughout Southern Africa and beyond as its graduates dispersed.[50]

Emerging African Leadership in Livingstonia Mission

Before the establishment of the Overtoun Institution in 1894, the kind of education that the missionaries were giving to the original inhabitants of the land was quite basic. However, after the establishment of the institution, there was a dramatic change in the kind of stuff to which scholars in mission schools were exposed. In the words of John McCracken:

> By the beginning of the 1890s Laws had become convinced that the creation of a viable Christianity in northern Nyasaland could be achieved only if African teachers, pastors and

---

47. McCracken, 171.
48. McCracken, 173.
49. Thompson, *Ngoni, Xhosa and Scot*, 102.
50. For a discussion of the contributions of this institution see Nyambose, "Establishment and Contribution of the Overtoun Institute."

evangelists were given a more substantial training than that which individual missionaries had been able to provide.[51]

This thinking meant that Laws and the other missionaries had come to a realization that the people they were serving had the potential to achieve greater things if given an opportunity and the necessary support. It was this turn of events that saw the first indigenous African theological students enrolling at Livingstonia, some of whom were to become the first ordained African pastors of the Livingstonia Mission.[52]

Ironically, though, the first generation of Livingstonia missionaries did not want to give full authority to indigenous pastors so that they would be on the same level with the missionaries with regard to pastoral work. In the words of Hamish McIntosh, "It took a long time for Laws and his fellow missionaries to give to the Africans in practice what they readily conceded in words to be their due."[53] I argue that it was this attitude of the Livingstonia missionaries that made the Mission delay the ordination of most of its accomplished and promising scholars, to the frustration of many. It is on record that it took Livingstonia Mission thirty-nine years to ordain its own indigenous pastors from the time of its establishment in the country in 1875. The first Livingstonia indigenous pastors (Yesaya Zerenji Mwasi, Jonathan Chirwa and Hezekia Tweya) were ordained in 1914. This means that despite the participation of Africans in church life, the church within the jurisdiction of the Livingstonia Mission was largely led and controlled by Europeans before 1914 and, to some extent, even beyond as indigenous pastors continued to experience what they perceived to be oppression.[54] On the part of the Scottish missionaries, it was their general belief "that the African is most efficient as an evangelist when guided and controlled."[55]

The behaviour of the missionaries towards emerging African leaders was quite intolerable in certain respects. In the thinking of some of the

---

51. McCracken, *Politics and Christianity in Malawi*, 171–172.

52. See McIntosh, *Robert Laws*, 152.

53. McIntosh, 156.

54. McCracken, *Politics and Christianity in Malawi*, 240. See also "Letter of Yesaya Chibambo 1921 to Livingstonia Mission Council," reproduced in Ross, *Christianity in Malawi*, 155–159.

55. Fraser, *Future of Africa*, 206.

indigenous leaders the behaviour of the Mission was even unchristian in the way it treated African Christians. For example, Charles Domingo lamented:

> Though Christ had dwelt only three years among His disciples and after these times left whole responsibility to them . . . White fellows have been here for nearly 36 years, and not one of them sees a native as his brother, but as his boy, though a native is somehow wiser than he in managing God's work.[56]

I argue that the position which the missionaries had taken put the indigenous pastors in an awkward situation vis-a-vis their missionary counterparts. It is therefore not surprising to find that some of the early African leaders of the Livingstonia Mission, such as Charles Domingo, Kenani Kamwana, the rightfully ordained Yesaya Zerenji Mwasi and others, "rebelled" against the Mission and founded their own denominations, independent of white missionary supervision.[57] Practically, most missionaries saw themselves as superior to Africans, perhaps because of the cultural and technological advancement of their own societies, though some, with the advantage of hindsight, saw things differently as reflected in Alexander Caseby's testimony after he had left the mission field:

> Men and women, mostly from Scotland, became missionaries and travelled to Africa, not to exploit but to explain; not to parade as superiors but to prove equality; not to demand but to share; not to cause friction but to show unity, goodwill and peace. In all my work I treated the African honestly and in deepest faith and in so doing my burdens were eased and all under me knew I, and most missionaries, had dedicated ourselves to uplift every African in sincere work, patient perseverance

---

56. Charles Domingo to Joseph Booth, 19 September 1911, quoted in McCracken, *Politics and Christianity in Malawi*, 259.

57. Yesaya Zerenji Mwasi put his ideas in a document that has been published (with an introduction by Kenneth R. Ross) as a booklet under the Kachere Text series. See Mwasi, *Essential and Paramount Reasons for Working Independently*. One of the Livingstonia indigenous pastors who left the Mission Church was Charles Chidongo Chinula (1885–1971), though, unlike his colleagues, he rejoined the CCAP Synod of Livingstonia before his death. See Phiri, *Chidongo Chinula*, and Ndekha, "Chinula, Charles Chidongo." For a view of some of the notable graduates of this institution see Nyambose, "Establishment and Contribution of the Overtoun Institute."

and all the time prove we were Christians with Christ's love for everyone.[58]

The most important thing at this stage, though, is the observation that, notwithstanding some racial tensions between white missionaries and the emerging Malawian leadership, the Livingstonia Mission, which was by now a Presbytery (since 1899), was ready to come to an amalgamation with the other presbyteries to form the Church of Central Africa Presbyterian (CCAP).

The Blantyre Mission

Just as was the case with the UMCA and Livingstonia Mission, the establishment of Blantyre Mission was also a result of the life and work of Dr David Livingstone in Africa. We have already noted that the enthusiasm on the part of the would-be volunteers for the Blantyre Missionwas not as fervent as is often imagined. However, it can be argued that for its organizers the enthusiasm was just as good as that of the organizers of the Livingstonia Mission. It was actually Dr Macrae who was at the forefront of organizing the recruitment of a missionary party for the establishment of what was to become the Blantyre Mission. Even the identification of Lt. Edward D. Young as the leader of the party, due to his experience in the area of destination, was first made by Dr Macrae. When the Livingstonia Mission people contacted Young for the same purpose, he suggested a joint Scottish mission but his suggestion was not supported by the churches.[59] Eventually, Young had to transfer to the Livingstonia initiative when they appeared to be ready ahead of their Blantyre counterparts. However, the organizers of the two missions remained friendly with each other and continued with cooperation for the success of the two missions' work.

The First Phase of Blantyre Mission History

Due to the cooperation that was taking place in preparation for the establishment of Livingstonia and Blantyre Missions, the departure of the pioneer parties of the two missions would almost have taken place at the same time. Owing to the delays of recruitment of the Blantyre Mission

---

58. Caseby, *Going with God*, 194.
59. MacDonald, *Africana or Heart of Heathen Africa*, 19.

volunteers, the missionary party was not yet ready when their Livingstonia Mission colleagues were ready to depart for the field. However, in the spirit of cooperation, Henry Henderson, an experienced farmer and scout, was recruited in order to accompany the Livingstonia Mission pioneer party so that he could search for a suitable site for the establishment of the mission in preparation for the arrival of the pioneer missionaries of what would become Blantyre Mission.[60]

In October 1875, Henry Henderson arrived with the Livingstonia party in the area where he was to scout for the site of a mission for the established Church of Scotland. With the aid of some interpreters, especially Tom Bokwito, Henderson toured the Shire Highlands and settled for an area under Chief Kapeni. It is significant to note that Chief Kapeni, just like Chief Mponda of the Lake Shore area in whose land the Livingstonia Missionary party had established themselves, was supportive of the "English" settling in his area because he thought they would provide some kind of protection for him from the raiding Ngoni who were terrorizing the area at the time.[61] To be established in an area where the locals, including their traditional leadership, wanted its presence was an advantage for Blantyre Mission.

While Henry Henderson was already in Africa, there was not yet a group of missionaries to follow him as the Blantyre missionaries. This made the Church of Scotland Foreign Mission Committee anxious about the recruitment of the pioneer missionary party. Consequently, they softened considerably on the qualifications of the people who were to go out for missionary work at Blantyre, with disastrous consequences during the mission's formative period due to the behaviour of some personnel with less, if any, Christian convictions.[62]

The pioneer missionary party of Blantyre Mission was composed of Dr T. Thornton Macklin, John Buchanan, George Fenwick, Jonathan Duncan, William Milne and John Walker. Thornton, a medical doctor, was the leader of the party and he and John Buchanan are described as dedicated Christian men.[63] The unfortunate thing with the Blantyre party, though, was that it

---

60. Ross, *Blantyre Mission*, 19.
61. McCracken, *Politics and Christianity in Malawi*, 72.
62. Ross, *Blantyre Mission*, 19.
63. Ross, 19.

had no ordained minister in its midst, a thing which made the spiritual direction of the mission a very challenging job despite the Christian zeal of the leader. This problem was accentuated by the unbecoming behaviour of some members of the party, especially Walker and Fenwick, who became notoriously evil in their dealings with the locals, putting the mission and the church in general in a very negative light in the midst of "heathenism."[64]

Between late 1876 and 1878 the Blantyre missionaries had to rely on the services of their sister mission of Livingstonia for spiritual leadership and other responsibilities which the Blantyre team could not manage on its own.[65] This explains the presence of Dr Robert Laws, Dr James Stewart of Lovedale, Mr James Stewart (civil engineer), and the two Xhosa missionaries, Mapassa Ntintili and William Koyi, at Blantyre Mission during some periods of this time.[66] It was actually Henry Henderson himself who appealed for assistance from the Livingstonia missionaries – and this was quite in agreement with the foresight of the organizers of the missions back in Scotland who had envisaged a time when cooperation in the field would be needed.[67]

The Foreign Mission Committee of the Church of Scotland considered it a humiliation that up to 1877 there was not even a single ordained minister coming forward to volunteer for the work of Blantyre Mission.[68] Relief came to the organizers of the Blantyre Mission in November 1877 when the Rev Duff MacDonald accepted their request to go to Blantyre.[69]

The arrival of the Rev Duff MacDonald was a great relief to both the Livingstonia leaders, who had shouldered the responsibility of caring for the two missions, and the Blantyre missionaries, who did not have a spiritual leader of their own. Immediately after his arrival, Duff MacDonald set to work, and he was able to make a lot of progress with the Yao language, which was the dominant language in the area then. He also committed himself to

---

64. Ross, 20–21.
65. Ross, 21.
66. Thompson, *Touching the Heart*, 59–73.
67. Ross, *Blantyre Mission*, 40.
68. Ross, 21.
69. Ross, 63.

the preaching of the word, making sure that the mission was able to do that for which it had been established.[70]

The biggest problem for the missionaries at Blantyre during this time was the precarious position they found themselves in due to the questions of civil jurisdiction as they had no real government to relate with. Prior to MacDonald's arrival, some of the Blantyre missionaries were already involved in scandals of beating people and relating to the surrounding chiefs in a manner that was not expected of Christian missionaries. Since they did not see the "native chiefdoms" of either Chief Kapeni or other chiefs as properly constituted government, these Blantyre missionaries took the law into their own hands, as it were, and dealt with civil matters as they saw fit, often ending up in abusing their position as Christian missionaries.[71]

Due to this background, it is not surprising that when one Mr Andrew Chirnside, a traveller, visited the area and the mission in 1879, he was horrified by the floggings and abuses that were taking place at the mission. When he went back to Scotland, Mr Chirnside published his experiences of the Blantyre Mission visit, highlighting the issue of executions and floggings which he witnessed or heard about.[72] This publication caused a scandal in Scotland and the Church of Scotland had to do something about it. Consequently, the Church of Scotland appointed Dr D. J. Rankin of Muthill and Mr Alexander Pringle, a lawyer from Edinburgh, to go and find out about the issues as Commissioners of Inquiry.[73]

The result of the Commission of Inquiry was the dismissal of Duff MacDonald, John Buchanan and George Fenwick from the mission. The two notorious fellows, Macklin and Walker, had already left their missionary employment, and so they could not be punished by merely dismissing them from the mission. Since the United Kingdom's government, which had been informed of the atrocities, left everything in the hands of the church, nothing could be done against those who had left the church's employ.[74]

---

70. Ross, 47.
71. MacDonald, *Africana or Heart of Heathen Africa*, 82.
72. Chirnside, *Blantyre Missionaries*.
73. Ross, *Blantyre Mission*, 56.
74. Church of Scotland, *Assembly Reports*, 78.

The sub-committee of the Foreign Mission Committee of the Church of Scotland was aware of the exercise of civil jurisdiction by the Blantyre missionaries as it had instructed them on many occasions earlier on that they were to establish a mission station as a kind of Christian colony, which means that they could not run away from exercising a measure of civil jurisdiction.[75] Ironically, Duff MacDonald was opposed to that policy and he attempted to extricate himself from such responsibilities by refusing to act as a magistrate. The same was true concerning Henry Henderson, who also could not happily "don a magistrate's robe."[76] MacDonald's practice of handing over runaways who were seeking refuge from the mission station in his bid not to burden himself with civil matters coincided with Chirnside's visit, who, without understanding the situation, felt sending people back to the local native authorities was more like signing their death warrants.[77] MacDonald was therefore punished for the bad which he did not do and was not praised for the good which he was doing, which eventually became the new policy, emphasizing that the missionaries of Blantyre were to have nothing to do with civil jurisdiction. This was a point which the church authorities later admitted had been vague and yet they seem to have supported it as a policy earlier on prior to the atrocities that are reported to have taken place. As Andrew Ross argues, "One can come to no other conclusion than that Duff MacDonald was made scapegoat for the African mission sub-committee, whose policy he had consistently opposed."[78] In 1882, the Commission of Inquiry's report and the facts of the Blantyre Mission atrocities were revisited, and it was found out that Duff MacDonald was not to blame, though the damage had already been done and there were no further follow-ups on the issue. This saga in a way marks the end of the first phase of Blantyre Mission, and it is significant to note that in the year 1882 there came new leaders for both the Mission and the sub-committee of the Church of Scotland's Foreign Mission Committee by the names of David Clement Scott and Dr Archibald Scott of St George's, respectively.[79]

---

75. Ross, *Blantyre Mission*, 56–57.
76. Ross, 56.
77. Ross, 57.
78. Ross, 57.
79. Ross, 61.

Blantyre Mission "Re-founded"

It is generally believed by many church historians that the year 1881 marked the re-founding of the Blantyre Mission. In any case, the negative stories of the past had to go and a new foundation had to be established. However, it can be argued that, had the Rev Duff MacDonald remained at Blantyre, he could perhaps have done great things for the Mission. If we consider his zeal and abilities, his short stay in the country brought to an end what would have been a great missionary career; perhaps, if he were to live and stay long enough, a career not very different from that of Robert Laws.

It was David Clement Scott whose mark on the history of Blantyre Mission was to have lasting results. Andrew Ross has observed that D. C. Scott saw the task of the missionary as being both a bearer of the gospel and of modern culture.[80] This was so because he considered the culture brought by the missionaries not simply as European culture but as modern culture in which all the peoples of the world were to participate. Despite his mistakes in certain instances in regard to his understanding of African culture, Scott was a champion of the Africanization of the church in order for it to be grounded in African forms. He thus expressed himself: "Our purpose we lay down as the foundation of all our work that we are building the African Church – not Scotch or English – but African. Rather we should say the African portion of the 'one Catholik and Apostolik Church.'"[81] After the unfortunate incidents referred to as the Blantyre Scandal, some authorities in the Church of Scotland were of the view that the Mission should have nothing to do with industrial development or a civilizing role except the preaching of the gospel to the natives. This position was reached, especially, through the recommendations of the report of the Commission of Inquiry mandated to investigate the Blantyre atrocities. Though Rev Scott was fully aware of this position, he pursued an agenda that was in many ways contrary to this view – continuing with industrial activities and the civilizing role of the mission. His argument was that unless the missionary "cut himself from all that is human and declare himself an ascetic, or unless he falls below the

---

80. Ross, 63.
81. *Life and Work in British Central Africa, April 1895.* Quoted in Ross, *Blantyre Mission*, 146.

appreciation of culture, he must perforce take an interest in and develop the people around him to the best of his ability."[82]

Some of D.C. Scott's most significant contributions to the church in Central Africa were the building of St Michael's and All Angels Church, which still stands today as an icon of the success of the nineteenth-century missionary endeavours in Malawi, and his publication of the *Cyclopaedic Dictionary of the Mang'anja Language*, considered by many scholars to have been no mean achievement at the time.[83] Scott is also fondly remembered for the training of many African evangelists who were to form the nucleus of the future church.[84]

Scott's leadership of Blantyre Mission was, however, not without controversy. While he was regarded by the indigenous Africans as a very religious and friendly person who had the welfare of the African at heart, he had no sympathy from many European settlers in the Shire Highlands who were planters and traders. The other quarter of animosity against Scott came from the Foreign Mission Committee of the Church of Scotland and from some missionaries of Blantyre Mission who did not like his style of leadership, especially in the way he administered the Missionary Council and his accommodating attitude towards native customs. He was also criticized for promoting black leadership in the church. It seems there were just so many things that Scott was enthusiastic about which did not please many quarters except the target of missions in the catchment area of Blantyre Mission.[85]

Andrew Ross has observed, in line with Stephen Neil's argument, that the second half of the nineteenth century was the period of a fundamental shift in the way missionaries operated in the field. Whereas before this time there was a lot of freedom on the part of missionaries in the field to act independently of the home committee with regard to the administration of the mission church, that freedom was now being minimized, with the home committees gaining a lot of supervisory influence on what was happening

---

82. *Life and Work in British Central Africa, December 1893*. Quoted in Ross, *Blantyre Mission*, 145.

83. Ross, *Blantyre Mission*, 143.

84. Ross, 151–153. See also Ross, "Vernacular Translation in Christian Mission," 107–126.

85. For a detailed discussion of these issues see Ross, *Blantyre Mission*, 158–159.

in the field, with the result that there was less leeway for innovation on the part of the missionaries.[86] This was also the period when the mission council gained prominence in the mission field as it formed a link between the home committee and the church of the mission field.

Ross argues that Scott's way of doing things at Blantyre was totally different as the Mission Council was not active, to say the least. This means that Scott was the sole leader of the mission and he directed most if not all things according to his own thinking. This arrangement seems to have been fine with the missionaries who were in one way or another close to Scott – and they were in the majority during the early years of Scott's administration.[87] However, when new missionaries who were not related or somehow personally close to Scott arrived on the scene they resented his leadership style and reported home negatively about him and sometimes even caused trouble for him in the Protectorate. The response of the FMC on this issue, after instituting a Commission of Inquiry, was that there should be more regular meetings of the missionary council and that it should be active in its work. This obviously had a negative effect on Scott who, in many ways, was used to his own way of heading the mission, with results that satisfied him in as far as the growth of the church in Malawi was concerned.[88] During David Clement Scott's tenure, the work of Blantyre Mission spread to many places where other mission stations were opened, such as Domasi and Zomba (1885), Chiradzulu (1887), Mulanje (1890) and Ntcheu (1893).[89]

On the issue of Scott's sympathy towards African cultural elements, he was accused of tolerating what was not holy enough in the church. On this point it can be argued with the advantage of hindsight that Scott was ahead of most of his contemporaries in understanding the importance of African cultural elements for the growth and vitality of the church in Africa. His belief in the ability of native leadership made him ordain some of his outstanding students to the position of deacons in order to prepare them for ordination as full church ministers. It has been observed that the ordination

---

86. See Neil, *History of Christian Missions*, 510; and Ross, *Blantyre Mission*, 143–144.
87. See Robertson, *Martyrs of Blantyre*, 148–149; and Ross, *Blantyre Mission*, 158–159.
88. Andrew Ross does not hide his admiration and defence of D. C. Scott. See Ross, *Blantyre Mission*, 163.
89. Abale-Phiri, "Interculturalisation as Transforming Praxis," 41.

of Scott's deacons was not, as generally understood in the Presbyterian sense, that of lay servants in the day to day running of the church's activities under the leadership of elders but more akin to the Anglican understanding, where deacons are just below the position of priests on the way to their own priestly ordination. It was to this "Deacons' Court," as it has come to be known, that Scott frequently resorted in order to discuss matters affecting the African church. This tendency, plus some innovations he initiated in the liturgy for the African church, made Scott to be accused of being a "traitor" of the Presbyterian system while subtly introducing High Church Anglicanism. This was quite anathema for most Scots at the time who felt that their Presbyterianism should be guarded at all cost whether at home or abroad.[90]

Another important issue on which Scott differed with most of his contemporaries was that of racial unity in the church. While most Europeans during this time considered themselves superior to Africans and therefore not free to associate with them on the same level, Scott was encouraging European members of the church in the Shire Highlands to mingle with their African brothers and sisters in matters both social and religious. To that effect, Scott promoted the mixing of races in both the local language church worship and in that of the English service, for to him it was a true mark of Christianity if black and white Christians fellowshipped together.[91] The conservative white party did not like that idea and tensions continued in the church until it became inevitable later for the white Christians to separate from their African brothers and sisters in congregational life.

Due to the pressure of opposition to his ideas from the FMC and unwilling colleagues in the field, coupled with his personal crisis after the loss of his wife and brother within a month, Scott's health deteriorated and he was forced to resign from Blantyre Mission and head for Scotland in 1898. After staying home for a short time, Scott proceeded to another missionary posting among the Kikuyu in Kenya where he died in 1907. It is not surprising

---

90. Ross, *Blantyre Mission*, 165.

91. D. C. Scott was very much for the idea of an African Church that was free from the "isms" of Europe.

that Scott was greatly missed by the African church in the jurisdiction of Blantyre Mission.[92]

After Scott's tenure of leadership, the Blantyre Mission was led by Alexander Hetherwick who for a long time had been Scott's right hand man in the work of the mission. As a member of Scott's inner circle, Hetherwick did not completely break with Scott's views though it was very difficult for him to continue with the way Scott was doing it. It became obvious to Hetherwick that in some situations he just had to bow down to the inevitable. He was, however, able to utilize the solid foundation laid by Scott in such a way that the church continued to flourish under his leadership. The stations opened during Scott's leadership continued to grow, and the Henry Henderson Institute was opened in 1909.[93] Another significant event was the ordination of the first Blantyre Mission Malawian pastors in 1911, by the names of Harry Kambwiri Matecheta and Stephen Kundecha.[94] It is Hetherwick who is credited with the success of steering Blantyre Mission towards the formation of the CCAP during the early and mid-1920s.[95]

The Dutch Reformed Church Mission

The Dutch Reformed Church Mission, which eventually evolved into the Nkhoma Synod of the CCAP, was formally established in the country in 1889 through its first missionary, A. C. Murray, who arrived in the country in 1888.[96] It is interesting to note how even the establishment of the DRCM in Malawi was intricately connected with the Scottish Presbyterian missions of Livingstonia and Blantyre.[97]

---

92. An obituary of D. C. Scott that appeared in the *LWBCA* of September/October 1907 by Mungo Chisuse expressed the sorrow the people had at the news of the passing of D. C. Scott. Chisuse, however, rhetorically explained that the people were amazed at the news of his death since they had been mourning him since 1898 when he left Blantyre. For a later appreciation of Scott's ministry see Ross, "*Wokondedwa Wathu*," 2–7.

93. McCracken, *Politics and Christianity in Malawi*, 171.

94. Weller and Linden, *Mainstream Christianity to 1980 in Malawi, Zambia and Zimbabwe*, 119.

95. Ross, *Blantyre Mission*, 193–194.

96. Pauw, "Mission and Church in Malawi," 59–61.

97. Pauw, 45–56.

Due to the influence of the Foreign Mission Committee of the Free Church of Scotland, which was responsible for the establishment of the Livingstonia Mission, the leadership of the Dutch Reformed Church in South Africa came to a consideration of starting their own mission in Malawi near where the Scottish Presbyterian missions had already established themselves for over a decade.[98] Further encouragement came from Dr James Stewart of Lovedale, who even proposed that the South African Mission could be hosted by the Livingstonia Mission and use that mission as a base for their own establishment in the country.[99]

The body that became responsible for this initiative was the newly founded *Predikanten Zending Vereniging* [Ministers' Mission Union(MMU)] which was a semi-independent organization of the Dutch Reformed Church with the aim of sending out missionaries for the work of evangelization in distant places.[100] The founding of this union by pastors, who wanted to spread the faith using an organization that was parallel to the church's own Foreign Mission Committee, is in total agreement with the observation that it was missionary societies rather than churches or denominations that promoted the work of missions.[101] In the case of the MMU, the Foreign Missionary Committee had given them a go ahead in their work on condition that they would not burden the committee with requests for funds and that they would be sending reports to the committee and consulting it before making any important decisions.[102]

The Rev A. C. Murray was ready to sail for Malawi in June 1888 after returning from Scotland where he had gone to train himself in the science of medicine in preparation for work in the mission field.[103] When A. C. Murray arrived in Malawi, he had to spend some time at the Church of Scotland's Blantyre Mission while waiting for the steamer to take him up north from Matope to Bandawe, which was then the headquarters of the

---

98. Pauw, 55.

99. *Die Kerkbode*, 25 June 1886, 203–204, cited in Pauw, "Mission and Church in Malawi," 56.

100. Pauw, "Mission and Church in Malawi," 56.

101. Walls, "Missionary Societies and the Fortunate Subversion of the Church," 141–155.

102. Pauw, "Mission and Church in Malawi," 59.

103. Pauw.

Livingstonia Mission. Murray's stay at Blantyre Mission was his first exposure to how mission work was being carried out in the country. He was greatly assisted by the generosity of his hosts, the Rev and Mrs D. C. Scott, from whom he also learned some approaches of missionary work even if his own approach was to be different from what he had observed, as evidenced from the following quote:

> We are not sent out, I think, to civilise peoples, but to convert them. Not to give them a high secular education, but to "teach them to keep all things" which our Lord and Master commanded. Let those who will be our helpers as evangelists, catechists or teachers, learn what is necessary for their work, but as far as the people in general are concerned, let us impress the Word of God upon them in all possible ways, and furthermore teach them to read the Bible for themselves in their own language.[104]

Afterwards, Murray left Blantyre Mission for Bandawe station of the Livingstonia Mission where he was supposed to be hosted while searching for a suitable site for the establishment of a mission station for the DRCM. After spending some days at Bandawe, Murray, accompanied by Mr Bain and other Livingstonia missionaries, headed farther north in search of a place for a mission station, and he did find what he thought would be a suitable site at the village of Kararamuka.[105] However, after staying for some time at this place, he fell sick and was not able to move for some days. The Livingstonia missionaries transported him back to Bandawe, and Robert Laws was making plans to have him repatriated to South Africa, when, all of a sudden, his health returned back to him.[106] Because of the improvement in his health the plan to have him repatriated was abandoned. Instead, he was sent to Njuyu Mission, which was under Dr and Mrs Elmslie, to continue with his recuperation since the place was considered healthier than Bandawe. His stay at Njuyu provided A. C. Murray with more opportunities to learn how the Livingstonia Mission was doing its missionary work.[107]

---

104. Murray, *Nyasaland en mijne ondervindingen*, 79, translated from the Dutch and quoted in Pauw, "Mission and Church in Malawi," 60.
105. Pauw, "Mission and Church in Malawi," 61.
106. Parsons, "Scots and Afrikaners in Central Africa," 24–25.
107. Pretorius, "Introduction to the History," 122.

DRCM Stations Established

Due to his experience of ill health, A. C. Murray felt the place in the north of the lake was not good enough for the establishment of a mission station, so he decided to go to a different place, towards the southwest of the lake from Bandawe, farther into the interior. Apart from the unhealthiness of the place, there were Arab slave traders in the area which also made the area quite unsafe at the time. Besides, Murray was of the view that the area was under Livingstonia Mission's influence. While Murray was at Njuyu, Dr Robert Laws communicated to Murray's authorities in South Africa that there was need for another missionary to come and be colleagues with Murray. The missionary who came in response to this suggestion was the Rev T. C. B. Vlok who arrived at Bandawe in 1889, and from there they set off for another search for a suitable site for the establishment of the Dutch Reformed Church Mission.[108]

After many an adventure travelling southwards towards what is now the Central Region of Malawi, A. C. Murray and T. C. B. Vlok pitched their tent in the area of Chief Chiwere. Here they waited for the chief to grant them permission to settle in his country, and once permission was granted, they established their station near a hill called Mvera. Choosing from various options of a name for their mission, they settled for the name Mvera, which had some connections to their purpose of preaching the gospel as the name means "to listen or obey."[109]

The DRCM missionaries set to the task of establishing themselves in the field by opening a school at Mvera and attending to village evangelistic meetings. A medical practice was also established at the station with A. C. Murray treating the patients.[110] The first teacher of the school at Mvera was Tomani, who had been trained by Rev J. H. Bain of the Livingstonia Mission and had come from Cape Maclear. Later, many school teachers and assistants came from the Livingstonia Mission station of Bandawe to work with the DRCM.

---

108. Pauw, "Mission and Church in Malawi," 62–53.

109. Tracing the origin of the name "Mvera," P. A. Cole-King argued that it was named thus because it was a rallying point whenever the chief called his people to arms by drumming from his headquarters. See Cole-King, "Lilongwe," 17. Also Pauw, "Mission and Church in Malawi," 66.

110. Pauw, "Mission and Church in Malawi," 69.

It was observed that attendance at church services both at the station and in the surrounding villages was at first very high but later on it went down. Consequently, the missionaries made a rule that whoever was employed by the mission or wanted to deal with the mission in matters of medicine and trade had to be attending the morning prayers at the station. This policy retained a good number of people who continued to listen to the preaching of the gospel.[111]

The first permanent church was built at Mvera in 1898. Work progressed well, so much so that by the year 1900 the number of baptized Christians in the mission register reached 151 names.[112] The first children of Christians are recorded to have been baptized on 13 November 1898.[113] More missionaries were also added to the original number as the years progressed. The first to arrive was Robert Blake in 1892. Later J. S. Cridland and Miss Martha Murray also arrived. Miss Martha Murray was the first lady worker of the DRC Mission in Malawi. In 1894 W. H. Murray, who was to succeed A. C. Murray, arrived. Among the first band of missionaries to work for the DRCM in Malawi three had died before 1899. These were Mrs Vlok, who died at Livulezi in 1895, Rev Koos du Toit, who died at Nkhoma in 1897, and J. S. Cridland, who died at Kongwe in 1898.[114]

In 1896 a mission was opened in Chief Mazengera's area at the foot of Nkhoma Mountain. This event was very important in the history of the DRCM as this station would eventually become the headquarters of DRCM in Malawi in 1912.[115] More mission stations were opened after 1896 in Chief Mpezeni's area in what is now the eastern province of Zambia. The pioneer missionaries sent there were Revs P. J. Smith and J. M. Hofmeyr who opened Magwero Mission in 1899. The next decade saw four more stations being opened – namely, Madzimoyo in 1903, Chipata in 1905, Nyanje in 1905 and Nsadzu in 1907.[116]

---

111. Pauw, 67.

112. Pauw, 70.

113. CCA, "Mvera Mission Log Book," S5 15.6.11.4., 13 November 1898, cited in Pauw, "Mission and Church in Malawi," 70.

114. Pauw, "Mission and Church in Malawi," 72.

115. Pauw, 74.

116. Pauw, 76. It has to be noted that the mission stations established in Zambia did not become part of the CCAP. The work of the Malawi DRCM in Zambia was taken over

Separation from Livingstonia Mission

From the beginning of its establishment the DRCM was founded as a separate mission, but due to circumstances of lack of capacity during its formative years it operated as a department or a branch of Livingstonia Mission until 1898 when it formed its own Mission Council. This was after the Home Committee had given the missionaries in the field the mandate to do so in the previous year. From then onwards, the DRCM would continue to cooperate with the Livingstonia Mission but was no longer required to report to its Council. One area of cooperation that continued for a time was the training of the workers of DRCM at the Overtoun Institution until 1903, when the DRCM institute was built at Mvera. In the same year, another significant development happened. Previously, all aspects of the work of the mission had to be discussed at the Mission Council meeting, but a special council of congregations was formed with the mandate of dealing with matters concerning the ecclesiastical development of the work and to advise the council.[117]

Christoff Martin Pauw disagrees with John McCracken's interpretation of the separation of the two missions. Whereas McCracken explains the independence of the DRCM from Livingstonia as a mission pluralism challenge in the sphere of the Scottish Presbyterian missions, Pauw considers the event a natural sequel to the developments that had taken place up until this time and also argues that this was what was agreed upon right from the beginning. Indeed, it is strange for McCracken to explain it the way he does. I totally agree with Pauw that the DRCM had to wean itself from the Livingstonia Mission at one time, and there were no ill feelings about it as the plans of the two missions were not a guarded secret. Besides, one is tempted to conclude here that McCracken did not take much time to study the Livingstonia/DRCM relationship during the formative years of the DRCM (which was not his aim anyway) and consequently made unfortunate

---

by the Synod of the Orange Free State of the DRC and these eventually separated from the Malawian work, later developing into the Reformed Church in Zambia. See also Pauw, 101.

117. Pauw, 82.

statements concerning the DRCM missionaries whom he had to mention in passing in his reconstruction of the Livingstonia Mission story.[118]

Challenges Unique to the DRCM

In the years that followed, the Dutch Reformed Church Mission experienced challenges as well as blessings that were unique to them, owing to their South African origin. On the side of challenges, the mission found itself in a very awkward position between 1899 and 1902 and immediately after. This was the period during which the Afrikaners and the British fought in South Africa in what has come to be known in history as the Anglo-Boer War. Since the DRCM was an Afrikaner mission, it meant that they were operating in enemy territory in Malawi as the country was at the time under British colonial rule. A cloud of suspense, therefore, hung on the DRCM missionaries as they could not know what the Colonial Government's move could be against them, given the circumstances. Apart from this uncertainty, this was also a period of rapid missionary turnover due to deaths and illnesses in the midst of a financial crisis.[119]

The MMU Hands over Responsibility to the General Mission Committee of the Cape DRC Synod

In 1903 the MMU handed over its responsibility of the DRCM in Malawi to the newly created General Mission Committee of the Cape DRC Synod. At its first meeting this committee elected a Malawi sub-committee to be specifically responsible for the DRCM in Malawi. However, the MMU was not abolished as it continued to exist, functioning as a supporting body which could make annual contributions to the General Mission Committee fund.[120]

From 1904 onwards the mission experienced unprecedented growth and it expanded its work in various activities, for example, education, agriculture,

---

118. See McCracken, *Politics and Christianity in Malawi*, 216; Pauw, "Mission and Church in Malawi," 80–81. It has to be noted that Pauw quotes McCracken's words on this issue as appearing on page 175 while the present research is quoting page 216. The reason for the difference of page number being that the current research is using the 2000 edition published by CLAIM and Kachere (ISBN 1025-0964) whereas Pauw used the first edition published by Cambridge University Press in 1977 (ISBN 0-521-2144-0).

119. Pauw, "Mission and Church in Malawi," 82–86.

120. DRC, *Acta*, 1903, 44–45, 60–62 and CCA, S5 1.1.2, 1 November 1903. Both sources cited in Pauw, "Mission and Church in Malawi," 85.

medical work and industrial activities. It must be noted here that though A. C. Murray and other pioneer missionaries were, in their missionary policy, generally against playing a civilizing role, even the DRC Mission evolved into an industrial mission as circumstances dictated that it respond to needs as they arose in the mission field. This position was reached long before the DRCM joined with the other Presbyterian missions or presbyteries to form the CCAP.

The Formation of the CCAP

When the CCAP was finally formed in 1924 with the union of the two Scottish Presbyterian missions, it was a fulfilment of the dreams of men like Robert Laws and David Clement Scott who had the vision of an African church unencumbered by European divisions right from the dawn of their missionary work. It will, however, be shown that the union achieved did not go all the way to fulfil the dream of the early missionaries.

David Clement Scott of Blantyre Mission was of the view, which was later inherited by his successor, Alexander Hetherwick, that a church created by African evangelists should have some freedom to develop in its own way.[121] To this end Scott wanted very much to have a church that would be fully in the hands of Africans. This desire of Scott's was fully in line with the thinking of Robert Laws who, as early as 1893, had propagated the formation of a United Presbyterian Church out of the congregations of the Church of Scotland's Blantyre Mission, the DRC Mission and the Livingstonia Mission. He thus expressed his wish: "I do not believe . . . that we should merely be a presbytery of the home church; we should work towards a Central African Presbyterian Church, which would include Blantyre and the Dutch."[122] The ideas of a unified church which had been conceived in the late nineteenth century were to develop further and bear fruit in the twentieth century. As early as 1900, there were several efforts at cooperation among the missions that were in the Malawian field. At the General Missionary Conference of 1900, which took place at Livingstonia, the missionaries agreed that their

---

121. Ross, *Blantyre Mission*, 174.
122. Livingstone, *Laws of Livingstonia*, 260. See also Pauw, "Mission and Church in Malawi," 265.

aim should be the establishment of a self-supporting and self-propagating native church.[123]

In 1903 Hetherwick revived Dr Laws's proposal for a united church which he had proposed earlier on. More discussions were to take place at the 1904 Missionary Conference between the representatives of the two Scottish Presbyterian presbyteries of Livingstonia and Blantyre, which had been established in 1899 and 1902, respectively. Though encouraging, the discussion between the two presbyteries still had some areas to be ironed out. Some of the questions raised had to do with the issue of theological basis, the number of missions to be involved and the disciplinary code to be established.[124] Another complication at this stage was the fact that, whereas Blantyre Presbytery was a presbytery of the home Church of Scotland, the Livingstonia Presbytery had a greater level of autonomy as it was not under the home church. A compromise was proposed, suggesting that the new synod to be formed should be a purely African synod, with the European missionaries remaining members of their home churches as separate congregations.

During the third Missionary Conference of 1910 at Mvera Mission, a formal meeting took place between the Blantyre and Livingstonia presbyteries, with the DRCM missionaries A. L. Hofmeyr and A. G. Murray acting as observers. The meeting agreed to have the two presbyteries united into one synod of a common church or denomination.[125] Opinion, though, was divided with regard to the actual name of the new church to be formed. Donald Fraser of Livingstonia Mission was of the view that the name of this church should just be "The Church of Central Africa," but he was opposed by Alexander Hetherwick who wanted the word "Presbyterian" added at the end. After voting, those that wanted the name Presbyterian won the day and from that time onwards the name has remained like that. Upon the presbyteries communicating with their mother churches back in Scotland, both the United Free Church of Scotland's General Assembly and that of the Church of Scotland agreed to the proposal, paving way for the establishment of the Synod of the CCAP.

---

123. Pauw, "Mission and Church in Malawi," 266.
124. Pauw, 267.
125. Pauw, 268.

The Church of Central Africa was open to other missions that were willing to join the union. During the early days Robert Laws hoped that the London Missionary Society in Zambia and the German missions in Tanganyika would join, but later historical events took a different direction.[126]

While most arrangements for unification had been completed by 1914, the actual amalgamation was to wait for another decade, mostly due to the disturbance caused by the First World War. A few more years passed after the war before the union could be consummated on 17 September 1924, with Livingstonia and Blantyre presbyteries becoming one synod of the Church of Central Africa Presbyterian (CCAP).[127] The most obvious candidate to join the union within Malawi after the two Scottish presbyteries was the DRCM Nkhoma Mission, owing to its cooperation with and affinity for the Scottish Presbyteries both in terms of theology and history. It has to be noted that the DRCM had three spheres of work in this region of Africa – namely, Malawi, Zambia and Mozambique. It was the intention of the DRCM to amalgamate its presbyteries of Zambia, Mozambique and Malawi into a Synod before joining the CCAP. However, the end of the DRCM's mission work in Mozambique in 1922 and the handing over of Livingstonia's Kasungu station to the DRCM were factors which, according to Christoff Martin Pauw, "swung the pendulum in favour of the Nkhoma section of the DRCM joining the CCAP."[128]

It took two years for the Nkhoma Mission to join the union. The reasons for this delay were many. First, it was the reluctance of the DRCM to accept the wording of the first article of the statement of faith for the united church.[129] Though this could not be changed, the DRCM was given leeway to interpret the statement according to its own taste, which was more of a compromise. Second, there was the issue of the influence of the DRC on the union. There was a proposal that the DRC should reserve the right to pull Nkhoma out of the union if it deemed it necessary to do so in certain

---

126. Bolink, *Towards Church Union in Zambia*, 194–196; Pauw, "Mission and Church in Malawi," 265.

127. Pauw, "Mission and Church in Malawi," 270.

128. Pauw, 271.

129. The article reads: "The Word of God, which is contained in the Scriptures of the Old and New Testament, is the supreme rule of faith and conduct." CCAP, "Extracts of Minutes of Synod 1924–1945," 4.

circumstances. This proposal could not be accepted by the Scottish missionaries who wanted all the presbyteries to have the full rights of continuing or withdrawing from the union without undue pressure from the mother churches. The last issue was the fear of Scottish liberalism on the part of the DRCM, whose theological position was conservative (in the evangelical sense of the word). The DRCM needed some kind of assurance from their Scottish colleagues that the Church in Central Africa would not be influenced by the so-called modernistic teaching of the Christian faith which, according to them, was not in tandem with orthodoxy.[130]

Once these issues had been ironed out, the way was open for the Nkhoma Presbytery to be received into the union, and this was officially done in 1926. The presbyteries were now free to discuss issues pertaining to the African church independently, though the mother churches of the missions retained some jurisdiction over their missionaries. Pauw has noted:

> Although now united in one Church, the three presbyteries still retained a large degree of independence and autonomy in such matters as the training, licensing, ordination and appointment of ministers as well as oversight and discipline over them, while the function of the Synod only included "matters pertaining to the general welfare of the Church."[131]

This in essence meant that the CCAP had more the character of a council or consultative body than an organic single denomination. With no legislative and enforcement powers as far as the work of the presbyteries was concerned, it was effectively excluded from imposing any change in the basis of faith or the Terms of Union upon the presbyteries.[132] Pauw argues that had this not been the case, the union would definitely not have lasted. He has not elaborated on this statement, but I understand him to mean that any meaningful union beyond the level reached would not have been achievable in the case of the CCAP. What then was achieved in this union? I argue that what was achieved was a loose federation of three distinct denominations

---

130. Bolink, *Towards Church Union in Zambia*, 197–199; Also Pauw, "Mission and Church in Malawi," 273.
131. Pauw, "Mission and Church in Malawi," 278.
132. Pauw, 278.

and a safeguard for any further development of these former missions into an organically unified denomination since the union had no powers of its own to decide the direction it would go without the blessings of the presbyteries which remained independent of one another.

Related Developments to the Formation of the CCAP

The formation of the CCAP in 1924, with the union of Livingstonia and Blantyre presbyteries, was not an entirely isolated phenomenon in the history of the church at the time. This was the time when many denominations were talking about unity or cooperation among Christian denominations, a concept otherwise known as ecumenism. While this unity was not as easy in the old Christian countries of Christendom, it was considered a bit easier or more desirable in the mission field where some missionaries did not want a repetition of the divisions of Christendom among indigenous peoples who, through the work of missions, had come to embrace the Christian faith in several parts of the world. Cooperation was, therefore, largely encouraged in the mission field.

Among the Scottish Presbyterian missions, it must have been pleasing to note that the home churches that were responsible for the sending of the missionaries in the field were themselves re-uniting. Robert Laws, for example, was a minister of the United Presbyterian Church of Scotland loaned to the Free Church of Scotland's Livingstonia Mission in Malawi, but in 1900 the two denominations united to form the United Free Church of Scotland. In 1929 the United Free Church of Scotland re-united with the established Church of Scotland. By this date, the CCAP had already been formed (in 1924), but there can be no doubt that activities taking place in Scotland accelerated or influenced the unity of the mission churches in the field, especially when one considers that for the CCAP the initiative was wholly that of the missionaries. The indigenous pastors were at this time not powerful enough to make such decisions. In any case, the discussions towards unity had actually started long before the indigenous pastors were even ordained as ministers.

In the mission field outside of Malawi, good examples of different churches coming together to form a single denomination can be seen in Zambia,

Kenya and India. In Zambia, several denominations of various denominational and missionary backgrounds united to form the United Church of Zambia (UCZ) on 16 January 1965.[133] It has to be noted, however, that this was a union that had its genesis in the early 1920s, the same time the CCAP was being formed. For the UCZ, the negotiations that started in the 1920s led to the formation of the Church of Central Africa in Rhodesia (CCAR) in 1945. This developed further into the United Church of Central Africa in Rhodesia (UCCAR) in 1958 after further unifications.[134] In the case of Kenya, a similar development to the formation of the CCAP was the establishment of the Presbyterian Church of East Africa (PCEA) between 1936 and 1956.[135] While this was a limited union, like that of the CCAP in Malawi, there was also a wider attempt to form a united native church which was attempted in the Kikuyu Conferences of 1913–14.[136] Another interesting union of churches around this time took place in India when several denominations from different denominational backgrounds such as Anglican, Methodist, Presbyterian and Congregational came together to form the Church of South India in 1947.[137]

The above examples squarely place the formation of the CCAP within the wider movement of ecumenism, which makes one understand that the field was ripe for such a development as changes were taking place in many corners of the world where the Christian faith was advancing.

---

133. See Weller and Linden, *Mainstream Christianity*, 148.

134. Weller and Linden, 149. See also Bolink, *Towards Church Union in Zambia*, and Chuba, *History of Early Christian Missions*.

135. World Council of Churches, "Presbyterian Church of East Africa," http://www.oikoumene.org/en/member-churches/presbyterian-church-of-east-africa, accessed 15 Oct 2013. See also www.pceaheadoffice.org.HiSTORY.html, accessed 15 Oct 2013.

136. Here, the Anglo-Catholic position of the UMCA(which did not even have a mission in Kenya, but Bishop Frank Weston of Zanzibar nevertheless participated), made it clear that an Anglican Mission could never join a United Church. He even accused Bishop John Jamieson Willis of Uganda and Bishop William George Peel of Mombasa for heresy because of their involvement in the unity talks with other denominations. So the conferences settled for no union but cooperation in Missionary Council. See Luce, "Kikuyu Scheme of Federation," 186–199. Also Schneider, "Kikuyu and Ecclesia Anglicana," 37–65; "No Kikuyu Heresy Trial," *New York Times*; and "Kikuyu Controversy," *The Morning Post* (London).

137. See Sundkler, *Church of South India*, and Webster, "Church of South India Golden Jubilee."

The Concept of Comity and Its Application in Malawi

Missiologically the word comity refers to the agreement of different missions on the boundaries of their spheres, which are supposed to be respected and maintained on the understanding that the missionary work of neighbouring missions is equally valid Christian witness. Practically, this means that the missionaries of one sphere cannot cross their boundary and go into their colleagues' sphere to preach the gospel without the approval of the owners of the sphere according to their comity agreement. Additionally, Christians converted by a mission that is different from one's own but with whom there is a comity agreement are accepted as such upon production of their membership evidence.

In the Malawian situation this agreement was initially only among the Scottish Presbyterian missions and the DRCM. The other missions that came later, especially the Roman Catholic missions and evangelical missions, did not enter into or respect this agreement. This meant that the three Presbyterian missions had to face competition from other missions within the areas they had designated to themselves. This, in many cases, caused a lot of conflicts among Christians of rival missions. For example, the presence of Joseph Booth's Zambezi Industrial Mission within the vicinity of Blantyre Mission was not a welcomed thing. Even when there were no direct clashes, such missionary rivalry was the cause of many suspicions and accusations, especially when those missionaries that were latecomers in the field were perceived to be coaxing mission boys with higher pay in order to employ already "educated" personnel.[138]

From its beginning to the mid-1890s, Blantyre Mission enjoyed cordial relations with the UMCA, especially during Bishop Charles Alan Smythies's and Bishop John Edward Hine's times. However, in later years there was no love lost between them.[139] The UMCA did not seem to value any cooperation at all with the Blantyre Mission and there were many tensions between the two missions, especially during the time leading up to the First World War.[140]

---

138. See Ross, *Blantyre Mission*, 179–180.
139. Ross, 180.
140. Ross, 180–181.

Nkhoma Mission also had some unpleasant experiences with the Roman Catholic missions in the upper regions of the Central Region. The situation was the same with the UMCA in the Nkhotakota area, which somehow disturbed the Livingstonia Mission's relationship with them since the latter expected them to expand from Likoma towards the eastern shore of Lake Malawi and not the western shore which they considered their own territory.[141]

These observations show that the issue of comity in Malawi was initially practiced only among the Presbyterians. On the part of the Roman Catholics there were two groups that brought the faith into the country – namely, the Montfortians and the White Fathers, but the agreement between the two groups in spreading the Catholic brand of Christianity cannot be termed comity since they were both serving the same denomination.

It has to be noted though that there was some cooperation among Protestant missions for the sake of the gospel, even if that cooperation did not entail unity or comity. For example, as early as 1900 the missions in the Malawian field agreed to have some cooperation in the area of education, especially in order for them to have one voice when lobbying the government in its support for activities related to missionary education. They also cooperated in the translation of the New Testament into Chinyanja (Chichewa). In 1910 the Consultative Board of Federated Missions (CBFM) was formed, which brought even more cooperation among the Presbyterian missions and some evangelical missions such as the Zambezi Industrial Mission, Nyasa Mission and the South African General Mission.[142] The areas of cooperation were in such fields as education, hymnal compilation and, more importantly, Bible translation. The cooperation in Bible translation led to the publication of the first full Chinyanja (Chichewa) Bible in 1922, under the leadership of William Murray of the DRCM.[143] It can be argued that through this body there developed some kind of practical comity among the member churches, especially when one looks at the fourth clause of their agreement, which emphasized "the recognition of each other's church membership and church discipline."[144] Ross has observed that due to the cooperation engendered

---

141. See McIntosh, *Robert Laws*, 132.
142. Pauw, "Mission and Church in Malawi," 40–43.
143. Retief, *William Murray of Nyasaland*, 96–106.
144. Ross, *Blantyre Mission*, 180.

by the CBFM, "the squabbles that had from time to time in the past taken place over encroaching on one another's areas or bribing away teachers by offering higher wages were now at an end."[145]

The above discussion has shown that cooperation among missions in Malawi for the sake of mutual benefit was widely promoted, especially among Protestant missions and later their churches. However, cooperation for the sake of eventual unity was a thing envisaged only among the Presbyterian missions. Nevertheless, even in their case unity did not mean going all the way to creating an organically unified single denomination. Hence, the CCAP remained a federative denomination without real unity. It is this federative denomination that the newly formed synods of Harare and Zambia joined to make the five synods in the CCAP General Assembly, as we know them today. Below is a brief explanation of the histories of those two synods in order to appreciate their positions in the CCAP General Assembly.

Harare Synod

The Harare Synod of the CCAP is the result of the development of the Harare Presbytery, which was formed out of the congregations that were under the presbytery of Nkhoma in Zimbabwe following the establishment of immigrant congregations there between 1905 and 1956.[146]

The first members of this church were immigrants from Malawi, Zambia and Mozambique who had decided to go to Zimbabwe for the sake of economic opportunities since they could easily find jobs in the Zimbabwean mines, farms and industries.[147] Apart from those that just wanted employment, many Malawians trekked to Zimbabwe during this time because of the hut tax the colonial government had introduced in the Protectorate.[148] The church was established as a response to the pastoral need that had developed due to the immigrant community's lack of pastoral supervision in Zimbabwe.[149] Consequently, several volunteers from the synods of

---

145. Ross, 180.
146. Gunde, "Church Historical Enquiry," 31.
147. Verstraelen-Gilhuis, *From Dutch Mission Church to Reformed Church*, 55.
148. Gunde, "Church Historical Enquiry," 32–34.
149. Chilenje, "Origin and Development of the Church of Central Africa Presbyterian."

Nkhoma, Livingstonia and Blantyre went to serve the migrant community in Zimbabwe.[150]

In the year 1912, the Rev T. C. B. Vlok took over the leadership of the church, bringing with him twenty-three years of missionary experience, as he had been a founding missionary of Nkhoma Mission together with A. C. Murray back in the late 1880s.[151] Rev Vlok was to lead Harare Synod during its formative years from 1912 to 1936.[152]

The Rev J. Jackson succeeded T. C. B. Vlok when the latter retired in 1936. Rev Jackson served the church from 1936 up to 1952. It was Rev Jackson's wife who initiated the establishment of the Women's Guild (Chigwirizano cha Amayi) in Zimbabwe.[153] She led the group from 1940 to 1952 when her husband retired.[154]

Between 1935 and 1965, the CCAP church in Zimbabwe grew under the two presbyteries of Harare and Gweru. The two presbyteries joined into one synod in 1965 under the name of Harare Synod, thus becoming the fourth independent synod in the CCAP at that time.[155] Later, the Gweru Presbytery became the Gweru and Bulawayo Presbytery, while Harare Presbytery became the Harare Highfield Presbytery. Currently, there are four presbyteries in this synod – namely, Harare, Gweru, Highfield and Bulawayo.[156]

The synod celebrated its centenary in 2012, recognizing the formal existence of the church in Zimbabwe since 1912 though it attained its synod status in 1965.[157]

---

150. Cronjé, *Born to Witness*, 27.
151. See Paas, *Faith Moves South*, 222–223.
152. Gunde, "Church Historical Enquiry," 39.
153. Gunde, 39.
154. Gunde, 39.
155. Daneel, *Mbiri ya CCAP Sinodi ya Harare 1912–1982*, 49; Cronjé, *Born to Witness*, 112.
156. CCAP Harare Synod, "CCAP Harare Synod," http://www.ccaphresynod.com, accessed 10 Jul 2015.
157. Gunde, "Church Historical Enquiry."

Synod of Zambia

The Synod of Zambia developed from the evangelistic efforts of the Livingstonia Mission as early as the 1880s.[158] The first mission station to be opened in Zambia was Mwenzo in 1882, followed in the same year by Chitheba, and thereafter by Uyombe in 1889, Tamanda in 1894, Kamoto in 1896, Kazembe in 1897, Lubwa in 1904 and Chitambo in 1907.[159]

After a break of some time, two more stations were opened, one at Chasefu in 1922 and one at Lundazi in 1962.[160] Since all the missions in Zambia were under Livingstonia Mission, it followed that when Livingstonia Mission became a presbytery in 1899 it was also responsible for all the congregations in Zambia.[161] This continued even after the Livingstonia Presbytery had become a synod in 1956, up to 1984 when the Synod of Zambia was constituted. Just as was the case with the DRCM stations in Zambia that originated from Malawi, some Livingstonia Mission stations did not become part of the CCAP but joined other Reformed churches in Zambia.[162]

Plans to have a separate CCAP synod in Zambia started way back before 1984, but the General Synod blessed the plans to go ahead with the establishment of the Zambia Synod at its 1982 meeting.[163] In 1984 the Zambia presbyteries which had developed over the years were given the status of a synod, thereby bringing the number of the CCAP synods to five. The first general secretary for the Synod of Zambia was Rev Dr Wyson Moses Kauzobafa Jele who previously served in several capacities under the Synod of Livingstonia.[164]

---

158. For a thorough treatment of the history of the Synod of Zambia see Chilenje, "Origin and Development of the Church of Central Africa."
159. Chilenje, 49–50.
160. Chilenje, 81–87.
161. Chilenje, 128.
162. See Chilenje, 111–115.
163. CCAP, "Minutes of the General Synod," 24–27 August 1982, min. 14(b), p. 4.
164. Bwalya, *Life of Dr Wyson Moses Kauzobafa Jele*, 46–48.

Conclusion

This chapter has shown how the three original missions that led to the formation of the CCAP came and established themselves in Malawi. It has been shown that through cooperation among them, starting with Livingstonia and Blantyre in Scotland and later with the DRCM both in South Africa and Malawi, the three missions' histories are intricately intertwined. One can even be tempted to say that they were destined to belong to one denomination.

It has, however, been shown that even though all efforts were leading towards the unification of the missions into one Central African Church in the 1920s, the actual unity did not go all the way to making one denomination but rather a kind of federation of denominations that largely remained independent of one another. This observation shows that even though there were ecumenical feelings among the missionaries, they were not completely free from the influence of the home churches with their emphases on denominational distinctives, which were not only influenced by theological emphases but also by cultural and historical factors. The other issue had to do with the lack of the African voice in the whole project despite the fact that the future of the church was to be entrusted into the hands of indigenous leadership in later years.

It was this lack of the development of a full-blown denomination that nurtured within the CCAP's unity the seeds of discord that would be a thorn in the flesh of the three original synods and, eventually, the five synods that included the Zimbabwean and Zambian congregations once they reached synodical status and were incorporated into the General Assembly.

CHAPTER 3

The CCAP: One Denomination, Several Independent Synods

Introduction

This chapter discusses the inner life of the CCAP from its formation to the present in terms of its liturgy and other denominational and congregational practices, in order to highlight the points of unity and diversity within the denomination. Significantly, this chapter also looks at the church-state relations and evaluates how the various synods have cooperated or differed in their responses to the various political situations obtaining in their contexts. For example, there have been times when the CCAP synods have cooperated in their prophetic voice towards the government but also times when some synods felt it necessary to voice out issues through pastoral letters and press releases individually without involving their sister synods in a bid to highlight societal ills from the perspective of a particular synod. Diversity has also been traced in developments like educational policies, theology and theological training.

This chapter also looks at the position of women in the five synods in order to appreciate the similarities and differences with regard to the way women have fared and continue to fare in the history of the CCAP. It also discusses several similarities and differences between the synods in the unity that is the CCAP.

It will be seen that, though the three presbyteries of Livingstonia, Blantyre and Nkhoma came together in the years 1924 and 1926, the process of becoming one denomination did not go all the way, thereby creating room for the perpetuation of distinctive characteristics of the missions which made them develop differently.[1] It is this fact that has made the CCAP one in name but five distinct "denominations" practically. Some would even argue that in Malawi the synods are actually three separate regional denominations as their areas of influence roughly correspond to the country's regional administrative divisions.[2]

Constitutional Matters

The five synods differ first and foremost in their constitutions in that they are recognized as separate legal entities despite sharing the same General Assembly Constitution. During the formative years of the CCAP, the original three groups that came together were at the level of presbyteries. As such, they had their own constitutions independent of one another and still affiliated to their own home churches under whose synods they were operating. It therefore became necessary for the united denomination to come up with a constitution that could be agreed upon by all three original missions. Blantyre and Livingstonia agreed upon this constitution in 1924 while the DRCM of Nkhoma waited for two more years to consider, but they were also finally comfortable with the agreement by 1926.[3]

Right from the beginning of the CCAP as a united denomination, differences were seen in the way many things were left to the jurisdiction of the presbyteries so that the autonomy of all the presbyteries was respected to the extent of rendering the synod powerless on many issues. The presbyteries were left with all the power to deal with their former churches as they pleased. This meant that the synod could not be completely free when the presbyteries' relationships with their mother churches could not be monitored by the synod itself. One could imagine that a lot of things

---

1. CCAP, "Minutes of First Meeting of Synod," 17–22 September 1924.

2. Malawi is divided into three regions: north, centre and south. The Synod of Livingstonia is in the north, Nkhoma in the centre and Blantyre in the south. The actual boundaries of the synods, however, do not necessarily follow the regional boundaries. Due to the border dispute between the synods of Livingstonia and Nkhoma, some borders are no longer being followed as the two synods are opening congregations beyond their traditional boundaries.

3. CCAP, "Entrance of Nkhoma Presbytery into Synod," in "Minutes of Second Meeting of Synod," 13–15 October 1926, min. 5, pp. 4–6.

could actually be taking place behind the synod's back. In a way, the presbyteries even had the powers to veto a decision of the synod as proposed in the Barrier Act of 1926:

> That before the Synod passes any Act which is to be binding Rule or Constitution to the Church, such Act before passing into law shall have been passed by no less than three quarter (¾) majority of members present, and shall therefore be remitted by them to the presbyteries, who may consult their respective sessions, and opinion of Presbyteries and consent thereto be reported to next Synod, who may then pass the Act as a law of the Church, if the more general opinion of the Church thus obtained agree thereto.[4]

This clearly shows that the synod as established then could not make any binding legislation and go to sleep expecting that the presbyteries would adhere to the policy. Even though the Barrier Act was there to safeguard the interests of the presbyteries over and against the wishes of the synod, it made the process of coming up with new ways of doing things in the synod very slow. The synod could not conclude anything at any sitting, since matters had to go the presbyteries first for their scrutiny before the synod could have a go ahead to formalize the decision.

Since the establishment of the CCAP the nomenclature of the union has been changing over the years in order to respond to historical realities. When the three original missions came together, their churches were at the level of presbyteries in the structure of the Presbyterian System. This means that the union of the three presbyteries resulted in the formation of the Synod of the Church of Central Africa Presbyterian. The union under the name of synod operated from the year 1924 to the year 1956, some thirty years later, when the three presbyteries were promoted to the status of synods. This development made the former synod to be referred to as the General Synod.[5]

The unity of the three synods in Malawi together with their sister synods in Zimbabwe (Harare Synod) and Zambia (Synod of Zambia), who

---

4. CCAP, "Entrance of Nkhoma Presbytery into Synod," in "Minutes of Second Meeting of Synod," 13–15 October 1926, Blantyre: Blantyre Mission Press, min. 27," pp. 12–13.

5. See "Constitution of the Church of Central Africa Presbyterian 1956," 8–9.

joined them in 1965 and 1984 respectively, existed as the General Synod from 1956 up to 2002 when the CCAP adopted another constitution with some changes to suit the modern era.[6] This constitution became not the Constitution of the CCAP General *Synod* but rather of the CCAP General *Assembly*. It is this General Assembly that now continues with the union or federation of the CCAP.

This therefore means that the CCAP denomination has practically six constitutions: the five constitutions for the synods and that of the General Assembly. This allows for diversity while providing room for some kind of unity. My observation is that there is more diversity than unity even at the level of constitutions. For example, on the issue of women's ordination the constitution of the General Assembly explains it in such a way that any synod can do what it deems fit.[7]

It can thus be argued that at the level of constitutions the CCAP is both one and five denominations. While oneness is still an ideal to be fully realized, practically the five synods are existing in the same way as other denominations that are not in any union but in some kind of agreement or association. This observation agrees with this book's presupposition that the CCAP is actually a loose federation of five denominations, notwithstanding their similarities in other respects.

Liturgy

Despite some similarities, the five synods have differences in the way their liturgies are performed to such an extent that if one moves from a congregation of one synod to another congregation belonging to a different synod, one feels like a stranger in the congregation of the new synod. The differences in liturgy are minor between Livingstonia and Blantyre but more similar between the synods of Livingstonia and Zambia. Nkhoma and Harare synods are quite close but pronouncedly different from their three colleagues. This can partly be explained due to differences in the liturgies of the synods' mother churches back in Scotland and South Africa, which, though

---

6. See "Constitution of the Church of Central Africa Presbyterian General Assembly."

7. "Constitution of the Church of Central Africa Presbyterian General Assembly." See "CCAP General Assembly Constitutional Schedule," 6.12.1 and 6.12.2.

removed geographically and culturally, still influence their daughter churches in Malawi through historical connections and contemporary interactions. Besides, the closeness of the Synods of Livingstonia and Zambia can be explained in the sense that it was the Synod of Livingstonia that gave birth to the Synod of Zambia. In the same way, Harare Synod is closer to Nkhoma Synod because the latter produced the former.

In the history of the CCAP attempts have been made to make the liturgy uniform in all five synods, but practically all the synods have continued with their particular liturgies. It seems people prefer to continue with what they consider to be familiar than embracing something new and unfamiliar. On the other hand, it can be argued that the General Assembly is lacking the capacity to implement this decision. It can also be argued that one of the reasons for the synods to continue with different liturgies is conservatism. The CCAP church as a whole is well known for its conservative stand on points of spirituality, including the issue of liturgy. One of the reasons for breakaways or individual attrition from the CCAP in recent years is the inability of the CCAP to embrace new ways of doing things, especially in the liturgy. Some youths and young adults leave the CCAP because they feel that the CCAP is quite rigid when it comes to changing its liturgy. These youths and young adults eventually find themselves in the Pentecostal and charismatic churches, whose styles of worship are considered lively and appealing to them.[8]

It has to be appreciated, however, that of late the CCAP, at least in its three Malawian synods of Livingstonia, Blantyre and Nkhoma, has adopted what it calls "contemporary worship." This type of worship or liturgy is quite charismatic, and it is attracting a section of the church that was being pulled towards the Pentecostal and charismatic denominations. However, even with this development the contemporary service is looked upon as not being "the real thing." For example, in the Synod of Livingstonia the contemporary service in many congregations is conducted in the afternoon from around 2:00 p.m. or immediately after the formal services. This can mean that the actual Sunday morning service, which follows the old way of worship or liturgy, is still taken to be the real thing. In most cases people associate

---

8. Munyenyembe, *Christianity and Socio-Cultural Issues*, 89–90. See also Mayaya, "Deconstructing Conversion."

Sunday worship with morning services. This means that afternoon services are mostly taken to be optional services for those that need an extra-service after the "real thing" that takes place in the morning.[9]

The main church of Blantyre Mission, St Michael's and All Angels, holds its contemporary services in the multi-purpose hall as one of the many services that the church conducts on Sundays. The contemporary service is never held in the "cathedral." This, in itself, may give the impression that the charismatic contemporary service is more of an entertainment kind of thing than a serious service of worship as is the case with the traditional worship that is reserved for the more "sacred" church building.[10]

As for the Synod of Livingstonia's practice of holding the contemporary worship in the afternoon, or late morning after the normal English and local language services, the negative observation is that it is sometimes waved whenever there are other programmes planned for Sunday afternoon. For example, whenever there are choir festivals, the afternoon contemporary services are postponed, as people are encouraged to patronize the choir festivals. This is equally true of any other programme that may need the participation of the same people who are attending the contemporary service. Consequently, the contemporary service is failing to attract a large number of participants as it is not considered to be in the mainstream of things in the church's culture.[11]

Another liturgical difference among the synods is in the area of the sacrament of Holy Communion. My observation is that the strictness of preparation for partaking of Holy Communion differs greatly among the five synods. In the synods of Livingstonia and Blantyre, a full communicant can decide to go and partake of the Holy Communion – or even discover

---

9. Personal observation, Mzuzu, 2014.

10. Mr Henock Chakhaza, in discussion with the author, Blantyre, 14 February 2014. The idea of holding the contemporary service in the multi-purpose hall may also be for the purpose of preserving the old church which appears not to be a very strong building after standing for over a century.

11. Personal observation, Mzuzu, 2014. I must, however, mention that in the course of the research there have been improvements taking place. For example, I have seen changes in the times allocated to the contemporary service in some congregations in order to allocate the right hour even for this new innovation. For instance, at Chibavi congregation in Mzuzu City in the Synod of Livingstonia the contemporary service time has changed from 2:00 p.m. to 11:00 a.m.

upon his or her arrival at the church that Holy Communion is being administered – and join the rest of the communicants without any problem. In the case of Nkhoma Synod such a thing cannot happen because people who want to participate in the Holy Communion on Sunday are first of all supposed to commit themselves to the rite by coming to church on Saturday for preparation. These preparations are spiritual on the part of the communicants and logistical on the part of the congregational leadership so that they have a picture of what to expect during the communion service the following day.[12]

When one looks at these differences in something that is so central to the life of a Christian congregation, it explains the frustrations many Christians experience when they transfer from one synod to another. Within Malawi, for those that go to the Central Region from either the North or the South there is now a choice between joining a Synod of Livingstonia congregation or that of Nkhoma Synod. The same is true when one goes to the North where Livingstonia and Nkhoma synod congregations now exist side by side in some areas.

In certain cases, the differences in liturgy among the synods are accentuated by the differences in culture and language as it is a given fact that the cultures and languages of the synods differ in accordance with the places in which they are found. For example, in the Northern Region of Malawi, where the Synod of Livingstonia has its headquarters, the dominant language is Chitumbuka. This means that most services in this synod are conducted in the Chitumbuka language except in urban areas where they also have English services alongside the Chitumbuka ones. But in the rural areas it is mostly Chitumbuka or one of the northern local languages dominant in the area (such as Tonga in Nkhata-Bay district or Nkhonde in some parts of Karonga district) that feature in the worship service. For someone coming from the Southern Region or Central Region of Malawi, it is not easy to fully participate in the worship services within such a context, especially when one considers the singing of Chitumbuka hymns and the liturgical recitation of things such as the Lord's Prayer and the Apostles' Creed in a language very different from one's own.

---

12. Mr Nathaniel Kawale, in discussion with the author, Nkhoma University, 20 February 2014.

While Blantyre and Nkhoma synods use similar Chichewa hymn books and speak almost the same language of Chichewa/Chinyanja (but with different dialects), even between these two synods there are differences in culture and accent when one finds oneself away from one's home synod. It is for this reason that the English language services are quite popular among urban Christians of the CCAP as they are a unifying force among members of the congregations from different cultural and linguistic backgrounds.

Theological Training

The history of theological training in the CCAP is one of the most fascinating things in the history of this church because of all the incidences experienced in this area. It must be pointed out from the onset that, when the missionaries arrived in Malawi, they did not immediately set to teach the people with a view to ordaining some of them into pastors in the nearest future. Each mission at first taught its people whatever individual missionaries felt was appropriate without any structured plan of what theological content was supposed to be covered or for what purpose besides basic evangelism.[13]

Later, each synod formalized its theological education, paving way for the first crop of theological students to emerge, some of whom became the first ordained indigenous leaders of the church in the country. Despite cooperation in many areas, the synods did not have a single institution for the teaching of their theological students until after the union had come to fruition. It has to be mentioned, though, that during the early years of the Overtoun Institution some scholars came from other missions in order to obtain the advanced training that was being offered at the institution. For example, in 1897 the DRCM sent four Africans to be trained as teachers at the Overtoun Institution.[14] In 1904 the DRCM started its own school at Mvera which was transferred to Nkhoma in 1912.[15]

Even with the CCAP union in place, the different synods continued with their own theological schools. This remained the state of affairs throughout the period of missionary control of the church until closer to the time when

---

13. McCracken, *Politics and Christianity in Malawi 1875–1940*, 171–172.
14. Pretorius, "Story of the Dutch Reformed Church," 17.
15. Pretorius, 17.

indigenous leadership was about to take over the control of the synods. In response to an overture from Livingstonia and Blantyre, it was decided that a theological institution for the three original synods be established at Nkhoma Mission, the headquarters of Nkhoma Synod.[16] It was thought that Nkhoma Mission station, being at the centre of the country, was better placed in terms of the distance to be covered by the synods of Livingstonia and Blantyre.[17]

Consequently, the first truly joint theological institution for the synods was established at Nkhoma in 1963. This arrangement seemed to have worked well for the three synods until in the early 1970s when, due to political influence, the synods were divided, and the institution transferred from Nkhoma to Kapeni in Blantyre. The college was at Kapeni in Blantyre from 1974 to 1977 when it further moved to Zomba, assuming the name Zomba Theological College. The three Malawian synods continued to train their ministers at Zomba Theological College and were later joined by their sister synods of Harare and Zambia, which have also had some of their student ministers trained at Zomba Theological College. Apart from the CCAP synods, the ecumenical nature of Zomba Theological College was boosted by the joining of other churches such as the Anglicans, Churches of Christ (Gowa Mission) and individual Baptists.[18]

It has to be noted, however, that at a later stage some churches such as Nkhoma Synod and the Anglican Church decided to establish their own theological institutions. The Anglicans eventually pulled out, thereby reducing the ecumenical nature of Zomba Theological College. They opened their own theological institution named Leonard Kamungu Theological College less than a kilometre from Zomba Theological College on the way to Chancellor College Campus of the University of Malawi. Besides this college, they opened another one in Lilongwe known as College of Christian Ministries which has now evolved into Lake Malawi Anglican University (LAMAU). Nkhoma Synod also went on to open its own college, Josophat Mwale Theological Institute. In the case of Nkhoma it may not necessarily have been opening a new college as such but reviving the old one. It has to

---

16. CCAP, "Minutes of Eighth Synod," Nkhoma, 25–29 April 1956, min. 36.
17. See also CCAP, "Minutes of the Ninth Synod (Special)," Livingstonia, 18–21 April 1958, min. 25, p. 7.
18. Chikopa, "Rise and Decline of Zomba Theological College."

be noted that even during the time when Nkhoma was happily sending all its students to Zomba Theological College, they were still required to spend one more year at Nkhoma Mission after leaving Zomba Theological College in order to be fully immersed in the culture of Nkhoma Synod before going out to start heading up their own congregations. This training was done at an institution known as Nkhoma Institute for Continued Theological Training (NIFCOTT). The difference here between Nkhoma and other synods is that in the other synods the pastor who has just graduated from a theological college does not lead a congregation on his or her own but is put under the tutelage of an experienced pastor for one year before being given a congregation.[19]

With the opening of the new college under Nkhoma University, it meant that, in their very final year, Nkhoma Synod students from Zomba Theological College join their colleagues from Josophat Mwale Theological Institute in finalizing their synodical teaching. Some have observed that the extra one year that Nkhoma Synod pastoral students spend at Nkhoma Mission does not really introduce anything new to them since during the holidays they already serve under pastors who have congregations from which they learn the practical aspects of pastoral work as demanded by their synod.[20] It is also observed that in terms of theology they cover much while at Zomba Theological College – so much so that the theology they learn during their final year at Nkhoma Mission is in most cases a mere repetition of the material they learned in the preceding years. My observation is that the only important reason for the students to spend one more year at Nkhoma Mission before being sent to congregations is for them to absorb the ecclesiastical culture of Nkhoma Synod, especially with regard to certain liturgical practices and theological emphases that are particular to Nkhoma Synod.

On the part of Synod of Livingstonia, there are still students that go to Zomba Theological College, but, with the establishment of Ekwendeni College of Theology – now the Faculty of Theology at the University of Livingstonia – some pastoral students are now being trained at this

---

19. Rev Matalius Likhoozi, in discussion with the author, Nkhoma, 20 February 2014.
20. Rev Dr Winston R. Kawale, in discussion with the author, Mzuzu, 8 May 2014.

institution.[21] It is obvious that for Synod of Livingstonia it is easier to train their pastors at Ekwendeni than Zomba because of travel costs. Ekwendeni is near most of the areas in the synod's catchment area.[22] It is very likely that in the future Synod of Livingstonia will stop sending its students to Zomba Theological College altogether, if only due to logistical constraints. This may not be easy, though, due to the synod's stake in Zomba Theological College as one of the owners of the institution.[23]

With regard to Blantyre Synod, their sending of pastoral students to Zomba Theological College has remained largely unchanged since the establishment of the college. In the first place it has to be appreciated that Zomba Theological College is within the geographical area of Blantyre Synod's jurisdiction, making it very difficult for Blantyre Synod to disassociate itself from the college even if it wanted to. This means that even if all the other participating churches and synods were to withdraw from Zomba Theological College, Blantyre Synod would still remain and perhaps become the sole owner of the college.

The challenge of Zomba Theological College's inadequate capacity to accommodate a larger number of students has from time to time also affected Blantyre Synod. In order to respond to this challenge, the synod has sometimes engaged in crash programmes and parallel programmes in order to increase the number of pastors for its congregations. These have taken place at Zomba Theological College itself or at Chilema Lay Training Centre near Malosa in Zomba, which is jointly owned by the CCAP Blantyre Synod and the Diocese of Upper Shire of the Anglican Church as an ecumenical institution.[24]

---

21. The institution was known as Ekwendeni College of Theology until March 2014 when it became one of the faculties of the University of Livingstonia, Ekwendeni Campus. This happened because the college received some students from the main campus of the University of Livingstonia at Khondowe after their Faculty of Social Science was transferred from Laws Campus to Ekwendeni Campus. See Mlowoka, "An Investigation into the Establishment and Impact of Ekwendeni College of Theology."

22. Ironically, due to disagreements with Nkhoma Synod, the Synod of Livingstonia is now opening congregations in the Central Region of Malawi, which used to be Nkhoma Synod's exclusive territory. The synod also has congregations now in South Africa, Zimbabwe and Tanzania.

23. Rev Levi N. Nyondo, Mzuzu, 5 September 2014.

24. CCAP Blantyre Synod, "Chilema Ecumenical Centre," http://www.ccapblantyresynod.org/chilema-ecumenical-center.html, accessed 23 Jun 2015.

I conclude this section by arguing that there is no difference in terms of theology among the five synods. They are all Reformed in theological orientation and Presbyterian in church government, which indeed qualify them to be one denomination. Their differences, however, are in the emphases they make in certain liturgical items, ecclesiastical culture and approaches in dealing with contemporary logistical challenges in theological education, especially in view of the fact that Livingstonia and Nkhoma Synod are now situating their theological institutions within the synods' newly established universities.

Education in the CCAP Synods

In general, the policies of the synods on education do not differ much. In a way, all the synods have continued with providing educational services from the missionary era.[25] With regard to primary and secondary schools, the Malawian synods of Livingstonia, Blantyre and Nkhoma have many schools, and their efforts are co-ordinated through the Association of Christian Educators in Malawi (ACEM) of which they are members together, individually, with other Christian denominations that own primary and secondary schools in the country. These come under the umbrella bodies of the Episcopal Conference of Malawi, the Malawi Council of Churches and the Evangelical Association of Malawi.[26]

The CCAP Harare Synod has only one school, Nyabira CCAP School, which is a primary school offering education to children between five and thirteen years of age. This school was built in 1957, and it is one of the many schools that the CCAP built in Zimbabwe prior to the establishment of the Harare Synod. All the other schools were handed over to the government through the local councils. The Harare Synod does not have any secondary or tertiary institution. The church retained Nyabira School in its hands in

---

25. See Brown, "Development in Self Understanding of the CCAP Nkhoma Synod," 80–110.

26. Association of Christian Educators in Malawi (ACEM), "Mother Bodies," www.acemmalawi.wordpress.com/.

order to continue showing its concern for a holistic Christian ministry in a symbolic manner.[27]

The Synod of Zambia, just like its sister synods in Malawi, is making a significant contribution to education in its area of operation.[28] The history of this synod's contribution to education goes back to the missionary era when the Livingstonia Mission opened several schools in what is now Zambia especially in the Central, Northern and Eastern provinces.[29] Some of these schools were taken over by the colonial government in 1952.[30]

At its 2002 synod meeting, the Education Committee of the Synod of Zambia recommended the synod repossess some of its former schools.[31] In 2003 some of these schools were indeed repossessed by the synod. The synod now has a number of primary and secondary schools that it is operating. Some of these schools, especially primary ones, are community schools, meaning that they are operated like charity organizations in order to help the poor and vulnerable in society, especially orphans, and the teachers in these schools are volunteers.[32] The synod so far does not have a tertiary institution.

With regard to tertiary education, there is cooperation among the Malawian synods in medical schools and hospitals through the Christian Health Association of Malawi (CHAM) of which they are also members alongside other Christian denominations that equally serve Malawians in this sector. However, on other fronts, especially in general tertiary education, the three synods are acting independently. All three Malawian synods have their own universities: the University of Livingstonia, Nkhoma University and Blantyre Synod University.

While some observers are of the view that it could be better for the CCAP as a whole to come up with one university, others feel it is far better for all the synods to have their own universities. However, looking at

---

27. CCAP Harare Synod, "Nyabira School," www.ccaphresynod.com/ourschool.htm, accessed 11 Aug 2015.

28. Chilenje, "Origin and Development of the Church of Central Africa," 219–220.

29. See Snelson, *Education Development in Northern Rhodesia 1883–1945*.

30. Chilenje, "Origin and Development of the Church of Central Africa Presbyterian," 219.

31. Chilenje, 219.

32. CCAP Zambia Synod, "Community Schools," www.ccapzambia.org/community-schools.html, accessed 11 Aug 2015.

how the church-related universities are struggling (despite their tremendous contributions), I feel that having one CCAP university would have been a better idea for the sake of a wider base for resource mobilization and also for enhancing the oneness of the church, as is the case with the Catholic University of Malawi, which is not the university of a particular diocese of the Catholic Church in Malawi but of the whole Catholic Church. The idea of having one CCAP university in Malawi owned by all the synods could not work while the synods continue nurturing their autonomy and independence from one another. Obviously, the CCAP General Assembly does not have any plans to establish a CCAP university in the near future. The synods are therefore left to themselves on this issue, thereby being divided further with regard to unity of purpose in tertiary education matters.

Women's Ministry

Women have been involved in church work right from the beginning of the Christian faith in this part of Africa. Though not always well documented, women's contribution to the spread of Christianity even within the CCAP church cannot be overemphasized. Apart from the individual contributions that women have made in the five synods, their group contributions are most conspicuous through the organizations known as women's guilds. All five synods have women's guilds whose activities are almost similar across the synods.

Women's Guilds

Women's guilds are believed to be among the most active groups of Christians in the CCAP denomination. The women's guilds in the five synods are called Umanyano wa Ŵanakazi in the Synod of Livingstonia (simply known as *Umanyano*); Chigwirizano cha Amayi in Nkhoma and Harare synods (simply known as *Chigwirizano*); Mvano in Blantyre Synod; and Christian Women's Guild in the Synod of Zambia. Several names were suggested for these groups during their formative years before the current names were accepted by all.[33]

---

33. See Synod of Livingstonia, *Mdauko, Mendeskero na Milimo ya Umanyano wa Ŵanakazi*, 14.

The ideas that led to the formation of these women's groups were hatched in the late 1930s by women who were already active in church work. However, it was not until the early 1940s that the various women's groups in the presbyteries of the synods evolved into the women's guilds as they are now known. Among the many activities that women's guilds do are such things as conducting Bible studies, doing charity work and comforting the bereaved during funerals. But above all, these guilds are also there to spread the gospel. It is interesting to note that, in the history of the Women's Guild of the Synod of Livingstonia (*Umanyano*), the group at one time even sponsored an evangelist to go and do the work of a resident missionary in Marambo, Zambia, in the 1960s and 1970s. The first evangelist to do this job in the name of *Umanyano* was Mr S. M. Kumwenda, who worked in this capacity from 1964 to 1973 before being succeeded by another man, Mr M. A. Nkunika.[34] This was a rare case of the women's guild shouldering the responsibility of an evangelist's welfare for the sake of the spread of the gospel, but all this just shows the zeal and dedication that the women have towards the success of the Christian ministry in their synods.

The women's guilds have worked as avenues of women's ministries in CCAP synods for a very long time. There was a time when the highest position a woman could get in the church was through her ascendance in the administrative structures of the women's guilds. This is not surprising, though, since women could not be ordained as ministers in any of these synods until the recent past when some synods have reluctantly accepted the development.[35] This means that in the synods where women are now ordained as ministers, it is possible to have women in the leadership of the church as a whole, while other women are leading in the women's guilds.

The changes that have taken place in the church have not spared the women's guilds. As a result, we see that the women's guilds have also evolved with time in order to suit the modern context in which they are now operating. For example, changes have occurred in the manner of dressing and of

---

34. Synod of Livingstonia, *Mdauko, Mendeskero na Milimo ya Umanyano wa Wanakazi*, 14.

35. Though some synods have accepted the ordination of women it is not celebrated by many Christians because people are still prejudiced against women ministers. See Mlenga, "Women in Holy Ministry."

conducting Bible study and other church activities following the innovation that comes with trends of doing things especially as new generations take over from older ones.[36]

Women as Ordained Ministers

The five CCAP synods are coming from a background that used to take it for granted that men alone are supposed to be leaders in the whole church while women can be leaders among fellow women and children. This attitude can be traced back to the time of the missionaries when it was only male missionaries that could be mission heads and also serve in congregations as ordained pastors. Their wives were not recognized, as they were only known as the wives of missionaries irrespective of their educational qualifications.[37] The only women whose contribution could be appreciated were the unmarried women who came into the mission field in their own right as missionaries without being attached to a husband.[38] But even these could still be under a male missionary even if that missionary was junior to them in terms of age or experience. As Isobel Reid comments in view of the relationship between missionaries Jack Martin and Miss Mary Patrick at Livingstonia Mission's Bandawe station in the 1920s: "It was entirely expected that a young inexperienced man should have authority over a single woman missionary with seven years more experience."[39] On the part of indigenous women they, too, were not recognized as leaders in the church except among fellow women and children. Besides this lack of recognition, indigenous women were also belittled for their lack of education, especially during the first decades of the church. This situation continued even after the responsibility of the church's leadership was passed on to indigenous males.[40]

Due to changes in the secular world, especially as influenced by women's liberation movements, some churches began to get influenced, and, in so doing, they were forced to re-read their Bibles in order to find a justification for the ordination of women or to refute the view that appeared to put women

---

36. See Gondwe, "Continuity and Change of the Umanyano Women's Guild," 5–10.

37. See Mamie Martin's letter to her parents of 26 August 1923 in Sinclair, *Salt and Light*, 148–149.

38. Mamie Martin to her parents, 26 August 1923, cited in Sinclair, *Salt and Light*, 149.

39. Reid, "Myth and Reality of the Missionary Family," 35.

40. Chifungo, "Women in the CCAP Nkhoma Synod," 164.

in the church at some disadvantage vis-a-vis men. These developments led to changes in the way some members of the clergy in the CCAP viewed women leadership in the church. Consequently, the synods of Livingstonia, Blantyre and Zambia took courage to change their conditions for eligibility in becoming a pastor by allowing women, whether married or single, to join theological training for purposes of serving as ordained ministers in the church. Currently, there are women ministers in the synods of Livingstonia, Blantyre and Zambia. In the case of Blantyre Synod, one female pastor, Rev Mercy Chilapula, has even served in the position of synod moderator, which is the highest but not the most powerful position in the church.[41]

It can be argued that this trend is not likely to be reversed in the three synods of Livingstonia, Blantyre and Zambia. The question, however, is do women now flood the theological institutions in order to take advantage of the chance long denied to them? Contrary to many optimistic expectations, the number of women theological students in the institutions of the synods is very low.[42] There can be a lot of reasons for this scenario, but above all it has to be remembered that these churches are coming from a culture that never accepted women pastors due to reasons that range from biblical interpretation to traditional African culture to early missionary practices. It is therefore not easy to find many women joining what hitherto was perceived to be exclusively a man's calling in the church.[43]

Within Nkhoma Synod, the issue of women's ordination is still being discussed and the synod has yet to take a position.[44] However, among the clergy of Nkhoma Synod there are some who personally and theologically have no qualms with women being ordained to the ministry of Word and Sacrament although they would not dare opine like this while in the pulpit or in the synod's meetings.[45] Despite the presence of diverse views concerning women's ordination in Nkhoma Synod, many commentators feel the

---

41. See Mpaso, "Big Interview: Mercy Chilapula."

42. The numbers of female students doing ministerial studies or theology is generally smaller than the number of male students. See Fiedler, "Challenge of Theological Education for Women in Malawi."

43. See Mlenga, "Women in Holy Ministry."

44. See Banda, "Study of Assessment of Women's Rights in Nkhoma Synod."

45. Interview with retired Nkhoma Synod minister, Lilongwe, 20 February 2014 (name withheld).

synod is oppressive towards women because of its official stand, which has yet to give women a leeway to pursue theological education for the sake of ministerial ordination.[46]

This issue of women's ordination, therefore, is another instance in which the five synods of the CCAP differ at the level of synods though they are supposed to be one denomination in doctrine and practice. Their differences make some observers conclude that those synods that are acting differently from their sisters should be perceived to be oppressive if their policies appear to be negatively disposed towards women's rights and other considerations.[47]

Non-ordained Men's Ministry

Apart from the women's guilds in the synods of Livingstonia and Nkhoma, known as *Umanyano* and *Chigwirizano* respectively, there are groups specifically for men's fellowship. These are *Umanyano wa Madodana* (simply *Madodana*) for the Synod of Livingstonia and *Chigwirizano cha Amuna* for Nkhoma Synod. While the Synod of Livingstonia has had this men's guild for quite some time alongside the women's guild, the phenomenon is of recent origins in the Nkhoma Synod though it is now getting settled.[48] The synods of Blantyre, Harare and Zambia, on the other hand, do not have special guilds for adult males. While it is generally believed that Blantyre Synod and Livingstonia are closer to each other, with Nkhoma Synod being on the other side, it appears there are stronger similarities between the Synods of Livingstonia and Nkhoma in the issue of men's guilds over and against Blantyre Synod.

It is on record that Nkhoma Synod copied the men's guild phenomenon from Synod of Livingstonia where it was first established. But why would Nkhoma Synod copy such a thing unless it was advantageous to them? The testimonies of many members of Nkhoma Synod point to the fact that the church felt a need in the area of men's coordination whenever men were supposed to do some tasks in the church. This problem was not there among

---

46. Nyirenda, "Women Voice in Church of Central Africa Presbyterian (CCAP) in Malawi."

47. Cf. Phiri, *Women, Presbyterianism and Patriarchy*, 110–111.

48. Banda, "Role of Men's Guild in Relation to Women's Guild."

women because their *Chigwirizano* was able to mobilize them whenever there was a need. It therefore became necessary to come up with an organization that could be in a position to mobilize men in ecclesiastical responsibilities, especially when we consider that a good number of men are not very active in the church when they are just ordinary members.

The formation of the men's guilds on the part of both Livingstonia and Nkhoma synods is a contextually relevant development in these synods which came about without the influence of the original mother churches, which do not have such guilds. The presence of men's guilds in the two synods is enabling men, who would otherwise have been inactive, to be active participants in such things as Bible study participation, marriage seminars, charity works and evangelization through guild initiatives.

One interesting thing in the phenomenon of men's guilds is that they do not have a woman elder in their midst to check on their discussions in relation to the norms of the church. In the women's guild within Nkhoma Synod, there is the controversial position of a male member of the church leadership who sits in the midst of the women in order to make sure that all is well with the women in their group. This position is known as *Mkhalapakati* (literally, "he who sits in the midst or in between," i.e. between the women's guild and the church leadership). The absence of this office in the men's guild makes some people question the integrity of the church when it comes to its perception of women's groups.[49] This gives the impression that it is only women who need supervision in their spiritual gatherings and not men. As long as such practices continue, they will always be attracting the wrath of feminist theologians and other feminist scholars who are fighting for the implementation of the equality of the sexes in all spheres of life but more especially in the church.[50]

Youth Ministry

All five synods have their youth departments which are quite active in ministering to fellow youths, besides doing various church responsibilities that

---

49. Phiri, *Women, Presbyterianism and Patriarchy*, 90.
50. See Gondwe, "Possible Influence of Crucial Pauline Texts on the Role of Women."

can best be handled by the youth.[51] All five synods of the CCAP have youth organizations with representatives from synod level to congregational level. Due to the fact that the youth are energetic and quite conversant with contemporary developments, they, in most cases, fail to be edified by the ministrations of their elders. In view of this, the youth find it easier to engage in their spiritual exercises without elderly supervision. This sometimes clashes with the leadership of the church as they think that the youth are going astray. I argue that when such things happen, the youth are not going astray as such but are expressing their dissatisfaction with the lack of spiritual imagination and contextual innovation by their elders and leaders, who naturally are comfortable with the status quo.

With the establishment of contemporary services in CCAP congregations, this is the kind of worship that many youths want and it is not a surprise to see that these services are mostly attended by them. In all five synods of the CCAP the youth have been very much influenced by the charismatic movement's way of doing things in the church. For example, over a decade ago the leadership of the CCAP discovered that their youth were drifting away from the spirituality and ecclesiastical culture of the CCAP to that of the Pentecostal and charismatic churches through their involvement in the Student Christian Organisation of Malawi (SCOM) since it was this spirituality that had pervaded the organization. The leadership's solution to this problem was to establish a separate student Christian organization that could identify with the ethos of the CCAP as a denomination. Consequently, the CCAP Student Organisation (CCAPSO) was born. This means that the birth of CCAPSO was a reaction to the emphases of SCOM and other Christian youth organizations as influenced by Pentecostal and charismatic spiritualities, especially as most of the people that are invited to preach and teach in the gatherings of these organizations come from Pentecostal and charismatic backgrounds.[52]

It has, however, been observed that CCAP students who have been significantly influenced by charismatic spirituality continue to fellowship in

---

51. The term youth in the CCAP context may refer to anyone between fifteen and thirty-five years of age.

52. See Khonje, "A Historical Study of the Establishment and Contribution of the Student Christian Organisation of Malawi (SCOM)."

SCOM rather than in CCAPSO, while some have dual membership in these student Christian organizations.[53] It is partly because of this trend that the youth have wholeheartedly embraced the introduction of contemporary services in their congregations. My observation is that what is termed contemporary worship is actually the charismatic way of worship. It is known as contemporary in the CCAP because it is an innovation in this denomination, coming in after the manner of their charismatic neighbours, while among charismatic and Pentecostal Christians it is just a normal thing without any adjectives to qualify it as being new or contemporary.[54]

Within the Nkhoma Synod, there was born in the year 2005 another youth organization with overtly charismatic spirituality targeting urban youth. The name of this organization is CCAP Youth Urban Ministry (CCAPYUM) due to its emphasis on urban ministry, especially in reaching out to the urban youth whose lives are very fast and vulnerably exposed to all kinds of influences, especially due to the proliferation of information technology and urban culture. This organization works more or less like an umbrella organization for all the youth fellowships in the congregations of Nkhoma Synod known as CCAPYUFS (CCAP Youth Fellowships).[55]

It can be argued that the challenges that the youth face in the CCAP are basically the same across synodical boundaries though there is no uniformity in dealing with them as each synod approaches the issue from its own pastoral angle. This means that the unity of the CCAP as a denomination does not translate down to the youth who remain confined within the perimeters of their synods. I believe things would be different if there was an active youth desk at the General Assembly level with the task of coordinating all youth activities in the denomination. However, the state of the General Assembly is such that it cannot manage to bring leadership to the synods on issues affecting the youth in the denomination.

---

53. Personal observation at various college and university campuses in Malawi.
54. Cf. Munyenyembe, *Christianity and Socio-Cultural Issues*, 89–90.
55. Kamuyanja, "Impact of Church of Central Africa Presbyterian Youth Urban Ministry in Nkhoma Synod."

Church and State Relations among the Synods

This section discusses the varied ways in which the CCAP, both at the level of the General Assembly and at the level of the synods separately, has been responding to political issues over the decades that the church has been in existence, especially in Malawi. I have divided this section into four subsections – the colonial period, single-party era, transition period and multiparty era – in order to show how the different political contexts have been influencing the church in its responses to socio-political issues over the course of history up to the present.

The discussion in this section concentrates on the Malawian synods of Livingstonia, Blantyre and Nkhoma and the political issues in Malawi. This does not mean that there have been no church-state relations in Zambia and Zimbabwe where the synods of Zambia and Harare operate. There are three reasons for not treating these synods in this section: First, it has to be remembered that the Synod of Zambia was not there as a synod until 1984, which means that the synodical decisions discussed herein could not originate from Zambia until after the synod's establishment. The second reason concerns only the Synod of Harare, established as early as 1965, but for which engaging with the powers that be would not be as practical as is the case with the Malawian synods because of the immigrant status of its members. Lastly, it has to be remembered that these two synods were very small for a good part of their history; it is only now that they are growing, hence they were not able to exert any significant political influence in their past. In view of these reasons, it was not possible to find readily available information for their discussion under the title of this section, hence the concentration on the Malawian synods of Livingstonia, Blantyre and Nkhoma.

The Colonial Period

Church-state relations are one area in which the CCAP as a whole has had a challenge in regard to raising one voice on issues. During the colonial times, Presbyterian missionaries were suspected by the colonial government of pulling in the opposite direction because of their tendency to act as a kind of "opposition party" in certain circumstances.[56] And yet it was the

---

56. Cf. Ross, *Blantyre Mission*, 129. Also *Life and Work in British Central Africa, August–December 1897* and Ross, *Colonialism to Cabinet Crisis*, 16–19.

missionaries that desired the establishment of British colonial government as preferred to Portuguese colonial rule.[57] The Scottish missionaries were of the view that a British Protectorate would be a better alternative to Portuguese annexation which they believed would be injurious to their work and to the welfare of the native population.[58]

Besides other suspicions between the government and the church, the relationship between the DRCM missionaries and the colonial administration became quite sour during the Anglo-Boer War of 1899–1902 as the DRCM found itself in enemy territory since Nyasaland was a British Protectorate.[59] The DRCM missionaries were subjected to special suspicion by the colonial government because of their nationality.[60] This means that they suffered a double blow from British colonial administration in Nyasaland as they were both victims of suspicion and the ravages of war, especially back home in South Africa.

It can, however, be safely stated that during the fight for independence the synods were all on the side of the freedom fighters though more credit has been given to the Synods of Livingstonia and Blantyre than to Nkhoma Synod.[61] The reason for this state of affairs has been the observation that the education policy of the DRCM perpetuated peasantry in its area of influence and did not produce many highly educated Malawians at the time of the independence struggle, as was the case in the jurisdictions of Livingstonia and Blantyre.[62] This gave the products of Livingstonia and Blantyre mission schools an upper hand in terms of articulating issues during the fight for independence.

When the Federation of Rhodesia and Nyasaland was imposed in 1953, it was bitterly resented and opposed by the African population. The Blantyre Synod found it necessary to add its voice to the criticism levelled against this act of white supremacy by issuing a statement condemning the many abuses and the retrogression that the Federation had brought to Nyasaland:

---

57. See Warhurst, "Portugal's Bid for Southern Malawi, 1882–1891," 25.
58. Ross, "Crisis and Identity," 382.
59. Pauw, "Mission and Church in Malawi," 82.
60. Pauw, 82–86.
61. Cf. Ross, *Blantyre Mission*, 11–12.
62. Parsons, "Scots and Afrikaners in Central Africa," 31–32.

> Synod is aware of the need for moderation and careful speech in these difficult times. Sometimes, however, to say nothing is to deny the truth. Synod therefore feels it urgently necessary to say that it is unanimously opposed to Federation as it has been in practice over these years. We see no hope of a peaceful, and righteous future for all the people of this land (whatever their race) under the present form of Federal Government.[63]

Though this statement did not have much impact in Malawi, it did influence the Church of Scotland to plead with the British Government to consider taking Malawi out of the Federation of Rhodesia and Nyasaland, which later made it possible for the country to attain independence.

It is significant to note that even though race relations had become sour in society in general during this time, it was possible for black and white Christians to stick together during these trying times when the church was generally in support of African nationalism. During the State of Emergency of 1959, the colonial government wanted to protect the white missionaries and offered them protection if they were in danger. At Livingstonia Mission, the oneness of the races in the church became significant during this time when the missionaries indicated that they were not in danger in the midst of their black brothers and sisters, and they dramatized this by marking the words of Ephesians 2:14 with whitewashed bricks in the lawn, which government planes flying above could easily see.[64]

After observing the fellowship of black and white in the church as experienced during the independence struggle at Livingstonia Mission, the Rev Stephen Kauta Msiska remarked: "I think this is the beginning of church history in Nyasaland."[65] Kenneth Ross has observed in reference to these words of Stephen Kauta Msiska that it was in the heat of the crisis that the identity of the church became clear.[66]

---

63. Blantyre Synod, "Blantyre Synod Statement on the Present State of Unrest 1958," quoted in Ross, *Christianity in Malawi*, 200.

64. Eph 2:4 reads, "For he himself is our peace, who has made the two one and has destroyed the barrier, the dividing wall of hostility" (NIV). See Jackson, *Send Us Friends*, 78. See also Jackson, "Breaking Down the Wall," 46–51.

65. See Jackson, *Send Us Friends*, 68. See also Ferguson McPherson, foreword to *Golden Buttons*, by Msiska, 15.

66. Ross, "Crisis and Identity," 389.

The Single Party Era

Between 1964 and 1994, when Malawi was under the one-party system of government, all the churches, in a way, became silent. It was not possible to criticize the government and the ruling party because of the ruthless way in which the government machinery was dealing with suspected critics of the regime. It has, however, been observed that the Nkhoma Synod was closely aligned to the ruling party, the Malawi Congress Party (MCP). It can be argued that Nkhoma Synod's closeness to the MCP was not something that the synod consciously initiated but that the synod was actually overtaken by historical events. For instance, it happened that the state president then, Dr Hastings Kamuzu Banda, was Chewa by ethnicity from the Central Region district of Kasungu. According to the church boundaries of the synods of the CCAP in Malawi, the Central Region largely falls under the jurisdiction of Nkhoma Synod. Besides, it was generally believed that Dr Banda was a church elder in the Church of Scotland, which automatically made him an honorary church elder in the CCAP and more so in the Nkhoma Synod. This made the Nkhoma Synod view Kamuzu Banda as "its own man."

W. S. Zeze has argued that the relationship between Nkhoma Synod and the MCP-led government between 1964 and 1994 can be likened to a situation where Christianity became a state-sponsored religion.[67] Zeze develops his thesis by providing four instances to illustrate how Christianity became a state-sponsored religion in the way Nkhoma Synod related to the MCP during the single-party regime.[68] It is interesting to note that this write up by Zeze is quite critical of Nkhoma Synod's relationship with the Malawi Congress Party during the First Republic despite the author being a member of Nkhoma Synod, from whom one would expect some sympathy. The write up is therefore self-criticism at its best within the Nkhoma Synod in view of past historical realities.

---

67. Zeze, "Christianity: A State-Sponsored Religion in Malawi?"

68. W. S. Zeze outlines the following instances as examples that illustrate his point: Rev Dishan Chimombo Episode (1964), Nyau Episode (1965), Theological College Episode (1974), Prayers and Loyal Messages to President Dr H. Kamuzu Banda and Political Transition Episode (1992–1994). In all these instances Zeze is trying to show how the Nkhoma Synod collaborated with the MCP, sometimes even placing itself under the party by appealing to the party's arbitration even on purely ecclesiastical matters. See Zeze, "Christianity: A State-Sponsored Religion in Malawi?," 5–10.

While the Nkhoma Synod can be accused of aligning itself with the government and the party during the single-party regime, the synods of Livingstonia and Blantyre can equally be accused of being silent during this time so much so that many lives were lost without the synods saying anything because they had been rendered voiceless.[69] Here we see differences and similarities in the way the CCAP Synods related to the government during the single-party era. The Nkhoma Synod can be understood to have been co-opted, thereby rendering it very uncritical to whatever the ruling party was doing. On the other hand, Livingstonia and Blantyre, though not co-opted as was the case with Nkhoma, equally failed Malawians by maintaining a culture of silence for the sake of their own survival over and against exercising the prophetic role of the church in society.

The Transition Period from Single-Party to Multiparty Politics

Come the transition period from a single-party system to a multiparty system of government in Malawi, the differences among the three Malawian synods became clearly pronounced. While the synods of Livingstonia and Blantyre were in agreement with what was going on, especially in siding with the multiparty advocates, Nkhoma Synod took a very different stand, which made it appear as the sole defender of the MCP-led government among Malawi's ecclesiastical bodies.[70] Yet facts on the ground were indicating that the majority of the citizens in the country did not want to continue with that party's leadership in the country during the years 1992 to 1994.[71]

---

69. Ross, "Transformation of Power in Malawi 1992–94," 20.

70. Brown, "Development in Self Understanding of the CCAP Nkhoma Synod," 234–236.

71. Some commentators have observed that the coming in of multiparty politics exposed the regional and ethnic divisions that have always been there in Malawi. For some people in the Central Region, those advocating for the introduction of multiparty politics were viewed as enemies of the region and by implication of all the Chewa people, especially when we consider that the main political players on the side of multiparty advocates during this time were mostly people from the Northern and Southern Regions. It is suggested that due to these facts, the Nkhoma Synod felt it was also being attacked due to its association with the leadership of the then ruling Malawi Congress Party, which represented the region and the dominant ethnic group in the area of its jurisdiction. This partly explains why, in the Central Region, a majority (67.54%) voted against the introduction of multiparty politics in the 1993 June 14 Referendum in which Malawians were given a chance to choose either political pluralism or to continue with the single party system of government. See

When the Roman Catholic bishops issued their 1992 Lenten Pastoral Letter, which many believe was the match that sparked the fire to burn up the single-party regime, the synods of Blantyre and Livingstonia supported the Catholic bishops' letter and expressed their desire for change. Nkhoma Synod, on the other hand, did not support the Roman Catholic bishops' initiative. It actually even went so far as to distance itself from the agitations which the Roman Catholic Church and other Protestant churches were making in the country for the sake of political change.[72]

Nkhoma Synod's aloofness, or even its desire to pull in the opposite direction, led to the Malawi Council of Churches (MCC) suspending the synod from its membership until it was ready to mend its ways. All this shows that, though the CCAP is supposed to be one denomination, the plurality of its independent Synods sometimes made (and makes) it fail to speak with one voice on pertinent prophetic issues as a united denominational force. As Schoffeleers further comments, "This difference of opinion between the synods made a formal official position of the CCAP on the bishops' letter impossible."[73] This means that the synods remained divided during the transition period in Malawi, with Livingstonia and Blantyre synods on one side and Nkhoma Synod on the other. The General Synod was not powerful enough to provide a united stand of the CCAP synods during this crucial period in Malawian political history.

The Era of Multiparty Democracy

Some interesting things about the unity of the CCAP vis-a-vis political developments in Malawi have been manifested during the era of multiparty democracy as the country continues to conduct elections every five years in order to choose its leaders. One thing that has come with the new dispensation is the issue of freedom of expression, which was not there during the single-party regime. This means that the churches are now free to issue press releases in both print and electronic media in order for them to inform the general public on issues of national importance. It is in this vein that the

---

African Elections Database, "14 June 1993 Referendum," *African Elections Database,* http://africanelections.tripod.com/mw.html#1993_Referendum, accessed 27 Jun 2019.

72. See Schoffeleers, *In Search of Truth and Justice,* 190.
73. See Schoffeleers, 190.

CCAP has also sometimes seen fit to write pastoral letters to its faithful in order to enlighten them on the position of the church on any burning issue in the country. In this regard, the three Malawian synods have sometimes cooperated to produce the said documents through their General Assembly so that all members of the CCAP have felt that their church has spoken. It has also sometimes surprised the faithful to see that pastoral letters have been written by one synod alone on an issue of national importance in a way that has put the leadership of the other synods in a quandary.

One example of a time when the General Assembly (still known as the General Synod at the time) wrote a pastoral letter that was quite useful as a prophetic voice was in 2001 when the Malawi nation was engulfed in a kind of uncertainty concerning the stability of its constitution with regard to the provisions regulating the presidential tenures. The then President of the Republic, Dr Bakili Muluzi, was cunningly pursuing an amendment of the constitution in order to allow for the extension of the constitutional maximum of two terms for a president in order to allow a president to continue to contest in elections for as long as he or she wished. This was dubbed the Open Terms Debate. After the failure of this attempt, there was a second attempt by the name of the Third Term Debate where the argument was that the amendment would only give a president who has been voted into power twice the chance to stand again for a third and last time. This proposal was again defeated. It can be argued that the pastoral letter which the General Synod leadership wrote prior to the voting had sensitized the people to the dangers of such a constitutional amendment to Malawi's nascent democracy, especially considering the fact that the first person to benefit from such a constitutional amendment would actually be the very first president who had emerged victorious against a life president.[74] It was as if the country was put in a reverse gear in order to experiment with what it had just rejected in a period of less than a decade. The condemnation of such machinations was expressed in no uncertain terms by the CCAP General Assembly under the leadership of the Very Rev Dr Felix Chingota (Blantyre Synod), who was the moderator of the General Assembly at the time, and the Rev Y. A.

---

74. See Ross, "Some Worrisome Trends," 91–107.

Chiyenda (Nkhoma Synod), who was the senior clerk.[75] Many Malawians of good will supported this letter and agreed with it entirely. The only people who were against this letter were the ruling party cadres and some political mercenaries from other parties who intended to benefit from such a rape of the constitution for the sake of their egocentric tendencies.

Recently, during the time of President Dr Joyce Banda, the General Assembly also spoke on behalf of the synods in the country concerning what it saw as ills in Malawian society, especially with regard to the looting of public funds in government ministries, dubbed the Cashgate Scandal. The letter also pleaded with political leaders to campaign cleanly towards the 2014 tripartite elections that took place on 20 May 2014.[76]

Despite their cooperation in different forums such as the General Assembly, the Public Affairs Committee (PAC) and the Malawi Council of Churches – where they are represented – the synods have also been exercising their individual rights to engage the general public, or their own members, by going it alone in their criticism of the government or in guiding the faithful on political choices during elections. For example, in the year 2009 the Nkhoma Synod wrote a pastoral letter titled "Choosing the Right Leaders" in order to enlighten Christians on various issues in preparation for the 19 May 2009 general elections. The pastoral letter went further to even giving tips to Christians on how to identify God's choice of a leader.[77]

Come April 2012, Nkhoma Synod issued another pastoral letter in which, among other things, it indirectly criticized the government and the ruling party for some socio-economic ills that were being experienced in Malawi.[78] This was perhaps one of the worst moments in the history of Malawi since the dawn of multiparty democracy. Of special concern among the matters that Nkhoma Synod raised were such issues as the scarcity of foreign currency and fuel, which came about as donor nations vowed to

---

75. CCAP General Synod, "Some Worrisome Trends Which Undermine the Nurturing of Our Young Democracy."

76. Watipaso Mzungu, "CCAP General Assembly Calls for Peaceful Elections," http://mwnation.com/ccap-general-assembly-calls-for-peaceful-elections/, 26 Feb 2014.

77. Nkhoma Synod, "Choosing the Right Leaders," 3–4.

78. Nkhoma Synod, "Exercising Our Faith through Prayer in Our Time."

punish Malawi following the country's poor diplomatic relations with them.[79] Nkhoma Synod also lamented the proliferation of political violence which the political leadership of the time appeared to be promoting, considering the freedom which the youth wing of the ruling party had in terrorizing the masses.[80]

From a purely historical point of view, the Nkhoma Synod pastoral letter of 2012 was also significant in that it commemorated fifty years of the existence of the synod under indigenous leadership. The synod noted the significance of the year in this way:

> This year is very special one for CCAP Nkhoma Synod because we have clocked 50 years since the Dutch Reformed Mission handed over the Church to Malawi leadership in 1962. Therefore, let us join hands in thanking God for using our Synod to His glory. We have now grown to 150 congregations in 16 presbyteries. Glory be to God [sic].[81]

Thus the synod has found its voice in commenting on political matters without fearing any reprisals as was the case during the single-party regime. It can be argued that the synod's practice is actually very much in line with Reformed Theology, which looks at all professions as God's calling and therefore worthy of his praise whenever everything is going on well and liable to censure when human practice seems to be departing from the norm or the ideal. It is this kind of thinking that made the synod condemn the Joyce Banda administration, especially in relation to the infamous Cashgate Scandal that rocked the country in the year 2013.[82] Besides the Cashgate

---

79. Some observers are of the view that the scarcity of foreign currency was not due to donor punishments as such but the selfish attempt by the then President Bingu wa Mutharika to control the value of the Kwacha artificially. Klaus Fiedler, in discussion with the author, 27 August 2015.

80. There is documentary evidence on how the youth members of the DPP, also known as Youth Cadets by their leadership, were terrorizing those of opposing views. As an example, there are pictures of these youths in pickup trucks wielding panga knives on the eve of 20 July 2011 in order to threaten the CSOs and concerned citizens who had planned to demonstrate against the government. Twenty people died as a result of this demonstration as the police clashed with the irate demonstrators.

81. Nkhoma Synod, "Exercising Our Faith through Prayer in Our Time," 1.

82. Nkhoma Synod, "Renewal and Regeneration of Our Nation." The Cashgate Scandal refers to massive looting of government coffers by some civil servants and politicians that was revealed in the year 2013.

Scandal, this pastoral letter condemned other evils in society such as the lack of respect for the elders, lack of decency in dressing, promotion of secular humanism, homosexuality, abortion, prostitution and pornography.[83]

As can be seen above, it is now generally expected that the churches have to speak out whenever there is need for some voice of reason in society concerning negative socio-political developments. This is unlike in the past when silence was the order of the day amidst the suffering of the masses at the hands of political leaders through the party and the government machinery that was at their disposal. It is in view of this that the CCAP General Assembly is taking an active role in prophetically condemning the ills in society but also giving some kind of direction on what would be in tandem with the values of the gospel.

With regard to the individual synods, it is interesting to note that Nkhoma Synod has been quite active in the new political dispensation in openly criticizing the political leadership whenever things have been perceived to be wrong, especially with regard to the issuing of politically critical pastoral letters.[84] This does not mean that the other two synods have not been active. Their contributions through the voice of the General Assembly cannot be underestimated, as well as their own critical reflection as uttered from the lips of those in the synod's leadership.[85] It is, however, generally perceived that Nkhoma and Livingstonia have been more critical than Blantyre Synod as individual synods. Some see political bias in the way the synods respond to various political issues, especially when the voice of the synods is not coming through the General Assembly. Since the dawn of multiparty

---

83. Nkhoma Synod, "Renewal and Regeneration of Our Nation."

84. While this tendency of the Nkhoma Synod in appears to be a new practice, theoretically the synod arrived at this position as far back as 1960. See Nkhoma Synod, *Zolamulira, Zopangana ndi Zolangiza* (Buku 2), 3–4, especially Z.II–12, 2(d). In this passage the synod clearly states that it is the church's responsibility to protect Christianity in the country, and that the church has a God-given mandate to oppose anybody, including the government, when it acts or commands things that contradict the Word of God. Original Chichewa verbatim quote: *Ndi udindo wa Eklesia kusamala Chikhristu mdziko, Eklesia mwa mabwalo ake ali ndi mphamvu yopatsidwa ndi Mulungu kutsutsa aliyense kungakhale Boma lomwe likuchita kapena kulamulira zotsutsana ndi Mau a Mulungu.* See also Botha, *Mkhristu ndi Ndale za Dziko.*

85. In this regard the Rev Levi Nyondo, general secretary of the Synod of Livingstonia, was arrested by the DPP-led government in 2010 for uttering what the political leaders of the ruling party interpreted as sedition during the funeral of Professor Moses Chirambo, a former cabinet minister. See Jomo, "Church Warns of Malawi 'Dictatorship' after Leader's Arrest."

democracy, the presidents that have ruled Malawi have always come from the Southern Region, which is under the jurisdiction of Blantyre Synod according to synodical administrative boundaries. Can it be that Blantyre Synod is succumbing to the temptation of treating its own "children" with kid gloves? Can it be said on the part of Nkhoma Synod that since the Malawi Congress Party was ousted from the government more than two decades ago, the synod has never been able to find an ally in political circles, and it is therefore critical of any political party that is in government until "their own political party" regains power? What about on the side of Livingstonia? Is it because the Northern Region is regarded as a minority politically, so the synod is always resentful of the ruling parties that come from the majority Southern Region, who, together with their Central Region colleagues, tend to scapegoat the minority North? One cannot avoid pondering these questions as one tries to make sense of the synods' responses to political developments in the country, especially when one considers the fact that the synods are equally susceptible to socio-political pressures. The answers to these questions are not simple and straightforward since the personalities and political leanings of their leadership influence the synods, sometimes even leading to divisions within the synods due to political influences as the leaders succumb to the temptation of teaming up according to their political sympathies.[86]

Conclusion

The aim of this chapter was to appreciate the fact that though the CCAP is taken to be one denomination, the independence of the synods has made it appear as if there are actually five denominations. By tracing the similarities and differences of the synods from their genesis, it becomes quite clear that diversity outweighs unity in the CCAP.

From a theological point of view, we see that some of the differences are there because of different theological emphases, especially due to the traditions of the mother churches that gave birth to the synods. On political

---

86. These politically motivated teams usually come to the fore during the periods leading to synodical leadership elections. For a fresh example as reported in the local press see Nyirongo, "Blantyre Synod Moves to Reconcile after Elections."

issues, it has been seen that the geographical and cultural contexts in which the synods are situated do contribute to the synods' different perspectives on pertinent issues as they cannot be taken to be operating in a vacuum. These observations therefore underscore the fact that the five synods' unity under the General Assembly is merely that of a federation rather than an organic whole.

CHAPTER 4

Pangs of Unity in Diversity among the Synods

Introduction

This chapter discusses the growing tensions within the CCAP, supposedly a united denomination, from its establishment in 1924/26 to the time the synods came into the open concerning their differences. The chapter argues that the process of union did not go all the way to making the CCAP one denomination in Malawi and thereby sowed seeds of possible discord in the future, unbeknown to the otherwise well-intending missionaries and early African church leaders.

The chapter also discusses the wrangle between the synods of Livingstonia and Nkhoma and the precarious situation of the synods of Blantyre, Harare and Zambia vis-à-vis the unity of the CCAP in contemporary times.

Early Tensions in the Unity of the CCAP

The coming together of the synods of Livingstonia and Blantyre (presbyteries at the time) as one denomination in 1924 was received with a lot of jubilation by the members of the church in Malawi as well as the mother churches of the missions back in Scotland.[1] The same was true when Nkhoma Synod joined the union in 1926. However, with regard to the joining of Nkhoma Synod, the jubilation was short lived as the continued membership of

---

1. See United Free Church of Scotland, *Reports to the General Assembly of the United Free Church of Scotland*, 12, 75–82.

Nkhoma Mission in the CCAP remained unstable throughout the period when the first constitution of the General Synod was in effect. This means that for thirty years (1926–1956) the unity of the CCAP was threatened by the DRC's desire to have Nkhoma pull out of the union if the union appeared to be working contrary to the expectations of the mother church back in South Africa.[2]

There were specifically two things that threatened the withdrawal of Nkhoma Presbytery from the synod of the CCAP. First, there was the issue of the article concerning the word of God in the document regarding the agreement of the three presbyteries, which according to the DRC had not been worded to their satisfaction. Initially, the DRC's dissatisfaction concerning the article was expressed prior to Nkhoma joining the CCAP family in 1926. The response of the other sister presbyteries of Livingstonia and Blantyre was initially to leave the wording of the article unchanged but give Nkhoma Presbytery the liberty to interpret the article according to their own understanding.[3] At the time this concession appeared to have solved the problem, for Nkhoma eventually joined the CCAP family in 1926. It has, however, to be remembered that the concern about the wording of the article came in the context of the DRC's general suspicion of the theological liberalism of the Scottish ministers, whose perceived modernistic attitude to biblical interpretation was, according to the conservative position of the DRC, undermining the authority of the Scriptures.[4]

This issue resurfaced at the synod meeting of the DRC which took place in Cape Town in October 1945. The Rev J. F. Mentz proposed that the General Missionary Council of the DRC be advised to see to it that the wording of Article I in the CCAP's original Statement of Faith be changed to clearly indicate that "the Bible as such is the word of God and not that it merely contained the word of God."[5] This issue became so serious in the DRC Synod meeting that it was actually proposed that if this were not to be done, the Nkhoma Presbytery should withdraw its membership from

---

2. See Pauw, "Mission and Church in Malawi," 346–347.

3. CCAP, "Minutes of Second Meeting of Synod," 13–15 October 1926, min. 7 (last para.).

4. Pauw, "Mission and Church in Malawi," 273–274.

5. Pauw, 348.

the CCAP. When it was learnt that this was what was agreed upon during the Cape DRC Synod meeting, some members of Nkhoma Mission staff were greatly perturbed by the synod's decision. This decision had actually put Nkhoma Presbytery in a very awkward position vis-a-vis its sister presbyteries of Livingstonia and Blantyre concerning their union in the CCAP. Consequently, some missionaries from Nkhoma took it upon themselves to explain the issue to their Livingstonia and Blantyre counterparts, in order to show that they were not particularly in agreement with the decision of their mother church's synod on the issue.[6] For some Nkhoma missionaries, the DRC Synod had actually even acted illegally since the terms of the union as originally drafted gave the powers to the Presbytery of Nkhoma on the question of possible withdrawal.[7] This meant that even though the DRC Synod wanted to exert its influence on the presbytery by posing as the final authority, it was actually contradicting itself since it had already agreed to the autonomy of the presbytery in matters concerning the union. This issue could not be fully resolved until there was a new constitution governing the CCAP.

The second major issue that threatened the unity of the CCAP during this first thirty-year period of its existence was the question of the incorporation of the Zambian churches into the CCAP family. Certain elements of the DRC, especially as influenced by the Orange Free State Synod, did not favour the London Missionary Society (LMS) in Zambia even though this was the desire of the Livingstonia missionaries, who wanted the CCAP to include the Presbyterian missions working in Zambia as well as those of the LMS.

The DRC wanted to preserve the Presbyterian system of church government and also the distinctive theology that the CCAP had come to embrace without diluting it with amalgamations from other church traditions. Besides, it is on record that some decades before this time, the relationship between some LMS missionaries and the Dutch colonists had proved sour, and the DRC leadership of the 1930s did not feel encouraged to associate itself with the LMS, which to some DRC members was perceived to be more of a political party than a missionary organization because of its criticism of

---

6. Pauw, 349.
7. SeeCCAP, "Minutes of Second Meeting of Synod," 13–15 October 1926, min. 5.9.

Dutch political polices.[8] In view of this lingering possibility of the CCAP amalgamation with the Zambian churches, the view of the DRCM was that Nkhoma Presbytery should withdraw from the CCAP if the other presbyteries would go ahead with welcoming the Zambian churches into the CCAP fold. This meant that the presbyteries of Livingstonia and Blantyre were faced with two awkward situations: either lose Nkhoma and embrace the Zambian churches or risk losing the Zambian churches and consolidate the membership of Nkhoma in the CCAP family. As it happened, the need to preserve the membership of Nkhoma prevailed, so for some time the CCAP would include only the Presbyterian missions operating in Malawi. This threat to the unity of the CCAP would also be dealt with in the second constitution of the union.

Differences in Practice

Besides the major issues that threatened the unity of the CCAP during the first thirty years of its existence, there were also some minor issues which the synod then found it necessary to bring to the attention of the presbyteries from time to time, especially in a bid to make uniform the different practices of the three presbyteries.

The first issue to be considered was the issue of infant baptism. It is now generally assumed that there has always been uniformity in the CCAP concerning infant baptism. However, that was not the case during the formative years of the federative denomination because different presbyteries then had different practices, especially when there were differences in the spirituality and membership status of the infants' parents.[9] It took some time before a uniform practice could be established in the synod. Due to the problem of migrant labour in the catchment area of Livingstonia, it was not easy for the presbytery to confine Christian marriage to Christians only. Where one partner in a Christian marriage was non-Christian, the Christian parent was allowed to present the children for baptism, if there was reasonable expectation that the vows would be carried out.[10] This practice by Livingstonia

---

8. Pauw, "Mission and Church in Malawi," 342.
9. CCAP, "Minutes of Synod," 1932, min. 36.
10. CCAP, "Minutes of Synod," 1936, min. 28(4).

Mission or presbytery continued up to 1948 when it was reported in the minutes of the Sixth Synod that the Livingstonia Presbytery had agreed to "administer baptism to infants whose parents were both Christians, or one a Christian and the other a Catechumen, thus establishing a uniform practice in the Synod."[11]

For some time, it was also proposed that the disjunction certificates for the Christians should be uniform in all the three presbyteries. In this regard, Nkhoma Presbytery was in the forefront in implementing the new policy by being the first to use the new disjunction certificates. During the sixth synod meeting, it was reported that Blantyre and Livingstonia presbyteries had not yet exhausted stocks of the old certificates but would begin to use the new certificates as soon as present stocks were finished.[12] This means that the two presbyteries, though in agreement with the decision of the synod, did not consider it a matter for urgent implementation.

All this shows that it was the desire of all the three presbyteries to make sure that the unity of the CCAP was not only imagined but practically realized even if it were at a slow pace. For the Christians at the grassroots level, this meant that the differences in the presbyteries were being minimized, thereby bringing unity and uniformity in the family of the CCAP. However, it has to be noted that the emphasis on the autonomy of the presbyteries as they continued to cooperate with their mother churches clearly marked differences that would later prove negative to the unity of the CCAP vis-a-vis the relationship of the three presbyteries, especially Livingstonia and Nkhoma.

It is interesting to read from some authorities that the unity of the CCAP was actually successful because of its "disunity," as the parent churches of the missions that formed the CCAP would not allow their missions to be fully under the newly established united local church. As Pauw explains:

> In fact, it is probably true to say that had this not been so the CCAP would never have come into being in this particular position. It is highly unlikely that the DRC or the Church of Scotland, for that matter, would have granted permission

---

11. See CCAP, "Minutes of Sixth Synod," 7–15 October 1948, min. 14, p. 3.
12. CCAP, "Minutes of Sixth Synod," 7–15 October 1948, min. 15.

> for its mission church to join as a presbytery if all control and authority over doctrinal and church political matters were in future to rest solely with the Synod of the CCAP.[13]

This shows that the mother churches of the missions were interested in union only in as far as they were able to exert influence on their former missions. It is in line with this observation that this study pursues its thesis that the CCAP, though touted as one church or denomination, is (and has always been) in fact five denominations under a loose umbrella of federative denominational identity. Pauw has actually referred to the CCAP as a "Federated Church [rather] than a United Church."[14] It is this concept that this study is following in trying to understand the relationship existing among the current five synods of the CCAP.

This observation does not in any way ignore the successes that the union has achieved, first as an amalgamation of the presbyteries and later the three Malawian synods and eventually the maturing of the Zimbabwean and Zambian branches into the synods of Harare and Zambia, respectively. The union itself is acknowledged as one of the most significant events in the history of Christianity on the African continent.[15] This union therefore was and continues to be a cause for celebration in the history of the church in Africa in general and in Central Africa in particular. Moreover, among the synods themselves there can be no doubt that more has been gained through the union, despite its problems, than would otherwise have been the case. It has been observed that Nkhoma Synod was able to contribute an evangelical and spiritual emphasis to the union as well as provide a certain theological conservatism and orthodoxy not very much associated with the other synods.[16] On the other hand, the Scottish missions contributed to the

---

13. Pauw, "Mission and Church in Malawi," 339.
14. Pauw, 339.
15. Pauw, 398.
16. Cf. Pauw, 398. Even among the grassroots it is well known that Nkhoma Synod tows a stricter, if conservative, line than her sister synods of Livingstonia and Blantyre. A simple story illustrated this point quite well during the course of the search for material for this chapter of the study. It was reported in one of the online news publications that St Columba Church of the Blantyre Synod had banned the wearing of miniskirts by women during church services. While this thing had nothing to do with the rest of the congregations under Blantyre Synod, let alone Nkhoma Synod, one commentator saw in it what he considered to be Nkhoma Synod's influence on Blantyre Synod by commenting thus: "The *Nkhoma*

method and approach of the successful administration of the church which Nkhoma Synod emulated.[17]

It can, therefore, be argued that on the basis of the positive factors of the union, it would be prudent to uphold the union – especially by exploring more areas of cooperation and uniformity, thereby sealing the cracks that are currently visible in the edifice that is the CCAP. The cracks that are in the CCAP are not new in that, as we have seen, the seeds of possible discord were sown right at the time of the denomination's establishment when boundaries were drawn in order to maintain the distinctiveness of the founding missions and their mother churches against a more uniform union under local synodical leadership.[18] It is not surprising therefore to find that the greatest bone of contention in the CCAP today is actually the issue of synodical boundaries and how these are treated by the various CCAP synods in order to maintain or increase their areas of jurisdiction or pastoral oversight to the flock that is always on the move across synodical boundaries. It is therefore necessary at this juncture to turn to a discussion on the issue of boundaries vis-a-vis the unity of the five synods.

Border Disputes in the CCAP

One of the issues – perhaps the greatest of them all – that has rocked the unity of the CCAP in recent years is the issue of the borders demarcating the areas of jurisdiction for the member synods of the General Assembly. In a way, this issue concerns all five synods of the General Assembly – namely, Livingstonia, Blantyre, Nkhoma, Harare and Zambia. However, the dispute between the synods of Nkhoma and Livingstonia is so pronounced that differences in other areas and with other synods are significantly eclipsed by this single dispute. For instance, the presence of the synods of Livingstonia and Nkhoma in Zimbabwe is an issue in the General Assembly in relation

---

Synodisation of Blantyre Synod will amount to nothing. How far will we go to judge women's spirituality by the clothes they wear? No matter the argument; conscience and one's personal relationship with God are what matter!" See Nyasa Times, "CCAP against Women Wearing Mini Skirts," *Nyasa Times*, http:// www.nyasatimes.com/2013/05/20/ccap-against-women-wearing-miniskirts, accessed 20 May 2013 (emphasis added).

17. Pauw, "Mission and Church in Malawi," 398.
18. See CCAP, "Minutes of Second Meeting of Synod," 13–15 October 1926, min. 5.5.

to the jurisdiction of the Harare Synod. At issue, also, is the presence of Malawian synods operating side by side in South Africa without uniting and without considering placing these South African congregations under the responsibility of the Reformed and Presbyterian churches of South Africa. It is interesting to note that at one of the General Assembly meetings it was resolved that all synods should pull out of the areas where they do not have constitutional jurisdiction and hand over the churches and assets to their sister synods or churches of the Reformed and Presbyterian denominational family.[19] This resolve is yet to be honoured by the synods, but it is also interesting to note that it was actually during this meeting's deliberations that the delegates of the Synod of Livingstonia decided to act as mere observers, in protest, because they were, according to them, denied their constitutional and traditional turn to chair the assembly by providing a moderator from their synod.[20]

The Livingstonia – Nkhoma Border Dispute

The border dispute between the Synod of Livingstonia and Nkhoma Synod continues to make headlines even though the two synods appear to have closed the chapter by declaring that there are no more borders between them, meaning that each synod is free to establish churches in the other's hitherto exclusive territory and expect the other synod to do the same. Some observers and commentators are of the view that this stand by the two synods is not a solution to the problem but a mere sweep under the carpet, which, with the passage of time, may actually prove to be a time bomb as it does not give any guarantee that the issue has been solved once and for all.

In order to understand the current developments in the border dispute between the synods of Livingstonia and Nkhoma we need to go back in time to where things began so that we can appreciate the problem from its source. It has to be noted that prior to the coming of the DRCM, which is the mother mission of Nkhoma Synod, the missions of Livingstonia and Blantyre shared the whole country of what is now Malawi (and beyond into neighbouring countries) between themselves in as far as Presbyterian comity was concerned. This means that Livingstonia and Blantyre shared between

---

19. See CCAP General Assembly, Press Release, 25 January 2007, para. (d) and (e).
20. Synod of Livingstonia, "Issues of Concern in Regard to General Assembly's Request."

themselves what is now the Central Region of Malawi and largely the territory of Nkhoma Synod – except for Ntcheu District and some parts of the northern and southern regional boundaries.

When the DRCM missionaries came into the country, they were hosted by Livingstonia Mission and afterwards they were provided for and sent on their journey from the north of the country towards what is now the Central Region of Malawi. For some time, the DRCM was under the supervision of the Livingstonia missionaries, whose materials, including even stationery, they used for some years before the establishment of their own Mission Council.[21] During all this time the question of boundaries did not enter anybody's mind except assuming, in general terms, that the sphere of influence for the DRCM was to be between the areas targeted by Livingstonia Mission in the north and Blantyre Mission in the south. The question of actual physical boundaries, therefore, did not arise until the year 1904, at least in so far as recorded missionary history is concerned.

The year 1904 saw the boundary between Livingstonia and Nkhoma being officially drawn. The results of this boundary demarcation date from 1910 in as far as documentation is concerned, but it is faithfully recorded that there was a meeting of the representatives of the Livingstonia Mission and of DRCM at the Village of Chinkwiri on 29 July 1904, where the boundary between their respective spheres was agreed upon in the following details:

> From the highest point of Chipata Mountain the boundary line passes through the highest points of Mpasa, Kanjoka (a small knoll south of Chinkwiri's), Mpale, Mwanjezi; hence to the mouth of the Rusa River; from which point the boundary is the watershed between the Rusa and Bua Rivers passing the Kapirintiwa, across the Rusa on to Mbwabwa.[22]

---

21. It is on record that even the bricks used for the first permanent building at Mvera had the name Livingstonia engraved on them. See Parsons, "Scots and Afrikaners in Central Africa," 22.

22. An extract from *Notuen Uitvorenden Roads Der Ned Geref Kerk Zending Naar Mideee Afrika Book I* appearing as an attachment to a memo from Maurice Munthali (Acting General Secretary, Synod of Livingstonia) to all ministers of Synod of Livingstonia under the subject "Border Dispute," 1. It was proposed to change the name M'bwabwa to Kwingwinyembe by the request of Dr Prentice (the Livingstonia missionary at Kasungu) on 4 September 1904.

The Livingstonia Mission representatives who agreed to this boundary line were George Prentice and M. H. Henderson, while on the side of the DRCM there were W. H. Murray and A. J. Liebenberg.[23]

Perhaps if this original official boundary had remained, there would have been no (or less) disputes between the Synod of Livingstonia and Nkhoma Synod in the succeeding years. However, as it happened, the original boundary was not to remain forever, and in the year 1923 Livingstonia Mission officially handed over its Chilanga and Tamanda Missions to the DRCM, thus completing the handover of all the mission stations established by the Livingstonia Mission that were now in the DRCM's area of influence. It is interesting to note that this transfer was actually initiated by the Livingstonia Mission leadership, who, some two years prior to the handover, had asked the leadership of the DRCM if they could accept the responsibility of taking over the administration of Chilanga and Tamanda mission stations. After their deliberations, the council of the DRCM agreed to accept the offer of transfer of Chilanga (Kasungu) and Tamanda Missions into their hands. They appointed the Rev J. A. Retief, Rev G. De C. Murray and Mr W. F. van de Riet as a commission to negotiate the terms of the transfer with their Livingstonia counterparts in the persons of Mr C. Stuart, Dr Prentice and Dr Laws.[24]

It appears that this offer was made at the same time as the invitation to Nkhoma Mission to join the CCAP family, being the direction towards which Livingstonia and Blantyre were heading. In the wisdom of the DRCM missionaries, they saw fit to separate the two issues in order to deal with them on their own merits. They thus intimated their position to their Livingstonia colleagues: "In reference to joining the Church of Central Africa Presbyterian we would consider the matter entirely on its own merit."[25]

---

23. An extract from *Notuen Uitvorenden Roads Der Ned Geref Kerk Zending Naar Mideee Afrika Book I* appearing as an attachment to a memo from Maurice Munthali (Acting General Secretary, Synod of Livingstonia) to all ministers of Synod of Livingstonia under the subject "Border Dispute," 2.

24. "Minute of Meeting of Commissioners from the Dutch Reformed Mission and Livingstonia Mission," Kasungu, 8 October 1923.

25. "Minute of Meeting of Commissioners from the Dutch Reformed Mission and Livingstonia," Kasungu, 8 October 1923.

Having transferred the ownership of the two mission stations, it was now necessary to re-define the boundary between the two missions in view of the new situation. It was recorded eventually that the new boundary would follow the approximate tribal boundary as represented by the schools occupied by Kasungu and Loudon, thus separating the two missions but also the ethnic groups in the area.[26] According to J. L. Pretorius "this was the final stage of a movement to assign all the Chewa people to the DRCM and the Ngoni/Tumbuka to Livingstonia."[27]

According to Felix Chingota, scholarly research in the area has shown that after the end of Chewa/Ngoni wars the tribal boundary was the Mpasadzi River.[28] Chingota further claims that there is no other document that has superseded or abrogated the 1923 document concerning the boundary between the two synods, at least in as far as the upland boundary is concerned.[29] As for the lake shore area boundary, archival sources do not show any document indicating the actual boundary between the two synods in the Dwangwa-Bua area of Nkhotakota District. Be that as it may, the claim on the part of the Synod of Livingstonia is that the boundary has all along been considered to be the Bua River, except for a small strip of land along the lake shore between the Bua and Dwangwa Rivers, and that, apart from this strip, the border is the Dwangwa River. On the part of Nkhoma Synod the conviction is that the boundary is the Dwangwa River all the way to the lake without recognizing the strip of land along the lake as part of Livingstonia territory.[30]

This means that the areas of dispute in as far as the border issue between the Synod of Livingstonia and Nkhoma Synod are concerned are those areas between the Rivers of Dwangwa and Milenje in Kasungu (upper land) and Bua and Dwangwa in the lakeshore area of Nkhotakota District.[31] The uncertainty of the borders can therefore be described as an old problem in the

---

26. Kasungu and Loudon were both Livingstonia Mission stations but serving the two different ethnic groups of Chewa and Ngoni, respectively.
27. Pretorius, "Story of the Dutch Reformed Church," 16.
28. Chingota, "Lost Opportunities," 4.
29. Chingota, 4.
30. "Memorandum of Understanding on the Border Dispute," 2.
31. "Memorandum of Understanding on the Border Dispute," 2.

relationship of the synods, especially the relationship between Livingstonia and Nkhoma.

After the establishment of the General Synod in 1956, attempts were made in the succeeding years to resolve the differences concerning the border issue. Of special significance in this regard was the Chamakala Agreement of 1967. This agreement, which was ratified by the Border Committees of the two synods of Livingstonia and Nkhoma at a place known as Chamakala, proposed that there be a buffer zone along the disputed border so that the two synods could be establishing churches side by side within the buffer zone but not beyond it.[32] The buffer zone proposed was the area between Milenje and Dwangwa Rivers. When the decision of the two committees was referred back to their respective synods for approval, the synods did not approve it. First, when the issue was presented to Nkhoma Synod, the Synod Conference rejected it summarily, arguing that the synod could only accept it if there was another buffer zone beyond Milenje River. This means that, from the point of view of Nkhoma Synod, Milenje River was their perceived boundary, with the result that any proposed buffer zone on the southern side of the river was already in a territory considered exclusively their own. Second, when the Synod of Livingstonia learned about Nkhoma Synod's proposal to extend the buffer zone northwards of Milenje River, they also rejected the proposal, thereby halting the whole process of sorting out the border dispute at that particular time.[33] Had the issue been sorted out at that time, the border dispute would by now be just a footnote in the history of the CCAP.

The dispute between the two synods continued and escalated further between the years 1980 and 1996 when some Christians of the Matiki congregation of the Synod of Livingstonia in the disputed area of Dwangwa Sugar Plantation in Nkhotakota District decided to break away in order to form a Nkhoma Synod congregation which they called Majiga.[34] This was more like a rebellion against the administration of the Synod of Livingstonia while defecting to Nkhoma Synod with which they wanted to identify at that time for whatever reasons. When the matter reached the General Synod,

---

32. "Memorandum of Understanding on the Border Dispute," 2.
33. Chingota, "Lost Opportunities," 1.
34. "Memorandum of Understanding on the Border Dispute," 2.

the leadership decided that the said congregation should go back into the hands of the Synod of Livingstonia. They arranged that a special handover ceremony be held where officials representing the two synods would symbolically perform the act of handing over and receiving the congregation back into the hands of the Synod of Livingstonia.[35] When the General Synod's Standing Committee met at the Christian Health Association of Malawi (CHAM) secretariat to be briefed on how the handover ceremony had been carried out, they learned, to their shock, that the ceremony had actually ended in a fiasco due to congregational resistance. It was reported that the doors of the prayer house were sealed with logs of blue gum (eucalyptus) trees in order to prevent the officials of the two synods from performing the handover ceremony.[36]

In reviewing the incident, the General Synod's Standing Committee found Nkhoma Synod at fault and reiterated the earlier decision that Nkhoma Synod must facilitate the handover of the prayer house under dispute to Synod of Livingstonia without conditions.[37] As it stands, Nkhoma Synod did not comply with that decision as no further arrangements were made to implement the handover of the prayer house in question. After some years, a Nkhoma Synod minister was sent to pastor the same congregation.[38]

The unity of the CCAP was greatly tested in 1996 when the Synod of Livingstonia pulled out of the General Synod with the intention of embarking on the establishment of prayer houses across synodical boundaries. The decision to leave the General Synod was rescinded in the year 2000 when they eventually re-joined "in the hope that a lasting solution would be found to the border dispute leading to Nkhoma Synod's withdrawal from encroached territory."[39]

---

35. See "Minutes of the General Assembly Sub-committee on Dwangwa held on 9–10 September 1995," item 5 under "Closing," p. 2 and "Minutes of the General Assembly Standing Committee held at St Peter's Church on 17–18 July 1996," min. 2.7/96.

36. SeeCCAP General Synod, "Minutes of the Forum of the Standing Committee on Dwangwa Dispute."

37. Chingota,"Lost Opportunities," 1–2.

38. Synod of Livingstonia, "Minutes of the Operation beyond Borders Taskforce Committee," min. 06/2006, being matters arising from min. 08/2005(i).

39. Synod of Livingstonia, "Solution to the Border Dispute."

In the year 2005, the dispute was fuelled further owing to the failure of the synods to agree on one thing in the Standing Committee of the General Assembly. The meeting of this committee became so emotional that the delegates of the Synod of Livingstonia opted to walk out in a kind of defiance. According to Rev Chingota's testimony, the meeting was convened on 18 April with the aim of deliberating on only two things: reports from the synods and a way forward on the border dispute issue. After the synods of Livingstonia and Nkhoma had presented their reports on the issue, as asked, it was time to discuss the way forward, but, when questions were asked about the reports in order to get some clarification, the process developed into a match of accusations and counter accusations between the "belligerent" synods of Livingstonia and Nkhoma, leading the former to literally walk out of the meeting. This meant that the meeting could not continue as one primary stakeholder had walked out. This meeting, together with the behaviour of the synods, was heavily reported in the press and received criticism and condemnation from the general public at large as the behaviour shown, notwithstanding the grievances aired, was below what is expected of the church as the custodian of morality and the spirit of toleration and accommodation for those with contrary views.

In the year 2006, with support from the Church of Scotland, the General Assembly constituted a Commission of Inquiry to investigate issues relating to the border dispute in terms of causes and the identification of the true border between the Synod of Livingstonia and Nkhoma Synod. This Commission of Inquiry came in as a result of commitment to an action plan recommended by a Conflict and Management Skills Workshop facilitated by Mr John Sturrock, which took place at Kambiri Lodge in Salima District from 12 to 15 March 2006. Mr Sturrock was identified as an expert in mediation by the Church of Scotland which had convinced the General Secretaries of the three CCAP Malawian synods – when they visited Scotland towards the end of the year 2005 – that such a person and his skills was needed in the effort to bring the border dispute to an end.[40]

Though the Synod of Livingstonia was not adequately represented at the workshop, owing to the conspicuous absence of its moderator and the

---

40. Chingota, "Lost Opportunities."

moderator-elect, the recommendations of the workshop had to be carried out. Consequently, on 28 March 2006 the Standing Committee of the General Assembly set up the Commission of Inquiry comprising three commissioners from the Synod of Livingstonia, three from Nkhoma Synod and two each from Blantyre Synod and the General Assembly.[41]

It has been observed that the Synod of Livingstonia did not assist the Commission of Inquiry as expected; its three commissioners are said to have been absent during the work of the Commission. Besides, contrary to its promises, the Synod of Livingstonia failed to hand over to the Commission of Inquiry the necessary documents that would help them with the work of the inquiry.[42]

After the Commission of Inquiry had written its report, it was arranged that there be a meeting of the General Assembly's Standing Committee to officially receive the report. This meeting took place at Masamba. Apart from the leadership of the CCAP General Assembly, present at this meeting were Mr John Sturrock, the mediation expert, and the Rev Dr Kenneth Ross, a representative of the Church of Scotland. Guided by the findings of the Commission of Inquiry, the Standing Committee went on to determine the border line between Nkhoma Synod and the Synod of Livingstonia even though the moderator of the Synod of Livingstonia did not attend the meeting.[43]

Of special significance at this Masamba meeting was the realization that the issues to do with the border dispute were deeper than what had been imagined up to that time, as economic, political, linguistic and ethnic undercurrents were perceived.[44] Due to what had been discovered as the undercurrents with regard to the border dispute, it was decided that a meeting of moderators and general secretaries of the synods and the General Assembly be convened in order to discuss a memorandum of understanding and a code of conduct with regard to the practicalities of the transfer of property and congregations in view of the new proposed boundaries. This meeting was, however, brought to a premature closure because the delegates of the Synod

---

41. Chingota.
42. Chingota, 2.
43. Chingota, 3.
44. Zgambo, "Conflict within the Church," 52.

of Livingstonia did not continue with the discussions. Their argument was basically that the draft documents of the memorandum of understanding and code of conduct were ultimately based on the report of the Commission of Inquiry, which, according to them, contained wrong information. The meeting was stopped in order to give the Synod of Livingstonia a chance to present their views in the next Standing Committee meeting.

Synod of Livingstonia's Operation beyond Borders Stand

On the part of the Synod of Livingstonia, Nkhoma Synod's establishment of over eighty congregations in Livingstonia territory is intolerable. It is on record that the decision to ignore the boundary between itself and Nkhoma was agreed upon at a Synod of Livingstonia meeting held in Mzimba in 1990. However, the Synod of Livingstonia claims that this decision was not immediately implemented in order to give a chance for the General Assembly and Nkhoma Synod to consider Livingstonia's concerns.[45]

In a letter addressed to all ministers of the CCAP Synod of Livingstonia dated 16 May 2005, the then Acting Secretary General of the Synod of Livingstonia, the Rev Maurice C. E. Munthali, informed all the ministers and heads of department of the Synod of Livingstonia about the decision the synod had taken concerning the border issue. The letter explains the frustration experienced by the Synod of Livingstonia on the failure to amicably resolve the border issue at a meeting called by the moderator of the General Assembly on 18 April 2005 where only the three Malawian synods of the CCAP General Assembly were invited. Owing to this "frustration," the letter intimates that the moderator of the Synod of Livingstonia called for a Synod Executive Committee meeting on 20 April 2005 in order to seek some guiding mandate and way forward. It was at this committee meeting that the Synod of Livingstonia strengthened its position of not respecting any borders between itself and Nkhoma Synod. The letter reads in part:

> The committee noted that we will only be spending time fighting over a boundary which our counterparts actually disregarded years ago if we choose to keep negotiating for it. It was pointed out at the same meeting that we should remain as

---

45. Synod of Livingstonia, "Solution to the Border Dispute."

members of the General Assembly but that each of us will be free to establish churches without regard to any official border.[46]

The acting general secretary explained in the letter that the reason Nkhoma Synod is advancing into Livingstonia territory is that it is following its Chewa-speaking "children," who do not understand or are not interested in the languages spoken in the Synod of Livingstonia's sphere of influence.[47] One of the reasons for this communication was for the presbyteries to discuss the issue in their meetings and come up with their own independent opinion, even though the position of the synod was already reached.

It can be argued that the frustration which Synod of Livingstonia felt was because it perceived the new arrangement of the border to be favouring Nkhoma Synod in that, through the Commission of Inquiry's Report, the proposed upland boundary of Mpasadzi River was actually giving Nkhoma Synod more territory into the Synod of Livingstonia's sphere of influence. What is not known is whether the acceptance of the new boundaries as demarcated would indeed bring the border dispute to a rest in view of the undercurrents that complicated the otherwise simple issue of physical boundaries. The Synod of Livingstonia's press release of 24 September 2006 made it very clear that, in as far as it was concerned, the issue of borders with Nkhoma Synod was over. This decision was reached unanimously at the synod's 30th assembly held at Bandawe Mission from 22 to 27 September 2006. Interestingly, the press release reiterated the Synod of Livingstonia's commitment to peaceful coexistence with her sister synods in Malawi and beyond, including the "belligerent" Nkhoma Synod, and also upholding the unity of the CCAP General Assembly in the new context of post-border co-existence of the synods.[48]

The decision taken by the Synod of Livingstonia appears not to have been greatly challenged by the synod's clergy though it cannot be ruled out that there were some who did not agree with the decision.[49] On the part of lay

---

46. Munthali, "Border Dispute."
47. Munthali, 2.
48. Synod of Livingstonia, "Solution to the Border Dispute."
49. For instance, Rev H. K. Mvula, an ex-moderator of the Synod of Livingstonia expressed his concern over the manner in which the Border Dispute was being handled by the synod. He also did not agree with the idea that this critical issue should be discussed by the synod's Executive Committee. See Mvula, "There Is a Crisis in the CCAP Church."

people, however, the negative responses have been experienced as evidenced by some members of the synod who organized themselves into concerned groups and raised their reservations on the synod's stand through petitions. One example, a group in Zomba City calling itself "Friends of Livingstonia–Zomba," met at Zomba Theological College on 2 May 2005, where, after deliberations, they decided to write a letter to the general secretary of the Synod of Livingstonia, expressing their concerns regarding the relationship between Livingstonia and Nkhoma synods. They observed, among other things, that by building different CCAP churches from the Synod of Livingstonia and Nkhoma Synod in one town, the church would inevitably foment conflict amongst its members.[50] One of their recommendations, therefore, was that the decision to recognize only Blantyre Synod's boundary, and any actions arising from it, should not be implemented immediately in order to allow more people to understand the problem so there is further effort to resolve it.

Despite resistance from many quarters, the Synod of Livingstonia resolved to establish churches deeper into Nkhoma Synod's territory as a way, in their view, to make sure that the issue of border disputes was now water under the bridge. Consequently, the Synod of Livingstonia formed a taskforce committee with the mandate of planning and directing the logistics towards establishing churches in the territory that was hitherto unquestionably under the jurisdiction of Nkhoma Synod. The results of the labours of this taskforce committee were such that the Synod of Livingstonia was able to establish Livingstonia congregations in Kasungu, Nkhotakota and Lilongwe, a deep penetration into Nkhoma Synod's territory beyond the disputed border areas.

Resistance to the Synod of Livingstonia's stand to disregard the boundary with Nkhoma Synod, and to start building churches in Nkhoma's interior territory, continued even after the Synod of Livingstonia had already started seeing the mushrooming of some of her churches in Nkhoma Synod's territory. On 26 April 2006, concerned members of the Synod of Livingstonia wrote a letter to the synod's moderator expressing their concerns over the opening of CCAP Synod of Livingstonia churches inside Nkhoma Synod's

---

50. Friends of the Livingstonia Synod–Zomba to the General Secretary of the Synod of Livingstonia, "Relationship between Livingstonia and Nkhoma Synod," 2.

area of jurisdiction.[51] The letter was copied to the general secretary of the Synod of Livingstonia and the general secretary and moderator of the General Assembly. Interestingly, among these concerned members there were three ordained ministers: one expatriate and two locals.[52] What this means is that even though the Synod of Livingstonia has gone ahead with its decision of not recognizing boundaries with its sister Synod of Nkhoma, not all of its members, whether ordained or lay, are comfortable with the present developments. The general concern among those that were against the synod's stand at the time was that these developments were likely to lead to a breach of peace and preclude any attempts at reconciliation and unity.[53]

It is very clear that pulling out from encroached territories is not easy, though possible, but pulling out from inner areas such as Lilongwe would not be an easy task to execute. Besides, Nkhoma Synod has also taken a stand that they too will not recognize the boundaries with Livingstonia. Consequently, we are now seeing Nkhoma Synod churches not only along the disputed border areas but also right in the interior of Synod of Livingstonia territory, such as Mzuzu City, Mzimba, Karonga and other areas.

Synod of Livingstonia is fully convinced that when the Nkhoma Synod churches were established in her territory the border was abolished, and she notes that there is co-existence along the disputed areas and hopes that by disregarding the borders there can still be peaceful co-existence, which has so far been the case despite the synods establishing congregations in the interior of each other's territories.

Nkhoma Synod's Position

Following Synod of Livingstonia's position of not recognizing the borders with it, Nkhoma Synod has been forced to reciprocate in this initiative. Whereas before Nkhoma Synod only had congregations along the disputed border areas, now it is establishing congregations all over Synod of

---

51. Synod of Livingstonia Members to the Moderator of the Synod of the Livingstonia, "Concern over the Opening of CCAP Synod of Livingstonia Churches inside Nkhoma Synod Jurisdiction."

52. Among the signatories of this letter there was also one non-ordained missionary.

53. Synod of Livingstonia Members to the Moderator of the Synod of the Livingstonia, "Concern over the Opening of CCAP Synod of Livingstonia Churches inside Nkhoma Synod Jurisdiction."

Livingstonia's territory. However, it is being said that for Nkhoma Synod the issue of doing away with the boundaries is being considered beyond its dispute with Livingstonia alone. This means that, in principle, Nkhoma Synod is pushing for a "no border policy" that will affect even Blantyre Synod, as it does not want to have boundaries in the south while there are no longer boundaries (or no respect for them) in the north. Initially, Nkhoma Synod was known to operate in the Synod of Livingstonia's sphere of influence only in areas near the borders.[54]

Blantyre Synod's Position

The history of the border dispute and other differences among the three CCAP synods in Malawi has always been a concern to Blantyre Synod, which could not enjoy peaceful membership of the CCAP when its two sister synods in the country were drifting apart over the course of history, but it has also realized that, in general, the unity of the CCAP has ever been "superficial." More than fifty years after the formation of the CCAP, in 1977, Blantyre Synod was lamenting at what it perceived to be a lack of real unity in the CCAP as expressed in its "Life and Work Report" during the General Synod of 1977:

> The Synod of Blantyre deplores that the unity of the CCAP has remained superficial for so long and wishes to express its support for any move towards deeper and organic unity. The Synod rejoices that the theological college will move to Zomba this October under the auspice of the four synods. More fields of cooperation should be encouraged to join, for in working together the Church will present a united Gospel Message of its Master Jesus Christ through prayers that we should all be one.[55]

---

54. After this chapter had already been drafted there were reliable reports that a Nkhoma Synod congregation had been established at Mzimba, which is a long distance from the disputed areas into the interior of the Synod of Livingstonia's territory. Besides, a new Nkhoma Synod congregation is now officially established in Mzuzu (where the Synod of Livingstonia is headquartered) at Katoto Secondary School.

55. Sangaya, "Life and Work of Blantyre Synod," 17. See also CCAP, *Minutes of the General Synod Held at Chongoni from 16th to 17th August 1977*, min. 20.C. (xiii). The reference to four synods in the above quotation refers to Livingstonia, Blantyre, Nkhoma and Salisbury (now Harare). This was before the establishment of the Synod of Zambia.

This shows that Blantyre Synod has been concerned with the issue of differences in the synods, and the current border dispute between the synods of Livingstonia and Nkhoma is no mean thing in as far as the position of Blantyre Synod is concerned. Clerical members of Blantyre Synod have voiced the need to resolve the differences between Livingstonia and Nkhoma Synods. They have done so either in their capacity as ordinary church ministers or in view of their privileged senior positions in their synod or in the General Assembly.[56]

Owing to the current disagreements, Blantyre Synod finds fault with both the Synod of Livingstonia and Nkhoma Synod in their failure to resolve their differences and also to respect the decisions made by the General Assembly in a bid to sort out the issue.[57] Of special importance, the Blantyre Synod censured Nkhoma Synod's failure to implement what have come to be known as the Chamakala and Majiga Agreements. In the first case, Nkhoma Synod refused to abide by the proposed agreement concerning the buffer zone south of Milenje River, while in the second instance they did not bless the transfer of Majiga Prayer House which the General Assembly unanimously agree belonged to the Synod of Livingstonia.

Of great concern also to Blantyre Synod is the current position of the Synod of Livingstonia's policy of saying there should be no recognition of borders between Livingstonia and Nkhoma. Comparing the situation with other churches in the country, which have and do respect their borders, such as the Anglican Dioceses and Roman Catholic Dioceses, Blantyre Synod fears that the "No Border Policy" has the potential to breed confusion and anarchy.[58] Some observers feel that Blantyre Synod is wary of this issue because it fears that Synod of Livingstonia may declare the "No Border Policy" even with them as it is feared Nkhoma Synod has done, though practically it has not yet gone into the territory of Blantyre Synod.[59]

---

56. For instance, see Chingota, "Lost Opportunities"; Chitsulo, "Prophetic Message for Reconciliation between Nkhoma and Livingstonia Synods"; Mangisa, "Questions of Conscience on Livingstonia-Nkhoma Relations."

57. Blantyre Synod, "Blantyre Synod Response," 1.

58. Blantyre Synod, "Blantyre Synod Response," 1.5.

59. Synod of Livingstonia minister, in conversation with the author (name withheld).

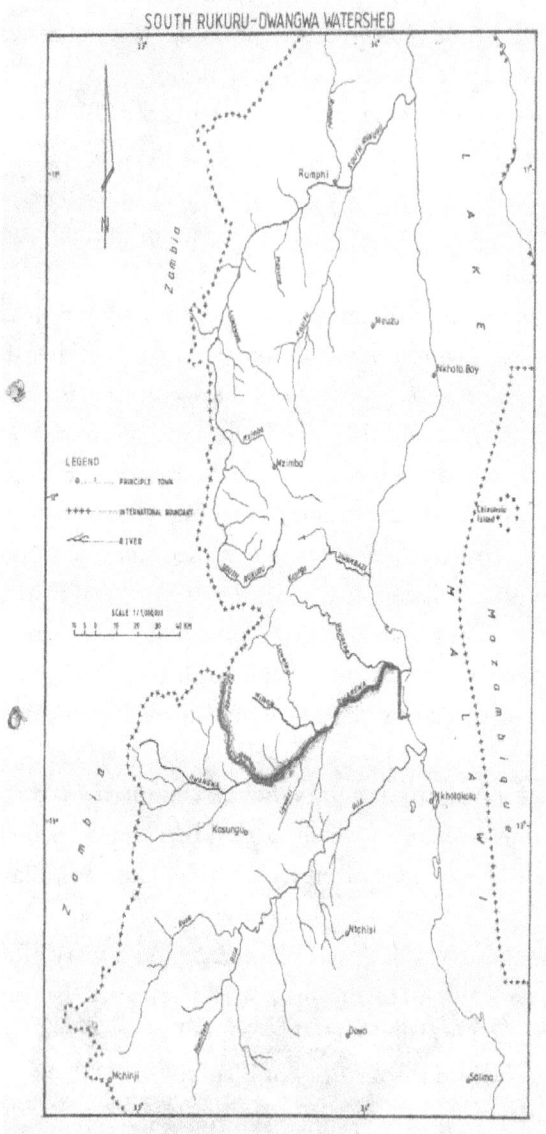

Figure 1: Map of South Rukuru and Dwangwa Rivers Watershed, showing the post Commission of Inquiry proposed boundary between Livingstonia and Nkhoma synods of the CCAP.[60]

---

60. Sourced from: Synod of Livingstonia, General Secretary's Border Dispute File, used with permission from Rev Levi Nyondo, the General Secretary of the Synod of Livingstonia.

Legal, Political and Theological Implications of the Border Disputes

The border dispute between the Synod of Livingstonia and Nkhoma Synod, especially in relation to the current stand that borders should no longer be recognized, presents interesting legal, political and theological cases. This is especially so in view of the church's need to adhere to its own constitution and theological position and the perceived failure to be able to do so within a given socio-political context.

Legal Implications

From a legal point of view, both the Synod of Livingstonia and Nkhoma Synod are at fault with regard to the constitution of the General Assembly as it currently stands. There are reports that a new constitution is being drafted which will take into consideration the current status of the synods' relationships. However, before that constitution becomes effective, the current constitution is still valid and the actions of the synods are supposed to be evaluated in light of what is stipulated therein. In the first place, the constitution does recognize boundaries among the synods as stipulated in the following provision: "The Church being one and only divided into Synods for administrative convenience each Synod shall ensure it lives in harmony with the Synod it shares a common border with and shall at all times respect the boundaries as existing or as prescribed herein."[61] This means that not to respect the boundaries is for the synods of Livingstonia and Nkhoma to act unconstitutionally. While it can be counterargued that the constitution does mention the boundaries but that they are not so clear and neither are they agreed upon by the synods, hence their violation, it would still be unconstitutional to declare that the boundaries shall no longer be respected when the constitution still mentions them and expects the synods to respect them. Besides, even if there were disagreements along the boundaries, the differences of opinion do not give the synods the mandate to go all the way into their sister synod's territory and establish churches where the question of boundary dispute cannot be justified. If the border lines could not be settled, why not just continue with encroachment in the disputed areas rather than going all the way to places that are farther removed from the disputed areas?

---

61. "The CCAP General Assembly Constitutional Schedule," 4.1.1.

Consequently, the actions of these synods and of the Christians who join the newly formed congregations further violate the constitutional order of the General Assembly, whose constitutional schedule stipulates as follows:

> The General Assembly shall, in the case of new Synods or Mission work areas, demarcate geographical boundaries of Synods and mission work areas and allocate authority to a particular Synod over the demarcated area. The geographical boundaries shall be set in such a way that all Christians within the bounds of that area will be under the jurisdiction of one Synod and no area or group of people within its bounds shall have the right to affiliate themselves with a Synod other than the one granted jurisdiction over that area by the General Assembly.[62]

This means that the General Assembly's constitutional provision that talks about boundaries among the synods is not just being violated but that it has been disregarded and abandoned altogether, making the two synods irredeemably culpable in as far constitutional adherence is concerned. Be that as it may, the General Assembly has no powers to punish the two synods; it can only plead with them to consider changing things for the better, but it has no enforcing authority to execute any punitive measures on the "wayward" synods.[63] This is to be most lamented because constitutionally the General Assembly is mandated to punish or discipline an offending synod as explained in the following provision:

> When a Synod or any of its lower courts wishes to open, establish or construct a new church or prayer house within three kilometres to the known Synod boundary it shall first consult the other Synod with which it shares a common border to confirm that such a site is indeed within the jurisdiction of the constructing Synod and failing such agreement the matter shall be

---

62. "The CCAP General Assembly Constitutional Schedule," 4.1.2.
63. In 2006, the then moderator of the General Assembly, the Rt Rev Dr Felix Chingota, was quoted in the press saying that the General Assembly would punish the Synod of Livingstonia for its violation of the provisions of the 2002 General Assembly constitution on border dispute issues, but the "threat," as it were, came to nothing. See Nyirongo, "General Synod to Discipline Livingstonia."

referred to the General Assembly whose decision shall be binding on the parties. Contravention of this provision shall lead to disciplinary action being taken against the offending Synod.[64]

While appealing to civil courts in border dispute matters may be a possibility, it is something that may not necessarily produce a lasting solution, since legality alone may not touch the core of the problem which has moral and theological dimensions besides other numerous undercurrents.

Political Implications

In most cases, the disagreements between the three synods in Malawi make people fear that they are likely to further disintegrate the country since the country is already divided along regional lines, and the synods, to a large extent, follow these regional boundaries. This observation is true in the sense that the three Malawian synods are naturally associated with the three regions of the country. While it may not be the intention of the synods to extend their differences into the political arena, politics is such a phenomenon that it makes the politicians not to leave any stone unturned in a bid to manipulate the situation for their own political gains.

It has to be noted that big political parties in Malawi take advantage of the people's differences along regional lines to consolidate their power bases by associating with particular regions as their strongholds and trying to make them "no-go-zones" for rival parties. Since the three Malawian synods have their areas of influence along regional lines, it is very easy to associate them with the political parties that consider those regions their strongholds. While this is not necessarily always the case, there is a temptation in the country to associate members of one synod with a particular political party, by implication making them rivals of their brothers and sisters from a different synod and, therefore, different region and different political party. This scenario gives confidence to politicians who are members of a dominant political party in the region that, come what may, they cannot lose an election in that particular region because it is "their" region. Consequently, even if this political party were associated with negative things, it cannot be censured by the synods of other regions because their position cannot be taken to be

---

64. "The CCAP General Assembly Constitutional Schedule," 4.2.

objective but as one based on regionalism or, worse still, as mercenary on behalf of rival political parties.[65]

It is because of such complexities that many feel a united CCAP is a guarantee for the unity of the country and a CCAP divided along synodical lines is likely to divide the country if not along ethnic lines at least along regional ones. It is in view of such observations that some of the concerned members of the CCAP Synod of Livingstonia who did not support the idea of opening Livingstonia churches in the Central Region pleaded with their synod to stop the trend and continue to trust that the General Assembly would arrive at an amicable solution to their differences with Nkhoma Synod, reminding the synod leadership that the "country is in bondage of regionalistic discriminations."[66] Even some members of the clergy from Blantyre Synod are afraid of the divisions in the church as seen among the synods, which they consider to have wider implications as Rev Master Jumbe observes: "This is dangerous not only to the church but to the nation that has enjoyed peaceful coexistence among its people throughout history. This development should be of concern not only to CCAP members but the government as well."[67] As it currently stands, there are no open hostilities among the Christians of the CCAP since the issue of borders or no borders is largely an administrative one though not immune from other influences. It is the fear of what may happen when other non-administrative and even non-ecclesiastical influences take over that makes many uneasy since the differences are already piling up like fuel for the spark that may come. Some are of the view that Malawian politicians are happy with the status quo because it, in a way, renders the church less critical ethically as it cannot speak with a united voice when it has a lot of issues to sort out in its own house. As Jumbe again rightly notes, "Unfortunately, any divisions, disagreements and schisms in the church is a cause for celebration among our politicians who for the last decades

---

65. It is due to this situation that sometimes a CCAP synod has been accused of being either a mouthpiece or a defender of a certain political party with which it is closely associated. On the other hand, a CCAP synod has also been accused of being an enemy of a certain party which has not managed, as it were, to charm the synod in question.

66. Synod of Livingstonia Members to the Moderator of the Synod of the Livingstonia, "Concern over the Opening of CCAP Synod of Livingstonia Churches inside Nkhoma Synod Jurisdiction," 2.

67. Jumbe, "When the Church becomes Tasteless."

have been threatened by the stand of the church."⁶⁸ Jumbe's sentiments are reminiscent of the fact that the churches in Malawi, and the CCAP synods in particular, have, to a certain extent, lost their prophetic role or mandate in society because of in-house fighting. Writing towards the end of 2008, as Malawi was approaching the 2009 General Elections, George Kasakula added his voice to the criticism levelled against the synods of Livingstonia and Nkhoma in relation to their moral authority to arbitrate between rival political camps: "In fact because of the way the two synods are conducting themselves, they have lost moral authority to pontificate to political leaders on what to do on anything although they will shamelessly attempt to do so especially with elections coming next year."⁶⁹ It therefore becomes obvious even to a casual observer that the CCAP synods are treading on slippery ground when it comes to the possible manipulation of their ecclesiastical issues by political stakeholders who may not necessarily be concerned with the general welfare of the country, let alone with eternal matters – matters which are of primary concern to the church. This calls for great prudence on the part of the CCAP leadership both in the General Assembly and in the individual synods so that the church does not become a victim of political machinations because of ecclesiastical disputes.

Theological Implications

From a theological point of view, it has to be mentioned first and foremost that one of the marks of a true church is that of catholicity. By catholicity we mean that the church is and should be universal. Practically, this means that the church should in no way show favouritism to some people or disregard certain people groups because of their colour, gender, language, ethnicity, social class status, level of education or otherwise. Any group that champions these things is not a true church. However, if such a group belongs to an acceptable church denomination we can conclude that it has started to develop heretical tendencies. Heretical tendencies are not just false positions theologically, but they are also quite destructive to the life, nature and work of the church.⁷⁰

---

68. Jumbe.
69. Kasakula, "Synods Mere Clubs."
70. Demarest, "Heresy," 291–293.

If we take the justification for Nkhoma Synod that it is encroaching into the Synod of Livingstonia's territory because it is following its "Chewa-speaking children," then it means that language is more important for Nkhoma Synod than the unity of the church. This would mean that Nkhoma Synod's position is heretical in the sense that its emphasis on language is interfering with the catholicity of the church.

In the same vein, the Synod of Livingstonia would also be culpable of heresy if her going into Nkhoma territory is for the sake of those members of hers who hanker for the "home" language in worship and music. It has to be pointed out, though, that this has not been mentioned as the Synod of Livingstonia's reason for going deeper into Nkhoma Synod's territory.[71] In any case, the situation would not be easier for the Synod of Livingstonia if that were the reason because the synod's catchment area in the Northern Region of Malawi has several languages, making it the richest synod in as far as linguistic diversity is concerned. Due to the fact that the Tumbuka language is considered the *lingua franca* of the Northern Region, there is always a temptation to associate the Synod of Livingstonia with the Tumbuka language, and sometimes even the leadership of the synod behaves as if that were the case. As a matter of fact, there are more ethnic groups and languages in the Northern Region of Malawi than in both the Central and Southern Regions combined.

If the Synod of Livingstonia is, therefore, not in the Central Region in order to follow its "Tumbuka speaking children," it should prove the point by not associating itself intricately with the Tumbuka language. For example, the programme for the launch of the Synod of Livingstonia congregation in Lilongwe on 17 September 2006 was a combination of the English and Tumbuka languages as opposed to Chichewa, which ought to have dominated the programme, considering the geo-linguistic position of the City of Lilongwe.[72] It is, perhaps, such observations that may tempt a neutral

---

71. On the part of Nkhoma Synod, it has been emphatically aired that their presence in the sphere of Livingstonia along the disputed borders is because they are following their Chewa-speaking children who cannot speak or understand northern languages. Whether this sentiment was made on an individual's basis or not, there has not been any statement from Nkhoma Synod to explain otherwise. See Kaonga, "History of the Birth and Growth of Livingstonia Synod's Congregation in Kasungu District," 8.

72. See Synod of Livingstonia, "Tentative Programme for the Official Launch of the Lilongwe." Cf. Kaonga, "History of the Birth and Growth of Livingstonia Synod's Congregation in Kasungu District," 28.

observer to conclude that the Synod of Livingstonia is also in the Central Region for the sake of its "Tumbuka-speaking children."[73] But even if that were not the case, the predominant membership of northerners in the Synod of Livingstonia's congregations in the Central Region would and does betray them as being segregative or being attracted to the home synod and fellowship with familiar peoples from one's own region, if not even district or village. By this chase, the argument makes both Livingstonia and Nkhoma synods culpable of heretical tendencies by emphasizing the differences between "we" and "them" in the body of Christ, which ought not to recognize or pander to differences of language and other socio-cultural distinctions among its members. Consequently, this compromises the catholicity of the church among the members of the two synods. Of course, this is something that can be remedied when the new churches recognize that it is important to show that they are not trying to be particular but ready to accommodate other members from whatever background.

Conclusion

In conclusion we can emphatically say that this chapter has highlighted the pangs that the CCAP is experiencing in its "unity," which actually makes the unity appear as a goal to be pursued but never fully attained. While the three synods in Malawi and their sister synods in Zambia and Zimbabwe want to continue existing as independent organizations, there can be no one organic denomination. I therefore argue that it is this prolonged independent existence of the synods that makes them separate denominations in the name of the CCAP federation. This, therefore, further illustrates the fact that the CCAP is actually a loose umbrella of independent denominations and not one church. The examples of the diocesan boundaries of the Anglican and Roman Catholic churches and the administrative boundaries of other denominations in the country do not make sense in the case of

---

73. Besides this apparently linguistic reason for the synods' encroachment into other synods' territories, there is also a monetary explanation because the people of a particular language in a different place are likely to contribute money to the synod of the language with which they associate. Actually, some feel this is the main reason for following the so-called "children" in other regions. See Kawale, "Biblical Analysis of the Impact of the Border Wrangle on CCAP," 7.

the CCAP synods, whose oneness, in the sense of singularity, has never existed.[74] Cooperation among the synods has existed, and sometimes very deeply, but this has been the case due to the leadership of the time or certain circumstances pertaining to the time but not the achievement of a truly united church. However, this observation does not mean that nothing can be done about it. After recognizing that the unity wished for has not been achieved over the years, more effort at unity can be exerted now with a view to changing the future history of the five synods. While that time awaits its fulfilment, the synods will continue to feel the pangs of unity in diversity.

Figure 2: A sample of newspaper cartoons depicting a caricature of the Border Dispute between the synods of Livingstonia and Nkhoma.[75]

---

74. In the churches mentioned here it is not doubted that they are single denominations despite having several dioceses or administrative boundaries. The uniqueness of the CCAP is in the fact that its oneness as a denomination is still subject to discussion.

75. Sourced from George Kasakula, "My Diary," *Weekend Nation 20–21 September 2008*; and Steven Nhlane, "On Saturday," *Malawi News, 4–10 October 2008*, respectively. Used with permission.

CHAPTER 5

Challenges Rocking the CCAP General Assembly

Introduction

In this chapter, I make an in-depth analysis of the position of the General Assembly (and changes in this position) vis-à-vis its synods in order to appreciate the challenges associated with the federative denomination's unity. The leadership of the CCAP acknowledges the problems that are there when it comes to enhancing its unity, and to that end several attempts have been made and continue to be made by the leaders of the synods in ensuring that the CCAP does not only appear to be one denomination but that it actually works as one.[1] Before going deeper into the discussion concerning the challenges rocking the General Assembly, there is need to provide an exposition of the body so that its structure and composition is known. After that, its evaluation can be ably handled.

---

1. From the days of the General Synod, the General Assembly is referred to, in some circles, as "a halfway house" because of its inability to bring all the synods together as a united denomination. The weakness of the General Assembly is seen in its lack of capacity to coordinate such things as ministers' salaries, theological education scholarships or even to oversee the various departments in the synods. See CCAP, "Minutes of Sixteenth General Synod," 43–47.

Constitutional Direction of the CCAP General Assembly

The unity of the CCAP has had three phases so far with regard to constitutional direction. Since the union started with the presbyteries, the initial coming together was at the level of the "Synod." When the presbyteries gained synodical status, they came under the General Synod. It is the General Synod that ushered the CCAP into the third millennium before paving way for the establishment of the General Assembly, even if the change was only in name.

Change of Name from General Synod to General Assembly

As alluded to earlier in this book, the General Assembly is the current umbrella body that strives to unify the CCAP with its membership of the five synods – namely, Livingstonia, Blantyre, Nkhoma, Zambia and Harare. The General Assembly as we know it today is the result of the evolutionary character of CCAP unity which started from its establishment in 1924. The constitution guiding the CCAP now is the 2002 constitution adopted on 8 December 2002. One of the most significant issues with regard to this constitution is the change in the nomenclature of the federative denomination. Whereas the CCAP union was previously known as the General Synod, the current constitution changed that name to General Assembly. As mentioned above, prior to the General Synod stage, the CCAP was only known as "Synod" as it was presbyteries that had joined together to form the union in 1924 and 1926.[2] This means that for a very long time (1956–2002) the unity of the CCAP was known by the name General Synod.[3] It is, therefore, important to know why the name changed from that of General Synod to General Assembly. The explanation for this change is that the name General Synod was a misnomer as it did not actually capture the composite nature of the unity of the CCAP. It was argued that, since the CCAP was made of several synods, the greater gathering of all the synods needed to have a better name than the singular General Synod. It was consequently decided

---

2. See CCAP, "Minutes of First Meeting of Synod," 17–22 September 1924 and CCAP, "Entrance of Nkhoma Presbytery into Synod," 4–6, in "Minutes of Second Meeting of Synod," 13–15 October 1926, min. 5.

3. See "Constitution of the Church of Central Africa Presbyterian 1956," 29.

that the term General Assembly was the most appropriate name with regard to embracing the diversity and totality of the synods. Besides, it was realized that actually the churches that had brought the Presbyterian system to Central Africa, especially the Scottish churches, had general assemblies for their umbrella bodies rather than general synods. This, therefore, explains the reason for the change of name from General Synod to General Assembly in 2002.

Changes in Some of the Names of the General Assembly's Leadership Positions

Further to the change in the name of the church's union, the new nomenclature also came with changes in the names and functions of some positions in the organisation. Whereas the position and powers of the moderator of the General Assembly have not changed since the General Synod days, as will be seen below, the names of the other positions have changed completely. In the General Synod the leadership comprised the moderator, the vice-moderator, the senior clerk, the junior clerk and the deputy clerk. The position of senior clerk in the General Synod has been changed to that of secretary general in the General Assembly. The position of junior clerk in the General Synod has changed to deputy secretary general in the General Assembly, while the position of deputy clerk from the General Synod has also changed to that of deputy secretary general in the General Assembly. This means that while, in the General Synod, there were three executive officers ranked in three different positions hierarchically, in the General Assembly there are still three executive officers but with only two ranks. The position of secretary general of the General Assembly has two deputies of the same rank, while in the days of the General Synod the senior clerk was the top most executive, seconded by the junior clerk, who was above the deputy clerk, the latter coming third in the ladder. The junior clerk was, by virtue of his position, also the treasurer of the General Synod.[4]

In the General Assembly, the deputies of the secretary general have specific areas for oversight despite their general role of deputizing the secretary general. The first office of deputy secretary general is for development, and it is responsible for education, administration, relief and development, health,

---

4. See "Constitution of the Church of Central Africa Presbyterian 1956," 29.4.

communication and advocacy.[5] The other office of the deputy secretary general is responsible for ministry work: mission and evangelism, interfaith relations, women, youth, church and society.[6]

Whereas in the former General Synod the treasurer was by default the junior clerk, in the General Assembly the office of treasurer is a stand-alone office, and it is filled by a person with appropriate qualifications and experience in accounts besides being a devoted Christian of the CCAP denomination from any synod.[7] According to the current constitution, this position is supposed to be filled on a permanent basis.[8] With regard to General Assembly meetings, the treasurer is not considered a commissioner and may not be allowed to vote, but he attends the meetings for the purpose of presenting reports.[9]

It was also necessary to change the names of the executive officers of the General Assembly because it was felt that, as they were in the General Synod, they were not appropriate for the chief executive officers of the General Assembly. In the hierarchy of the CCAP, generally the lowest executive officer is the session clerk, who with his or her deputy or deputies is responsible for the administration of the congregation under the spiritual supervision of the congregational moderator.[10] When we come to the presbytery level, which is normally the second level in the Presbyterian ladder comprising a grouping of several sessions/congregations, the executive officer is known as the presbytery clerk while, at the synod level, he is known as general secretary. It, therefore, did not sound proper to have the executive officer of the General Assembly called senior clerk, a term similar to the executives of sessions and presbyteries, when under him there were general secretaries of the synods, hence the change in the name of the office.[11]

---

5. See "Constitution of the Church of Central Africa Presbyterian General Assembly," 8.5.4.a.

6. "Constitution of the Church of Central Africa Presbyterian General Assembly," 8.5.4.b.

7. "Constitution of the Church of Central Africa Presbyterian General Assembly," 8.5.5.

8. "Constitution of the Church of Central Africa Presbyterian General Assembly," 8.5.5.

9. "Constitution of the Church of Central Africa Presbyterian General Assembly," 8.5.5.

10. In the Synod of Livingstonia they also have a Vestry Chairman who is responsible for the administration of a "vestry," meaning the governing body of a prayer house, which is a branch or outstation of a congregation. It is these vestries that form a congregation which is led by a session.

11. Rt Rev Dr T. P. K. Nyasulu, in discussion with the author, 20 November 2014.

The Office of the General Assembly Moderator

While the nomenclature and powers of this office did not change during the transition from the General Synod to the General Assembly, there is some dissatisfaction currently with the name in view of the contemporary understanding of the Presbyterian offices in the General Assembly. Since the name "moderator" is used from the session level to the synod level, there is a feeling that the moderator of the General Assembly should have a more appropriate title befitting his seniority among colleagues instead of merely calling him moderator. Since he happens to be the moderator of moderators in the hierarchy of the church, some are of the view that the term "moderator general" would be more appropriate for the moderator of the General Assembly in order to distinguish him from the other moderators who are lower than him in rank by virtue of the stage at which they preside in the hierarchy of the CCAP.[12]

It is my observation that the office of moderator of the General Assembly is not a conspicuous office compared to the moderators of the synods. In most cases, people recognize the presence of the synod moderators but not the presence of the General Assembly moderator. The General Assembly moderator becomes conspicuous only when the General Assembly is meeting or when the General Assembly has either authored a pastoral letter that appears to be critical of the government of the day or has made a comment that is considered sensational in the media. This is so because it takes four years for a General Assembly to meet, and whenever there are other impromptu meetings, the General Assembly moderator works behind the scenes. It is for this reason that many Christians do not know their General Assembly moderator. Even the other officers of the General Assembly are equally unknown to ordinary members of the CCAP who are only interested in their congregations, presbyteries and synods.

The moderator is elected by secret ballot from among the ministerial commissioners to the General Assembly meeting, and he and his deputy hold office for a period of four years, after which they are not eligible for re-election.[13] This position rotates among the synods and the constitution

---

12. Rt Rev Dr T. P. K. Nyasulu, in discussion with the author, 20 November 2014.

13. The pronoun for the moderator is masculine because some synods are yet to start ordaining women ministers. This means that for the sake of those synods that do not recognize

stipulates that the General Assembly or the Standing Committee shall by resolution determine the order of the rotation as it deems fit.[14] So far, the practice is that the positions of General Assembly moderator and secretary general come only from the three Malawian synods of Livingstonia, Blantyre and Nkhoma, though the deputies may come from the synods of Zambia and Harare. The reason for this is to ensure that the top most leadership of the General Assembly comes from Malawi because of the prominence of the CCAP church in the country compared to the presence of the other CCAP synods of Harare and Zambia in their respective countries.[15] This has the advantage of making the CCAP leadership always more ready to engage with the political powers within Malawi than would have been the case if the top most leadership of the church was not always Malawian.

The Meetings of the General Assembly

The General Assembly meets every four years, and it is convened by the moderator or, in his absence, by the vice moderator. Apart from the regular meetings taking place once in every four years, the General Assembly may be convened by the moderator, or vice moderator in his absence, in extraordinary session any time when matters arise requiring urgent attention and resolution.[16] In the absence of the moderator or vice moderator the General Assembly meetings may be chaired by a locum acting as chairman of the meeting.[17]

The General Assembly demands in its constitution that all its decisions and resolutions be implemented by each synod without further ratification at synod level. It further warns that failure to implement such resolutions shall be cause for disciplinary action against the failing synod. Realizing that the synods may not always be willing to bind themselves to a decision or

---

women pastors the moderator of the General Assembly at present can only be a man though in the synods that ordain women it is possible to have a lady pastor as synod moderator.

14. "Constitution of the Church of Central Africa Presbyterian General Assembly," 8.4.3.

15. Despite the autonomy of the Synods in the CCAP there is a silent recognition of the fact that the synods of Harare and Zambia are daughters of the synods of Nkhoma and Livingstonia, respectively.

16. "Constitution of the Church of Central Africa Presbyterian General Assembly," 8.7.2.

17. "Constitution of the Church of Central Africa Presbyterian General Assembly," 8.7.3.

resolution of the General Assembly, the constitution provides the following provision as a "safety valve":

> The General Assembly, however, may in some cases when passing a resolution or decision require and specify that ratification of the resolution or decision by at least a maximum of 3/5 of all Synods is necessary before the concerned resolution becomes binding on all Synods. The ratification or rejection by the Synod must be communicated to the General Assembly within six months of the resolution. Failure to notify within this period shall be taken as ratification.[18]

In between the meetings of the General Assembly, the executive work of the General Assembly is run by the General Assembly Standing Committee. This committee is composed of the General Assembly moderator, vice moderator, secretary general, the two deputy secretary generals, the moderators and general secretaries of each synod and two church elders nominated by each synod. All these serve for a period of four years. The treasurer of the General Assembly also attends the standing committee meetings in an ex-officio capacity without voting powers.[19]

Commissioners of the General Assembly

The people who represent their synods at the General Assembly are referred to as commissioners. In keeping with the Presbyterian tradition, which emphasizes the rule of the church by elders, the General Assembly delegates consist of equal numbers of ministers and elders from each synod. In the current constitution, different synods have a different number of delegates that they can send to the General Assembly meeting. The three Malawian synods of Livingstonia, Blantyre and Nkhoma are required to send forty commissioners each (twenty elders and twenty ministers) while the synods of Zambia and Harare are required to send ten commissioners each.[20] Section 8.3.2 of the Constitution of the CCAP General Assembly stipulates that the number of the commissioners as explained in section 8.3.1 may be

---

18. "Constitution of the Church of Central Africa Presbyterian General Assembly," 8.7.5.
19. "Constitution of the Church of Central Africa Presbyterian General Assembly," 9.4.
20. "Constitution of the Church of Central Africa Presbyterian General Assembly," 8.3.1.

changed from time to time by resolution of the General Assembly or its standing Committee. In the interview I had with the current moderator of the General Assembly, Rt Rev Dr T. P. K. Nyasulu, he mentioned that the synods of Zambia and Harare are now sending twenty delegates as commissioners to the General Assembly meeting.[21] It can therefore be assumed that the provision of section 8.3.2 of the constitution has been in use since the constitution was adopted in 2002. According to the current General Assembly moderator, the decision to have different numbers of delegates for different synods was reached based on the sizes of the synods. It is a well-known fact that the Malawian synods of the CCAP are much bigger than their sisters in Zambia and Harare.

The constitution also recognizes the General Assembly moderator, vice moderator, the secretary general and the deputy secretary general as commissioners from their particular synods for purposes of determining the total number of commissioners from each synod. Special church ministries such as the Women's Guild, Men's Guild and the Youth also have a representative each. However, their representative is supposed to be a church elder by rank.[22]

Attempts at Empowering the General Assembly

The General Assembly cannot be seen to have any powers if it is not engaging with the synods and the lower courts of the church down to the congregational level as an umbrella body of the CCAP. Its task would be better realized if it were possible for it to be coordinating all the functions of the synods. It has to be pointed out, though, that so far this has not been possible, partly due to inadequate funding on the part of the General Assembly as an umbrella body over the individual synods. There are constitutional provisions for the General Assembly to establish desks which would synchronize the various work of the federative denomination. So far none of these desks have been established. The functions for which the General Assembly would have established specialized desks include the following: Mission, Evangelism and Interfaith, Youth Work, Women's Work, Health, Church and Society Work,

---

21. Rt Rev Dr T. P. K. Nyasulu, in discussion with the author, 20 November 2014.
22. See "Constitution of the Church of Central Africa Presbyterian General Assembly," 8.3.1, 8.3.3.

Relief and Development Work, Education, Communication and Advocacy and Men's Desk.[23]

It is expected that if these desks can be established, the synods are supposed to support them with human, material and financial resources in such a form and to the extent that the General Assembly Standing Committee may determine from time to time.[24] The constitutional proposal is that these desks should be manned by ministers or lay people who are seconded by their synods or directly engaged by the General Assembly. With regard to their physical offices, they may either be at the General Assembly's secretariat or at the offices of the sending or sponsoring synod. It is expected that these desks should be holding church conferences with delegates from the synods and at the end of the day presenting their resolutions to the General Assembly or the General Assembly Standing Committee for consideration and action in its subsequent meetings.[25]

All this shows that on paper there are grand plans for empowering the General Assembly and that the aspirations of its members are thereby known. However, when it comes to implementation, things seem not to work according to the members' expectations. With regard to the individual synods making contributions of money and personnel to various desks of the General Assembly, it is a well-known fact that such contributions would be stretching the synods too much since some of the well-established departments in the synods themselves are greatly challenged by lack of personnel and inadequate funding. It would therefore not be easy for them to be making substantial contributions to the General Assembly when they cannot meet their own needs.

During the General Synod era the mandate of the General Synod in speaking on behalf of the whole federative denomination was confined to four areas as enumerated below:[26]

1. To warn the congregations of evils tending to invade the church
2. Marriage regulations

---

23. "Constitution of the Church of Central Africa Presbyterian General Assembly," 8.13.
24. "Constitution of the Church of Central Africa Presbyterian General Assembly," 8.13.
25. "Constitution of the Church of Central Africa Presbyterian General Assembly," 8.13.
26. "Constitution of the Church of Central Africa Presbyterian 1956," 30.4.

3. Relations with other churches
4. Legislation which conflicts with the word of God

On the above matters, according to the phraseology of the 1956 constitution, which governed the administration of the General Synod up to 2002, it was stated that "the synods shall . . . have power to delegate authority to the General Synod to speak in the name of the whole church on such matters."[27] By contrast, in introducing the issues alluded to above, the 2002 General Assembly constitution, which currently governs the General Assembly, states that "the General Assembly shall have power to speak in the name of the whole church on the following and other matters."[28] In the first place, the General Assembly gives itself power over and against the synods so that the synods do not delegate power to the General Assembly as was the case with the General Synod. Besides, by adding the phrase "and other matters," the General Assembly is leaving the door open to whatever other matters it may want to speak about on behalf of the synods in trying to enhance CCAP unity in ecclesiastical pronouncements. Moreover, the list in the constitution of the General Assembly adds a fifth item of a "serious matter of national interest or concern."[29] This last clause is the justification for the General Assembly's involvement in socio-political critique, especially when it comes to issuing press statements on some pressing issue in society or writing pastoral letters that comment on socio-political matters in the country in the church's bid to fulfil its prophetic role.

It is the intention of the General Assembly to see greater unity and uniformity among the synods of the CCAP. Its constitution, therefore, mandates the General Assembly to endeavour to achieve uniformity and harmony in such matters as the training of ministers; catechetical instruction; prevention of evils which corrupt the people, such as alcohol drinking, gambling, drug abuse, heathen initiations and other such things; education; medical work; ordering of public worship; dispensing of the sacraments; funeral rites; criteria for selecting church elders and deacons; women's guild; and recognition of church officers.[30]

---

27. "Constitution of the Church of Central Africa Presbyterian 1956," 30.4.
28. "CCAP General Assembly Constitutional Schedule," 4.5.
29. "CCAP General Assembly Constitutional Schedule," 4.5.5.
30. "CCAP General Assembly Constitutional Schedule," 4.5.

Besides the above areas, the General Assembly also intended in its 2002 constitution that the liturgies and rules of the synods be harmonized. In this regard, there was need to make uniform across the synods such things as the order of service and the various liturgical instruments. This was supposed to be done very quickly after the adoption of the 2002 constitution, and synods were asked to send their documents to the General Assembly for scrutiny and evaluation by the liturgy committee which had been formed to steer the process.[31] Practically this would ensure that when members transfer from one synod to another they would be subject to similar rules and regulations as the ones they are familiar with.[32]

What all this means is that the change from the General Synod to General Assembly wanted to completely transform the CCAP by re-aligning all the synods in a uniform manner in order for the oneness of the church to be enhanced. However, what is developing on the ground over a decade after these decisions were made and incorporated into the constitution is business as usual in the synods; all the synods are still doing their thing as they have always been doing it. No strides seem to have been made towards a practically more united CCAP under the General Assembly as it was intended from the 2002 constitutional change.

In concluding this section, I argue that though the General Assembly would like to strengthen itself and promote the unity of the CCAP under its umbrella, the reality on the ground is pulling against this direction. The root of all this failure by the General Assembly to take off with oomph is the autonomy of the synods. This means that insofar as the synods shall maintain their autonomy, it will be difficult for them to voluntarily place themselves under the authority of the General Assembly. Consequently, it becomes very clear that the direction the CCAP General Assembly wants to go cannot just be determined by constitutional provisions. Something needs to be done beyond or alongside constitutional provisions if true unity and uniformity is to be achieved. As it is, the constitution stipulates that the highest court of the church is the General Assembly and that it has authority to formulate policy for the church and to oversee and direct the synods and

---

31. "CCAP General Assembly Constitutional Schedule," 4.3.
32. "CCAP General Assembly Constitutional Schedule," 4.3.

lower courts.³³ However, without real power in its possession, the General Assembly shall remain "a toothless dog" and an auxiliary organization among the autonomous and relatively well organized synods.

The Efficiency of the General Assembly versus the Autonomy of the Synods

While the synods want the General Assembly to be efficient, it may be that they do not realize that it may not work that the CCAP can have a vibrant General Assembly while they are maintaining their autonomy. There are reminiscences among some senior ministers in the CCAP to the effect that the General Assembly secretariat was efficient and vibrant in the past during the tenures of Rev W. P. Chibambo and those that followed him. These ministers, therefore, hanker for this golden age gone by when the General Assembly (still known as the General Synod then) was vibrant and efficient and the secretariat was a true representation of CCAP unity. What these ministers forget, though, is that the General Synod did not bother much with the way the synods were being administered, and there was little effort to try and unite the synods by proposing some kind of radical uniformity as is the case with the current General Assembly constitution. One elderly minister of the Synod of Livingstonia confessed that during the General Synod era not many differences among the synods were known, and people did not care much whether there were differences or not.³⁴ He, however, notes that with the changes that were proposed in the General Assembly constitution of 2002, and the desire to initiate some uniformity, the synods realized that there were pronounced differences among them and they could not just easily sacrifice their long cherished traditions and distinctives for the sake of a uniform CCAP under the General Assembly.³⁵ This means that until the change to the General Assembly demanded true unity and uniformity of the federative denomination, the synods did not realize how much they were going to lose as individual synods while gaining as a General Assembly. No wonder there has been resistance (subtle, but effective) on

---

33. See "CCAP General Assembly Constitutional Schedule," 6.6.
34. Rev K. R. M. Nyirenda, in discussion with the author, Mzuzu, 12 December 2014.
35. Rev K. R. M. Nyirenda, in discussion with the author, Mzuzu, 12 December 2014.

the part of the synods, as can be seen by their reluctance to change towards a more unified and uniform CCAP identity and character. For example, to make the liturgy uniform would be a very easy matter for the synods, but that has not materialized though it has been a song over the decades that the liturgies be synchronized.[36]

Lack of Adequate Funding for the General Assembly

In accordance with constitutional provisions, the General Assembly is supposed to have its own budget in order for it to be able to support its operations within its jurisdiction for mission work abroad.[37] This budget is supposed to be approved by the General Assembly Standing Committee. It is interesting to note that synods are expected to make contributions towards the General Assembly budget annually. Constitutionally, these budgetary contributions by the synods are supposed to be made in two instalments in a year – that is, in the months of January and July.[38] This means that the sustainability of the General Assembly largely depends on the ability and willingness of the synods to make contributions to its budget.

Apart from the contributions from the member synods, the General Assembly also receives donations from well-wishers within the country and from foreign donors. With regard to money coming from foreign donors, the General Assembly benefits subject to good working relations among the synods. For example, the Reformed Mission League of the Netherlands has always funded the General Assembly, but due to inter-synodical wrangles, especially the dispute between the synods of Livingstonia and Nkhoma, which rendered the General Assembly inactive for some time, the funding stopped until the CCAP General Assembly was ready to put its house is order.[39]

A good amount of foreign funding also goes to Zomba Theological College, which is one visible sign of CCAP General Assembly unity,

---

36. The call for the synchronization of the liturgy can be seen even in the minutes of the General Synods meetings of the 1970s up to the 1990s. For example, see CCAP, "Moderator's Keynote Address," in Minutes of the General Synod," Chongoni, 9–13November 1994, min. F.2(f), p. 18.
37. "Constitution of the Church of Central Africa Presbyterian General Assembly," 8.8.
38. "Constitution of the Church of Central Africa Presbyterian General Assembly," 8.9.
39. Rt Rev Dr T. P. K. Nyasulu, in discussion with the author, 20 November 2014.

especially in the area of theological education, as a number of ministers from all the five synods of the CCAP train there. In recent years, some synods are establishing their own synodical theological colleges, but they are still sending some of their theological students to the ecumenical Zomba Theological College. This means that funding from donor partners has to go to three different places: synods, Zomba Theological College and the General Assembly. With regard to synods, each synod sends its own requests to partners in order to fund its budgets, and the same partners may receive budgetary support requests from various synods. At the end of the day, there is not much set aside for the General Assembly. Consequently, the General Assembly suffers from lack of adequate funding.

Lack of Adequate Infrastructure

While all the synods have relatively well-looked after places for their headquarters, the story is different for the General Assembly. The General Assembly headquarters, or secretariat, lacks well-furnished offices where the different departments or desks proposed for it could be working. While in the past a full-time secretary general was manning the office, now the place is nearly abandoned except for the presence of security personnel guarding what is left after several raids by burglars. For a very long time, Mr Kafumbi Njewa was the caretaker of the General Assembly building, but after his retirement the place seemed to have been abandoned, especially without the presence of the secretary general. The principal offices of the General Assembly are not able to operate from Lilongwe. Consequently, they remain in their synods and do General Assembly work as if it were an added responsibility.[40]

When the newly elected leaders of the General Assembly visited the General Assembly offices in 2014, after their election in December 2013 at the Lundazi General Assembly meeting, they reportedly cried because of the pathetic situation of the place they witnessed.[41] They saw the place in a state of abandon due to the fact that the offices were built some decades ago coupled with the fact that, due to the wrangles leading to the 2013 General Assembly meeting, the General Assembly secretariat was not fully functional.

---

40. Rt Rev Dr T. P. K. Nyasulu, in discussion with the author, 20 November 2014.
41. Rt Rev Dr T. P. K. Nyasulu, in discussion with the author, 20 November 2014.

This clearly shows that, with regard to the sense of ownership, the synods do not seriously regard the General Assembly offices as their own. The relative seriousness with which the synods look after their own mission stations or headquarters does not translate to the General Assembly secretariat, hence the neglect of the General Assembly premises.

The neglect of the General Assembly offices in Area 18 in Lilongwe is one of the signs of lack of unity and cooperation in the CCAP. The place and its infrastructure hardly qualify as the headquarters of the General Assembly of the CCAP. In his humour, the former general secretary of Nkhoma Synod, Rev Dr Winston Kawale, mused that the state of the General Assembly premises reflects the current picture of the CCAP.[42] At a closer look, though, the premises seem to be worse than the denomination itself, but one can be excused for making the comparison. Lapani Nkhonjera, a fellow researcher in this thematic area, testifies thus in his work concerning the General Assembly premises: "When I visited the place for the first time during my research work, I did not believe having reached at such a high office by looking at its structures which look worse than some congregational offices of the CCAP. But no wonder this is a sign of how ineffective the office has been [sic]."[43] The CCAP General Assembly premises tell the story of a body that is not taken seriously by its own members as they are busy running their own business, which looks more real and takes much of their time. The leadership of the CCAP, if truth be told, is mostly concerned with the synods and not with the General Assembly; the General Assembly suffers from lack of serious ownership. Consequently, the General Assembly office has not seen any development since the structure was originally built. Worse still, the place has all the marks of deterioration.[44] The structure is at an open plot with no fence and no security features whatsoever. No wonder the windows and other fittings have succumbed to plundering over the years. The situation at the General Assembly offices shows that it will take a very long time before the General Assembly can become an active player with a secretariat that is visible and working, with good infrastructure, and departments or centres

---

42. Rev Dr Winston R. Kawale, in discussion with the author, Lilongwe, 14 May 2014.
43. Nkhonjera, "Church of Central Africa Presbyterian," 47.
44. See appendix 3 for some pictures of the CCAP General Assembly office.

that are vibrant. Meanwhile, it is business as usual in the CCAP synods except for the occasional bad publicity due to in-house wrangles.

Lack of Adequate Personnel

Apart from the ministers who are elected into several positions of the General Assembly, there are no people so far to serve in the various proposed desks as provided for in the constitution. This is a direct consequence of lack of adequate funding because, where an organization is not well funded, it cannot employ the relevant personnel it requires. It has therefore remained the dream of the General Assembly, at least as provided for in its constitution, that several desks and projects be created and implemented, with many people coming in from their respective synods and other places to work for the General Assembly, but with no realization of this dream so far.

Inability to Implement Decisions

Another problem with the General Assembly is its inability to implement decisions that are made during the General Assembly meetings. For decisions that are likely to bring about change to be implemented, there is need for strong leadership; leadership that is not concerned with the plight of the individual synod but with the welfare of the church as a whole. One former general secretary of one of the synods laments the passivity of the General Assembly secretariat. According to him, this is due to leadership incompetency and lack of management skills among pastors, some of whom are tasked with the mandate of leading the General Assembly. He laments that no one is strong enough to initiate the change, so decisions gather dust without being implemented.[45]

I find it difficult for the General Assembly leadership to initiate much change since they all come from their respective synods, and they are expected to go back to them once their General Assembly responsibilities are over. It is therefore natural that they would very much be concerned with their synods, seeing that there is where their future lies, unlike the General Assembly which they are likely to leave soon once their tenures expire. Besides, because of the inactivity of the General Assembly secretariat, the

---

45. Former general secretary of one of the synods in Malawi in discussion with the author.

elected leaders have been operating from their synods where they also hold responsibilities in either administration work or as pastors running congregations.[46] In such a scenario, the position in the General Assembly leadership is looked upon as an extra responsibility on top of their most important synod work.[47] Consequently, it is difficult for such people to commit themselves fully to the work of the General Assembly, which, in any case, has its offices far away from them unless they are operating in Lilongwe.

Lack of Knowledge Concerning the General Assembly among Ordinary CCAP Members

The ordinary CCAP member is very much aware of his local congregation and the role of the moderator (who is always a minister) and the session clerk in the session which is the administrative body at congregational level. From the session, many Christians are aware of the presbyteries, though here the common Christian is not very knowledgeable. When it comes to knowledge of their synods, many know about them a great deal. This means that the ordinary members know about their congregation and synod but little of their presbytery. However, when it comes to the General Assembly, there is just too much ignorance among the CCAP Christians. Many do not even know that such a thing as the General Assembly exists. With regard to sister synods, they do know about them and know that they are all CCAP, but that there is a body known as the General Assembly above the synods many are not aware. Why is it so when the General Assembly has always been there since time immemorial? Besides, the unity of the CCAP as one denomination only makes sense in view of the General Assembly's existence. Explanations for this state of affairs vary, but they are basically condensed into three reasons as explained below.

Non-recognition of Something above the Synods

The synods have developed in such a way that they do not recognize something above them. The way the Presbyterian system operates in the CCAP,

---

46. Rev Colin M'bawa, in discussion with the author, 11 November 2014.

47. For example, the current general assembly moderator is the education secretary for the Synod of Livingstonia's Education Department, an equally demanding office. The general secretary was still pastoring a congregation in Blantyre Synod almost a year after he was elected when I contacted him.

it is generally assumed that the buck stops at the synod level. It is, therefore, practically not easy to pass on authority to a higher body which is not fully recognized as having superiority over bodies that may be understood to be lower in rank. I argue that this failure to recognize the superiority of the General Assembly is the result of the General Assembly's inability to monitor what goes on in the synods. In any case, its funding and personnel abilities are such that it cannot make its presence felt in the congregations, hence lack of its knowledge among the grassroots Christians.

Pronounced Sense of Synodical Uniqueness

While the leaders of the synods know that they are supposed to be united in one denomination despite belonging to different synods, there is always a tendency to emphasize what is unique about a particular synod. Usually these emphases go back to the culture of the founding missions with some feeling of pride that this synod, unlike its sister synods, was founded by such and such a church. For the Synod of Livingstonia, the emphasis is on the fact that its ethos is that of the Free Church of Scotland despite the developments that have taken place over the course of history. In the same way, Blantyre Synod prides itself in being a "child" of the established Church of Scotland, and Nkhoma Synod, too, finds its unique identity in the Dutch Reformed Church in South Africa's roots worth clinging to. These distinctives, whether consciously or unconsciously, do eclipse the people's understanding that all the synods belong to the General Assembly because much energy and time is spent emphasizing these distinctives to the neglect of what actually unites the synods into the CCAP today.

Lack of Civic Education on the Part of the Leaders and the Christians

As a corollary to the above reasons, it has also been observed that there is lack of civic education on the part of the Christians and even some leaders. The Christians are not taught about the General Assembly and its role. It is therefore not surprising to see that they do not know about it. During services of worship in the CCAP churches, there comes a time when one member in the congregation rises to say the intercessory prayer. In this prayer, many things are mentioned, and the synods are in most cases specifically mentioned. In Malawi, it is mostly the three Malawian synods that are singled out for specific mention in prayer while at other times all five synods are mentioned, depending on the knowledge of the person praying. In either case, the General Assembly is never mentioned. The surprising thing is that this happens not only when the person offering the intercessory prayer is an ordinary Christian but even when it is an elder, be it lay or ordained. In all the times I have been attending the CCAP Sunday worship in all three synods in Malawi over the years, I witnessed a church leader lamenting the lack of knowledge of the General Assembly among congregants only once. This happened in Zomba at Chinamwali CCAP congregation of Blantyre Synod where the Rt Rev Dr Felix Chingota mentioned it to the congregation that there should be a special mention of the General Assembly in the intercessory prayer, lamenting that it was regrettable that the General Assembly was never mentioned, unlike the synods, which were always mentioned and specifically prayed for during worship's intercessory prayer. This instance shows that the leadership has not made it their practice to tell Christians that they belong to the General Assembly, hence the ignorance.

Inter-Synodical Wrangles and the Stability of the General Assembly

On top of all the other challenges that the General Assembly faces, one of the biggest challenges is that of inter-synodical disputes, especially in relation to synodical boundaries. As already alluded to, though there are many disagreements among the synods with regard to boundaries, the most pronounced dispute being the one between the synods of Livingstonia and Nkhoma. In line with the adage which says, "united we stand, divided we fall," the efficiency of the General Assembly is very much tied to the unity and good relations of the synods. Whenever the synods are not in accord, the General Assembly suffers heavy setbacks. It is because of this realization that at each and every General Assembly meeting there are calls for greater unity and cooperation among the synods. While such calls are good for the sake of encouraging the members to seriously take care of their oneness in the General Assembly, the problem is that it becomes more like a song when there are no tangible results from the calls. From the beginning of the CCAP as a federative denomination, tensions have been part of the life of the General Assembly. What is surprising, therefore, is not that there are disputes among the CCAP synods, but that there is any unity at all.

While disagreements have always threatened the existence of the General Assembly right from the beginning, the real threat to this unity was manifested in the years between 1996 and 2000 and 2007 and 2013. According to the view of the Livingstonia Synod, NkhomaSynod rejected the General Assembly resolutions on the border issue in 1967 and 1996, which seemed not to have been in Nkhoma Synod's favour. In view of these prolonged disagreements and frustrations, the Synod of Livingstonia took a very negative step in the year 1996 by deciding to pull out of the CCAP General Assembly. This was a very heavy blow to the stability of the General Assembly. This initial pull out by the Synod of Livingstonia lasted up to the year 2000 when, "after a series of mediations," they decided to re-join the General Assembly after being out of it for a period of four years.[48]

The second heavy blow to the stability of the General Assembly began in 2007, when, owing to inter-synodical disputes, the Synod of Livingstonia opted out of the 21st General Assembly deliberations because, according to them, they were not given the chance to provide a moderator as it was their turn to do so. The position of Nkhoma Synod was that the leadership that was there should continue leading the General Assembly until the border dispute issue was resolved. Apparently, Nkhoma Synod was more comfortable to have a member of the Blantyre Synod leading the General Assembly as moderator than someone from the Synod of Livingstonia, with whom they were not in good terms owing to the border dispute. The General Assembly moderator at this time was the Rt Rev Dr Felix Chingota, and he continued chairing the meeting after the synods of Blantyre and Nkhoma had adopted the agenda of not starting the meeting with the election of new office bearers as was the practice. Due to their disappointment at what they considered constitutionally and traditionally un-procedural, the Synod of Livingstonia's delegates decided to make themselves mere observers of the deliberations. It is interesting to note that at this time the Synod of Livingstonia delegates felt "betrayed" by their Blantyre Synod colleagues whom they usually consider closer to them than those of Nkhoma Synod due to their Scottish

---

48. Synod of Livingstonia, "Solution to the Border Dispute between Nkhoma and Livingstonia Synods."

connections. The then general secretary of the Synod of Livingstonia did not hide his feelings when sharing the issue with their partner churches: "To the astonishment of the delegates from Livingstonia, the proposal from Nkhoma Synod was strongly supported and backed by Blantyre Synod. . . . All the delegates from Blantyre and Nkhoma Synods voted against passing the office to Livingstonia. Only one delegate from Blantyre voted that it was time for the chair to be passed on to Livingstonia."[49] On the fourth and the last day of this meeting, the General Assembly requested the Synod of Livingstonia to rescind its decision and participate in the election of new office bearers, but the Synod of Livingstonia delegates would have none of it. Since this was a stalemate, as the mandate and authority of the new office bearers could be questionable, the General Assembly resolved to appoint former moderators, who are life members of the General Assembly, to act as a team of interim leadership until the time when new office bearers would be elected. The former moderators appointed were: The Very Rev Dr S. S. Nyirenda from the Synod of Livingstonia, the Very Rev K. J. Mgawi from Nkhoma Synod, Rev G. J. Maseko from Nkhoma Synod and the Rt Rev Dr Silas Ncozana from Blantyre Synod.[50] The then serving moderator, Rev Dr Felix Chingota, was made part of the group, and it is actually him who handed over the mantle of the General Assembly moderator to Rev T. P. K. Nyasulu in 2013 when new office bearers were elected.[51]

The stalemate was also due to the fact that the Synod of Zambia declared that they would not participate in the election exercise because the General Assembly had denied the Synod of Livingstonia their turn to chair the assembly through the provision of a moderator. Consequently, the synods of Blantyre and Nkhoma could not form a General Assembly quorum since the Harare Synod did not attend this particular General Assembly meeting. Interestingly, the Synod of Zambia happens to be a "child" of the Synod of Livingstonia, as it was Livingstonia missionaries who established this brand of Christianity in Zambia. One can therefore argue that it was the affinity

---

49. Rev Howard Matiya Nkhoma, email correspondence to all partner churches, Mzuzu, 29 January 2007.

50. Rev Howard Matiya Nkhoma, email correspondence to all partner churches, Mzuzu, 29 January 2007.

51. Rt Rev Dr T. P. K. Nyasulu, in discussion with the author, 20 November 2014.

between the two that made the Synod of Zambia to sympathize and side with their Livingstonia colleagues.

The sad thing about the existence and efficiency of the General Assembly is that it had to take six years instead of four before another General Assembly meeting could take place. During this six-year period, the General Assembly, as it is known, became quite passive. As a result, even the General Assembly secretariat offices in Lilongwe were neglected. No wonder the newly elected leaders cried when they visited the premises during their familiarization tour.[52]

The current topmost General Assembly leadership has Rt Rev Dr T. P. K. Nyasulu from the Synod of Livingstonia as moderator ("moderator general") and Rev Collin M'bawa from Blantyre Synod as secretary general. These were elected at the General Assembly's 22nd meeting held at Lundazi in Zambia from 13 to 15 December 2013.[53] As would be expected, even during this meeting "differences of perspectives were acknowledged while the desire for unity was widely and repeatedly emphasized."[54] This observation by Nancy Collins is in line with the current study's general view that, whenever the General Assembly meets, there are calls for unity, which is not surprising given the unstable position of the General Assembly over the decades.

Though not much can or should be promised, it is pleasing to note that despite the differences in the stands of the synods, the 22nd General Assembly meeting revived the desire for the unity of the church and renewed the synods' commitment to the unity of the CCAP in the General Assembly. Some leaders have testified that even the atmosphere of this meeting was pleasing and uplifting, so much so that delegates felt that they really belonged to one denomination despite differences in their synods.[55] In a way, this meeting was also corrective of the past disagreements from the 2007 meeting when the Synod of Livingstonia missed its turn to chair the General Assembly by providing a moderator. Noteworthy is the fact that all the synods were present at this meeting, and the support for the election of the new office bearers was overwhelming even from synods that would otherwise have

---

52. Rt Rev Dr T. P. K. Nyasulu, in discussion with the author, 20 November 2014.
53. Chimpweya, "Reverend Nyasulu is General Assembly Moderator."
54. Collins, "Malawi: A Report on the Recent CCAP General Assembly."
55. Rev Levi N. Nyondo, in discussion with the author, Mzuzu, 5 September 2014.

been against candidates from their perceived rivals. In this regard, Nkhoma Synod's support for the Synod of Livingstonia's candidate, Rev Dr T. P. K. Nyasulu, as moderator was more than edifying.[56]

Partner Churches and the Stability of the General Assembly

A thorough discussion of the General Assembly vis-a-vis the synods and their foreign partners is treated in the next chapter. At this juncture the question is whether some of the foreign partners' policies do contribute to the unstable position of the General Assembly. In the words of some oral informants who happen to be leaders in the denomination, the foreign partners also share the blame for the failure of the General Assembly to be a vibrant union. The blame goes back many years to the time of the moratorium when the missions were handing over the leadership of the church to the indigenous leaders. According Rev Dr K. J. Mgawi, the first indigenous general secretary of Nkhoma Synod, the missionaries or mother churches of the missions contributed to the problems that the General Assembly is facing today.[57] Mgawi claims that the indigenous leaders inherited a church that was not fully united because the expatriate leaders had not dealt with the issue of total union of the synods fully before handing them over to the local leaders. The local leaders were therefore not able to initiate further unification, especially in view of the fact that the mother churches had committed themselves to keep on helping their former missions (now turned daughter churches) with money, personnel and other resources. This meant that even though the local churches were now independent, their independence was not total because they still had to rely on or expect assistance from their mother churches. In view of this, the synods do not fully face towards the unity of the CCAP but towards their various partners who still fund them and give them some direction even today. Some church leaders even claim that the foreign partners favour different synods so much that not all of them can be trusted in ensuring that the General Assembly ticks to the extent of eclipsing the individual synods. It has to be confessed that this is

---

56. Rt Rev Dr T. P. K. Nyasulu, in discussion with the author, 20 November 2014.
57. Rev Kilion Mgawi, in discussion with the author, Nkhoma, 21 February 2014.

a very tricky and complex issue and that it perhaps involves personalities more than the hidden agendas of the foreign partners in question. In any case, the fact still remains that "he who pays the piper dictates the tune," so the influence of the foreign partners cannot be ignored when we consider that theirs is the financial muscle.

Some CCAP leaders are of the view that this economic power of the foreign partners can and should actually be used to force the synods into more unity and uniformity under the General Assembly. When he was general secretary of Nkhoma Synod, Rev Dr Winston Kawale, in one of his meetings with fellow church leaders and delegates from partner churches, actually made this suggestion to the Associate Secretary of the Church of Scotland World Mission, Sandy Sneddon. His suggestion was that, just like the foreign governments which give aid to Malawi forced the single-party regime in the early 1990s to allow for political change in the country by freezing aid and imposing certain sanctions (and still do so to current governments), the partners of the synods should do the same to the synods by threatening aid freeze until the synods have sorted out their problems in the General Assembly or resolved their disputes. In response, apart from explaining to Rev Kawale that overseas partners would not do that for fear of hurting the common people who are the beneficiaries of aid and assistance from partner churches, Sandy Sneddon reiterated his position and that of his organization by writing a letter from Scotland to Rev Kawale saying:

> The dispute between Nkhoma and Livingstonia synods remain a major challenge for CCAP and the General Assembly and I hope and pray this issue will be resolved to the satisfaction of all parties. As I said when we met, this is an issue for the General Assembly and I do not believe overseas partners should use pressure or threats of sanctions against any synod.[58]

It is clear that many leaders in the CCAP would love to see greater unity among the synods under the General Assembly. To achieve that goal, some would even use desperate measures to force foreign partners to exert their

---

58. Sandy Sneddon (Associate Secretary, Church of Scotland World Mission Council) to Rev Dr Winston R. Kawale (General Secretary, Nkhoma Synod), letter correspondence, 14 August 2007.

influence on the synods if it were possible. However, as has been seen, the onus is still on the local leaders to move forward without relying on the foreign partners who have their own ecclesiastical problems to solve in their respective countries.

Political Machinations and the Stability of the General Assembly

It is a fact that the bigger churches in Malawi exert some political influence in the country which makes politicians try by all means to gain some sympathy or even support from these churches, especially their leaders. In situations where the government is not doing the right thing, the bigger churches sometimes write pastoral letters which end up damaging the reputation of the party in government or even in the opposition if it becomes very clear that the problems rocking the country are coming from the opposition parties. Politicians, therefore, realize the importance of endearing themselves to prominent church leaders, in the hope of lessening the critical stance of the churches on their governance performance. In view of this scenario, I have observed that the synods are sometimes forced to work in antagonism with each other because of the political pressure bearing on the churches' leadership. Of course, this comes as a temptation to some individuals in the leadership of the churches as sometimes they do not realize that they are being ensnared.[59] Consequently, the synods are divided when it comes to speaking out on pertinent issues in society. This explains why some synods have written pastoral letters on their own without involving their sister synods in the General Assembly in order to have a united CCAP voice. And the sister synods that have not issued the critical pastoral letter have

---

59. Moses Mlenga mentions an interesting testimony with regard to the tenure of Rev Dr O. P. Mazunda of the Synod of Livingstonia, who served between 1992 and 2000, that he left the office "a frustrated man because he was being accused of being too close to the President [Dr Bakili Muluzi] and the United Democratic Front (UDF)." See Mlenga, *History of Livingstonia Mission*, 24. Of course, the former general secretary does not hide the fact that he was and still is friends with Dr Bakili Muluzi (oral information, Ekwendeni, 2013). It was, therefore, not surprising to see Rev Dr O. P. Mazunda contesting as an aspiring councillor of one of the wards in Mzuzu City under the banner of the UDF party in the 2014 General Elections.

opted not to make any official responses to such pastoral letters as a sign of maintaining political neutrality.

An incident illustrative of political influence in the church happened in December 2010 in Blantyre Synod when the then moderator of the synod, Rev Reynold Mangisa, and his deputy general secretary were removed from their positions for addressing a press conference in the name of Blantyre Synod when they were actually expressing their own views, apparently in a bid to defend the then ruling party (to which they had become quite close) from the criticism published in a Roman Catholic pastoral letter of October 2010.[60] During this incident, the general secretary of Blantyre Synod, the Rev MacDonald Kadawati, was barred from seeking re-election, apparently due to slightly different reasons, even though he was not dismissed as the others.[61] In the same vein, there were allegations that the United Democratic Front (UDF) and the Democratic Progressive Party (DPP) supported and campaigned for certain individuals who were running for Blantyre Synod's leadership positions in the elections of 2009 and 2011.[62]

A similar incident happened in the Synod of Livingstonia in April 2013 when Rev Clifford Baloyi, a former moderator of the synod, wrote a critical "pastoral" letter against President Joyce Banda's regime, apparently in sympathy with the DPP which had been forced out of government a year earlier by the death of President Bingu wa Mutharika. In this letter, Rev Baloyi opined on issues such as homosexuality, the quota system of selecting students to public universities, Section 65 of the Malawi Republican Constitution – which bars members of parliament from crossing the floor – and on issues to do with civil servants' salaries among other things. The Synod of Livingstonia, however, disowned this "pastoral" letter saying that the synod had nothing to do with it.[63]

Such incidences have the potential to instil a sense of mistrust among leaders of the General Assembly who may suspect that some of their colleagues are not only doing church business but also serving their political

---

60. Nation Reporter, "Shake Up at Blantyre Synod," *The Nation*, 2 December 2010.
61. Nation Reporter, "Shake Up at Blantyre Synod," *The Nation*, 2 December 2010.
62. See Liponda, "Muluzi Sponsored Clergy Lose Polls." See also Muheya, "Blantyre Synod Elects Female Moderator, New SG."
63. "Livingstonia Synod Needs Discipline," *The Nation*.

masters. And since it is common knowledge that the synods sometimes differ when it comes to political leanings, it becomes inevitable for the General Assembly leadership to view one another as belonging to different political camps.

During the presidency of Dr Bingu wa Mutharika, some leaders in the synods even approached the late president in the company of some party gurus, asking him to intervene in the inter-synodical disputes by using his executive powers. In his wisdom, the late president is said to have declined to have anything to do with church disputes because, in his view, church disagreements are very volatile and have the potential to throw the country into chaos.[64] This was the president's official position. However, besides the official position, the president is said to have bared his soul to some church leaders on the inter-synodical disputes, explaining the advantage of it at that time to his party and thereby taking sides.[65]

It is obvious that politicians use divide and rule tactics to influence certain individuals in the churches. Once some of the church leaders have been co-opted by politicians, they tend to do things that are against the church's mandate because temptations to please their political masters become great. This, therefore, means that political forces, though quite subtle, have a significant bearing on the failure of the synods to fully unite for the effectiveness and efficiency of the CCAP General Assembly.

Private Initiatives at Reconciling the Synods and Strengthening the General Assembly

Many Christians who would rather see the CCAP fully united under the General Assembly have spoken out on the synods' failure to sort out their differences. Already mentioned in this book are such groups as the Friends of Livingstonia in Zomba who, in 2005, tried to persuade the Synod of Livingstonia to reconsider its stand on the border issue so that it would not go ahead with its plan of officially establishing churches in Nkhoma Synod's

---

64. Rev Levi N. Nyondo, in discussion with the author, Mzuzu, 5 September 2014.
65. Oral information from a minister who was present in the meeting. Name withheld.

interior territory.⁶⁶ Alongside these ones were the concerned Christians in the Northern Region, especially Mzuzu and Ekwendeni, who also did not agree with their synod's position and tried to persuade it to change its stand for the sake of the unity of the General Assembly.⁶⁷

Close to the end of the year 2011, there was also another group comprising of twenty members from all the three Malawian synods which also wanted to initiate some inter-synodical dialogue for the sake of unity in the CCAP. One prominent member in this group was Professor Kings Phiri, who at one time chaired the Commission of Inquiry which looked into the border issue between the synods of Livingstonia and Nkhoma under the auspices of the General Assembly. Other prominent members were Professor Kanyama Phiri, a renowned academician and the current Vice Chancellor of the Lilongwe University of Agriculture and Natural Resources (LUANAR), and Rev Takuze Chitsulo of Blantyre Synod, among others.⁶⁸

This group decided to call itself Forum for CCAP Unity (FCU) and it launched its activities in Blantyre in November 2011. Interestingly, the leaders of all three synods of the CCAP in Malawi expressed pessimism at the success of this group, fearing that it would be a tall order for all the concerned parties to reach a compromise on the issue under dispute.⁶⁹ According to the *Malawi News* of December 24–30, 2011, the general secretary of the Synod of Livingstonia, Rev Levi Nyondo, dismissed the legitimacy of this group, arguing that it did not follow Presbyterian channels and procedures when coming up with the initiative. When contacted by the said newspaper, Rev Takuze Chitsulo, the group's secretary, contended that the group remained focused and could not be blamed for breaking protocol. He thus argued:

> Our grouping is an independent entity. As such it would not be wise to align ourselves with structures of the same institutions that we are [mediating]. The most important thing is that we have alerted the leadership of all synods about our existence . . .

---

66. See Friends of the Livingstonia Synod–Zomba to the General Secretary of the Synod of Livingstonia, "Relationship between Livingstonia and Nkhoma Synod."

67. See Synod of Livingstonia Members to the Moderator of the Synod of the Livingstonia, "Concern over the Opening of CCAP Synod of Livingstonia Churches inside Nkhoma Synod Jurisdiction."

68. See Matonga, "Livingstonia Synod Snubs Dialogue Initiative," 1–2.

69. Kasakura, "Synods Giving Up on Border Row," 1, 3, 6.

we aim to see that at the end of the day our synods are working in harmony.[70]

Rev Nyondo, however, acknowledged the importance of the group's intention, though in his capacity as general secretary of the Synod of Livingstonia he could not appreciate the position of the group in the CCAP hierarchy.

As for Rev Davidson Chifungo, who was then the general secretary for Nkhoma Synod, he observed that the success of the FCU depended on their being accepted by all synods and also on the strategies that they would use.[71] For him it was important that some people could take such an initiative for the sake of having unity in the church, which he claimed Nkhoma Synod fully supported.[72]

Speaking on behalf of Blantyre Synod, Rev Alex Maulana, general secretary, believed that the emergence of such a group was complementary to the prayer for practical unity, which, according to him, Christ preached.[73] He, however, blamed fellow church leaders for failing to humble themselves in order for a solution to be found, lamenting that the gospel of unity and reconciliation seem to be falling off the church's spiritual agenda.[74] Predicting the challenges ahead of the group's task, Rev Maulana reasoned that "from a human perspective, the task of uniting the synods may seem impossible because one looks at the level of disagreements which has been escalating."[75] He, however, hoped that with God's help the goal may be achieved, provided church leaders decide to listen and be obedient to God.[76]

The above scenario shows that the failure of the General Assembly to experience practical unity is a thorn in the flesh in as far as the oneness of the CCAP denomination is concerned, hence the many attempts by individuals and groups to try and reconcile the synods. These attempts are happening in the context of the synods of Livingstonia and Nkhoma having already concluded that the solution to the border dispute is to ignore the borders so

---

70. Kasakura, 3.
71. Kasakura, 6.
72. Kasakura, 6.
73. Kasakura, 6.
74. Kasakura, 6.
75. Kasakura, 6.
76. Kasakura, 6.

that the General Assembly becomes a unifying factor irrespective of synodical boundaries, at least between Livingstonia and Nkhoma.

Current Trends in the General Assembly

Since December 2013, there seems to be some peace in the CCAP General Assembly, especially as there are no more squabbles or disputes among the synods worth reporting in the media. The synods of Livingstonia and Nkhoma continue to establish churches in each other's territory with less eye-brows raised now as the practice has been there for some time, and it seems people are beginning to consider it as something normal. This is so especially in the wake of Nkhoma Synod saying that they, too, would not recognize the boundary with Livingstonia. This reciprocal position by Nkhoma Synod, in a way, gives the Synod of Livingstonia some feeling of peace and confidence to go ahead with their planting of churches in what used to be Nkhoma Synod's exclusive territory as their position now becomes less radical.

The other synods of Blantyre, Zambia and Harare may not be very much supportive of the new trend of not recognizing synodical borders, but even for them peace in the General Assembly is something desirable. At present, the fear of Blantyre Synod that Livingstonia and Nkhoma may want to invade Blantyre territory seems to be unfounded. Synod of Livingstonia has made it very clear that she will not go into Blantyre Synod's territory. On the part of Nkhoma Synod, their message has not been very clear whether they would want to go to Blantyre as well or not. Despite sporadic differences that are experienced along the Blantyre-Nkhoma boundary, the dispute has not reached a boiling point where one can liken it to the Livingstonia-Nkhoma border wrangle. It is hoped that relations will continue to improve for the better.

With regard to having a united voice when commenting on socio-political issues in the country, it is now showing that there are some positive developments. For example, the General Assembly managed to issue a statement in the year 2014 expressing dismay at the failure of the government and the Malawi Broadcasting Corporation (MBC) to open up the public broadcaster to all political parties as the country was drawing closer to the May 20 tripartite elections. In the same vein, the General Assembly showed that the CCAP could sometimes unite when, on behalf of the synods, it further condemned the scandal of looting public coffers in various Government ministries – a scandal otherwise known as Cashgate – which saw many donor partners withdrawing their aid from Malawi between 2013 and 2014. The General Assembly also condemned homosexuality in the same statement, arguing that the church's teaching is clear that a man marries a woman and vice versa.[77]

It is therefore becoming clear that in the new understanding of the General Assembly, the synods are trying to co-exist and make the General Assembly work despite their differences. It is yet to be seen how far this positive development will go, but, with good leadership in the General Assembly, it makes sense to say that the CCAP has spoken, rather than the synods uttering their own individual statements. One CCAP leader is of the view that, without the borders being recognized, the CCAP synods can continue to work harmoniously under the leadership of the General Assembly.[78] An example is given of Scotland, where there are no geographical boundaries of ecclesiastical jurisdictions, but the church functions well under the General Assembly. The difference, though, is that in Scotland there are no synods; from the presbyteries they go straight to the General Assembly. This may explain why their General Assembly is not plagued with inter-synodical disputes.

Conclusion

This chapter has looked closely at the General Assembly, in the process showing that the changes that were initiated during the transition from the General Synod to the General Assembly were meant to foster a closer unity of the synods. Even the General Assembly constitution was drafted in such a way that the unity of the five synods would be more practical. However, looking at the developments from the year 2002 when the General Assembly constitution was adopted to the year 2013 when the most recent General Assembly meeting took place, it can be seen that the road to closer unity has been and continues to be a bumpy one.

---

77. See Namangale, "CCAP wants Govt to open up MBC."
78. Rev Levi N. Nyondo, in discussion with author, Mzuzu, 5 September 2014.

Figure 3: The first CCAP General Assembly leadership after the change from General Synod.[79]

Of special significance in the issues that divide the CCAP synods is the issue of the border dispute between the Synod of Livingstonia and Nkhoma Synod, which is indeed a thorn in the flesh that affects the whole body of the General Assembly. At the 22nd General Assembly meeting, it became clear to the rest of the delegates from all the synods that the positions taken by the synods of Livingstonia and Nkhoma would not be reversed. This means that the penetration of the Synod of Livingstonia into Nkhoma territory is likely to be permanent, and so, too, the penetration of Nkhoma Synod into Synod of Livingstonia Synod territory. This is a fact not to be forgotten when considering the future of the CCAP General Assembly. The delegates to the 22nd General Assembly meeting, realizing this fact, decided to elect a constitutional review committee. This committee would look into the issue of boundaries between the synods so that some provisions in the constitution can be amended in order to provide a legal framework for those synods

---

79. From left to right: Rev Daniel Tembo (Deputy Secretary General 2), Rev Jeremiah Chiyenda (Secretary General), Rt Rev Dr Felix Chingota (Moderator), Rev Kingsley R. M. Nyirenda (Deputy Secretary General 1) and Rev Joseph C. Juma (Deputy Moderator). Used with permission.

that do not want to have borders between them to operate freely wherever they want to go. Now the question would be: if this is given a constitutional blessing, is the CCAP still one denomination or several denominations that cooperate under the name CCAP? It is my argument that the CCAP General Assembly is only a loose umbrella organization of independent denominations, albeit under the names of synods.

I, therefore, conclude in this chapter that indeed the position of the General Assembly in the CCAP is an unstable one, and has been so over the years due to the autonomy of the synods, but much more so in the recent years because of the disputes among the synods. Though the 2013 General Assembly has somehow healed the tension, the future of the General Assembly is likely not to be a vibrant one as long as the synods do not fully surrender their autonomy to a body that is supposed to be above them administratively. And this appears not to be the synods' option in the nearest future.

CHAPTER 6

Foreign Relations and Current Developments in the CCAP

Introduction

This chapter explores the relationships of the five CCAP synods and their General Assembly with regard to foreign partners. What are the dynamics of foreign relations in view of the current challenges the CCAP is facing? How are these relationships impacting CCAP unity? These are some of the questions explored in this chapter so that the relationship of the five synods under the umbrella of the General Assembly can be appreciated when it comes to initiating and sustaining the various relationships that the synods have with foreign partners.

The Genesis of Foreign Relations

The CCAP as a product of nineteenth-century missionary activities has foreign relations that go back to the time of the establishment of the missions in Central Africa as initiated by the "mother churches" of the synods. This means that each synod has some kind of traditional partner from whom they cannot be separated as their histories are intertwined. Such relationships put some synods of the CCAP in the shoes of "daughters" while the missionary-sending churches are considered "mother churches." These mother churches were responsible for the welfare of the mission churches throughout the time that the synods existed as missions.

During the time of the transition from missions to churches, with the responsibility of the missionaries passed on to the indigenous churches, it was the same "mother churches" that handed over the leadership to the first generation of indigenous leaders. Even though leadership was handed over to the indigenous leaders, it did not mean the end of the presence of the "mother churches" in the life of the synods. These churches continue to help their "missions" in terms of money, personnel, and other resources, hence the presence of relations with them up to now. It can therefore be argued that the relationship of the "mother churches" and that of their "daughters" in the former mission fields is similar to that of former colonial governments with their colonies after the latter have attained independence. The difference being that, whereas in the political world foreign partners exert a lot of pressure on the local political leadership, among the churches there is a reasonable recognition of independence, so much so that it is not always that partner churches demand conformity to certain conditions in order for the relationship to continue. Actually, partner churches from the West are even reluctant to get involved in the politics of the synods though occasionally they try to assist in finding solutions to the problems the synods face, especially in relation to humanitarian assistance and their unity in the General Assembly.[1] All five synods of the CCAP have these partners, and it is my observation that, were it not for the assistance of these partners, there would be more problems in the synods, especially in issues to do with projects and other money-related activities.

The Development of Foreign Relations

It has to be noted that the CCAP synods' relations with different partners have not been static over the years. There have been many developments taking place in relation to foreign partners due to several reasons. One notable feature of this issue of foreign relations is the diversity of the partners. Apart from the traditional partners dubbed "mother churches," the synods have over the years explored possibilities of increasing their partners,

---

1. A case in point is the initiative taken by the Church of Scotland in bringing the synods together in 2005/2006 in order to resolve synodical differences that had surfaced due to the Livingstonia-Nkhoma boundary dispute. See Chingota, "Lost Opportunities." See also Chisambo, "Nkhoma, Livingstonia Spare Rev Lunan the Blushes."

especially from overseas countries. Another feature of these relationships is that apart from the loftier partnerships at General Assembly and synod levels, the different synods have also seen their presbyteries twinning with other presbyteries in countries such as the USA, Ireland, Scotland, Australia and Canada. This trend has gone down even to the congregations, so much so that now it is not surprising to learn that a certain remote congregation in one of the CCAP synods has a partnership agreement with a congregation in the USA or Scotland.

It must, however, be pointed out that in as far as church-related partnerships are concerned, the CCAP synods do not partner with churches that are outside the Reformed and Presbyterian family of denominations at the level of presbytery or congregation. Besides church-related partners, there are also partnerships with organizations that are neither church nor church-related though it can be argued that they are still motivated by the Christian faith.

It is also clear that in all the partnerships that are there, it is the African churches that are benefiting in terms of material sharing because the Western churches are not in lack when it comes to material blessings and therefore do not expect such blessings from their African partners. The benefits that Western partners gain from these relationships are therefore different from what they themselves give out.

The Synod of Livingstonia and Its Foreign Partners

The Synod of Livingstonia has had a very interesting story with regard to foreign relations, especially the relationship between "mother" church and "daughter" church. Besides the Church of Scotland, which is its currently recognized parent church, the Synod of Livingstonia has other partner churches such as the Presbyterian Church in Ireland (PCI), Myers Park Presbyterian Church, Eastern Oklahoma Presbytery, Presbyterian Church in Canada and others.

The Church of Scotland

It has to be remembered that the initiative to establish the Livingstonia Mission came from the Free Church of Scotland that was in existence between 1843 and 1900.[2] Besides, the man who eventually became the recog-

---

2. Finlayson, *Unity and Diversity*.

nized father of the Livingstonia Mission, Dr Robert Laws, was originally not a Free Church of Scotland member but someone loaned from the United Presbyterian Church (UP).[3] Since the Free Church and United Presbyterian Church joined together in 1900 to form the United Free Church of Scotland (UFC), Robert Laws found himself comfortably at home with the new development.[4] This meant that, whereas the Synod of Livingstonia was originally considered a child of the Free Church of Scotland, it became a child of the United Free Church of Scotland consequent to the amalgamation of the Free Church of Scotland and the United Presbyterian Church. One can imagine that this was very good news for Dr Robert Laws who, in a way, was already a member of the two denominations before their unification by virtue of his being a Free Church missionary loaned by the United Presbyterian Church. In the words of Hamish McIntosh: "He himself [Robert Laws] had for a quarter of a century embodied in himself the principle of such a union, although he had always felt that loyalty to his own UP church obliged him to remain a minister within it until such time as the union so many desired should come about."[5] Further developments happened towards the year 1929 when the United Free Church of Scotland decided to rejoin the established Church of Scotland. When this rejoining happened, a small section that had distanced itself from the union of 1900 between the Free Church and the United Presbyterian Church became the sole owner of the name Free Church of Scotland (also known as the "Wee Free"), but because of its minority status it had already lost some of the Free Church property and personnel though at first it was granted permission to own everything that had previously belonged to the main Free Church of Scotland. This settlement did not affect the Livingstonia Mission much because its revenues were raised independently.[6]

Since 1929, the Synod of Livingstonia has been a "daughter" of the Church of Scotland through the union of the United Free Church and the established Church of Scotland, considering that the union actually made the United Free Church of Scotland to be swallowed up by the established

---

3. See Laws, *Reminiscences of Livingstonia*.
4. Livingstone, *Laws of Livingstonia*, 327.
5. McIntosh, *Robert Laws*, 144.
6. SeeMcCracken, *Politics and Christianity in Malawi 1875–1940*, 166, fn. 65.

Church of Scotland. This means that the established Church of Scotland is the "primary" partner of the Synod of Livingstonia when it comes to foreign relations since the missionaries handed over the administrative responsibility of the church to the first Malawian general secretary of the synod, Rev Patrick Chaŵeya Mzembe, in 1956.[7] It is interesting, however, to note that due to contemporary controversial issues in the church and the world, the relationship between the two is not very rosy. For instance, the Church of Scotland has in recent years softened its stand on the issue of homosexuality to the extent of even accommodating clergy who are confessedly gay in their sexual orientation. The Synod of Livingstonia is very much against this view, and to that end it is not endearing itself to the Church of Scotland as was previously the case, though it has not completely severed ties.[8]

Against this background the Synod of Livingstonia is attempting to re-establish ties with the remnant Free Church of Scotland with which they have similar roots though historical developments forced them apart for over a century. The Free Church of Scotland has continued with an evangelical theology that borders on conservatism, and they have decided to openly oppose gay relationships in the church. This is where the two churches feel they are birds of the same feather over and against the Church of Scotland. Even in Scotland itself, some congregations and pastors from the Church of Scotland are crossing over to the Free Church because of the gay rights question, which has caused division within the Church of Scotland.[9]

Despite the differences with regard to the issue of homosexuality, the Church of Scotland still assists the Synod of Livingstonia in many ways in their partnership. The two partners run projects from which the partner with financial difficulties benefits. For example, the Church of Scotland assists the Synod of Livingstonia through direct support to the David Gordon Memorial Hospital at Khondowe, Ekwendeni Theological College

---

7. Rev Patrick Chaŵeya Mzembe served the synod in the position of general secretary from 1956 to 1978. For a thorough treatment of his leadership style and how he tried to avoid transferring the synod headquarters from Khondowe to Mzuzu, see Mlenga, *History of Livingstonia Mission*, 7–10.

8. Rev Douglass Chipofya, in discussion with the author, Mzuzu, 26 April 2015.

9. Rev Levi N. Nyondo, in discussion with the author, Mzuzu, 5 August 2014. See also Brown, "Anglican Minister to Take Free Church Congregation," *The Scotsman*, http://www.scotsman.com/news/scotland/top-stories/anglican-minister-to-take-free-church-congregation-1-2910003, accessed 20 Apr 2015.

(now Ekwendeni Campus of the University of Livingstonia) and in the Livingstonia Synod AIDS Programme (LISAP).[10]

Apart from funding these areas there are also exchange visits between the two partners' workers in what is known as the Faithshare visits. The current general secretary of the Synod of Livingstonia, Rev Levi Nyondo, is himself one of the beneficiaries of the Faithshare programme, as he went to serve as a minister for Pitlochry Parish in Scotland from 2000 to 2001.[11] Another notable minister who spent some time in Scotland owing to the Faithshare programme is Rev Mezuwa Banda.[12] This programme of the Church of Scotland does not only involve the clergy but also lay church workers.

Another area of cooperation in this partnership is in congregational twinning whereby congregations in Scotland befriend congregations in Malawi and exchange friendship visits between them. These visits have the significance of enlightening the peoples of the two churches in what takes place in the other's country, especially with regard to church life and cultural context in general. I observe that the relationship between the Synod of Livingstonia and the Church of Scotland is a very strong one and that it is likely to continue because of the history behind it despite the challenges currently rocking it due to the issue of gay rights in the church and in society in general.

The Presbyterian Church in Ireland

The testimony of the leadership of the Synod of Livingstonia is that of all its partner churches, the Presbyterian Church in Ireland (PCI) is the most active. It is claimed that even when it comes to the number of contemporary missionary personnel there are more missionaries coming from the Presbyterian Church in Ireland than from the other partner churches. Through its Board of Mission Overseas (BMO), the Presbyterian Church in Ireland sends missionary personnel to various organizations in Malawi and in other countries. In this section we only concentrate on the church's activities in its partnership with the CCAP Synod of Livingstonia.

---

10. The Church of Scotland, "Our Partner Churches," http://www.churchofscotland.org.uk/serve/mission_worldwide/our-partner-churches/africa/malawi, accessed 5 Apr 2015.

11. Rev Levi N. Nyondo, in discussion with the author, Mzuzu, 5 August 2014.

12. Mlenga, *History of Livingstonia Mission*, 29.

The Presbyterian Church in Ireland's BMO categorizes its missionary personnel into three categories. The first category, known as the Integrate Programme, has missionaries that serve in the mission field for a period of two or more years. The second category is known as the Involve Programme. In this category missionaries serve for a period of up to two years. The third category is known as the Ignite Programme and in it members render services of up to one year.[13]

Within the BMO there is a committee known as the Leadership Development Committee (LDC) which helps to train and equip leaders in PCI's partner churches. This committee also works to promote individual partnerships through a rotating emphasis on each region of the world and engagement by congregations in leadership development work. In 2012, the Executive Secretary of BMO, Uel Marrs, paid a visit to Livingstonia Theological College where he learned about the challenges faced by theological students at the institution.[14] Such visits enable their missionary organization to appreciate the challenges their partners experience so that they can be able to scratch where it itches when it comes to providing assistance.

It is argued that the Presbyterian Church of Ireland is closer to the Synod of Livingstonia in its ethos than the Church of Scotland, hence the close relationship between the two. The relationship between the two is an old one as it started in the 1950s, and it has been growing from strength to strength as evidenced by the presence of many Irish missionaries and their continued support in the synod.[15]

Focus on Malawi

Among the many overseas partners that help the Synod of Livingstonia is an informal group of volunteers in the UK, called Focus on Malawi, composed of both medical and non-medical personnel. These work in association

---

13. Matt Williams, in discussion with the author, Mzuzu University, 16 April 2015. He eventually left the country in August 2015.

14. Presbyterian Church of Ireland, *2013 General Assembly Annual Reports*, 134.

15. According to the testimony of Rev Andrew D. Kayira, the first Irish missionary to work with the Synod of Livingstonia in Malawi was the Rev Bill Jackson who initially came to work in Karonga in 1958. This was after Rev Andrew Kayira had asked Rev Dr A. A. Fulton of the Presbyterian Church in Ireland for a missionary helper when the former visited Malawi in 1957. See Andrew D. Kayira, foreword to *Send Us Friends*, by Bill Jackson, ii.

with the Raven Trust, which is a charity supporting needy communities in Malawi. The objectives of Focus on Malawi are to:
1. Support the hospital directors of Ekwendeni, Livingstonia and Embangweni in the development of permanent and self-sustaining eye-services.[16]
2. Raise awareness in the UK among friends, professionals and the general public concerning the needs and required support.[17]
3. Channel resources and expertise, and to support local training.[18]

This group was established in 2005, and it is headed by Sue Kevan, an orthoptist, and Dr Caroline Sheldrick, an ophthalmologist.[19]

The Raven Trust

Already mentioned above in connection with the Focus on Malawi group, the Raven Trust is a registered charity in Scotland as well as a company limited by guarantee.[20] Its name comes from the story of Prophet Elijah in the Old Testament (1 Kgs 17:6) to whom ravens brought bread and meat in the morning and in the evening when he was at the brook Cherith during a period of drought in Israel in the reign of King Ahab. The motto of this trust is "Serving communities in Malawi directly," and, just like the ravens in the Elijah story, they aim to bring provisions for the needy in Malawi.[21] Among the things this charity has been able to send to Malawi, in excess of £1,000,000 so far, are medical supplies, books of all kinds, tools and equipment, clothing and other items such as mattresses, sports equipment and other necessities.[22] This organization collects donations made by individuals and church congregations in the UK and sends them to the Synod of Livingstonia according to identified needs in the synod's institutions.[23]

---

16. The Raven Trust, "Focus on Malawi," http://focusonmalawi.blogspot.com, accessed 7 Dec 2014.
17. The Raven Trust, "Focus on Malawi."
18. The Raven Trust, "Focus on Malawi."
19. The Raven Trust, "Focus on Malawi."
20. Focus on Malawi (The Raven Trust), "Supporting the Development of Eye Care," http://www.theraventrust.org/about/, accessed 10 Apr 2015.
21. Focus on Malawi, "Supporting the Development of Eye Care."
22. Focus on Malawi, "Supporting the Development of Eye Care."
23. Focus on Malawi, "Supporting the Development of Eye Care."

The Presbyterian Church in Canada

The Presbyterian Church in Canada is another major partner of the CCAP Synod of Livingstonia as it assists the synod in various ways. This church mostly engages in relief and development work through its development arm known as Presbyterian World Service and Development (PWS&D) and through its Department of International Ministries, both of which are under the Life and Mission Agency Committee.[24] Through PWS&D the Presbyterian Church in Canada is helping the Synod of Livingstonia in such crucial areas as the Malaria Control Programme, through links with the synod's hospitals such as Ekwendeni Hospital, David Gordon Memorial Hospital and Embangweni Hospital.[25] Through this programme, in 2010 eight hundred bed nets were distributed and ninety-five volunteers were trained on malaria prevention, and they went door-to-door educating community members in the vicinity of the synod's hospitals concerning malaria issues. In the same vein, PWS&D has been providing households with nutritional supplements, fertilizers and feeds. In the same year of 2010, some 264 orphans were enabled to attend primary school by being provided with school uniforms and other supplies curtsey of PWS&D Ekwendeni Hospital HIV and AIDS Orphan Programme.[26]

PWS&D has also assisted in the construction of a community-based childcare centre at Ekwendeni and provided training and bicycles to volunteers for HIV and AIDS work. They have also helped the synod in capacity development for its Development Department, especially in the area of optimizing the use of computers and strengthening the monitoring and evaluation systems of the Development Department in its bid to provide effective programming.[27]

Through its Leadership Development Programme, the Presbyterian Church in Canada helps a number of students from different places in the world who study either in Canadian institutions or in institutions within their own countries. From the Synod of Livingstoniathere was one

---

24. Presbyterian Church in Canada, "Mission," http://presbyterian.ca/pwsd/mission/, accessed 11 Apr 2015.
25. Presbyterian Church in Canada, "Mission."
26. Presbyterian Church in Canada, "Mission."
27. Presbyterian Church in Canada, "Mission."

beneficiary of this programme during the period of this research by the name of Rev Greyson Munyimbili who was studying for a Master's Degree in Theology and Religious Studies at Mzuzu University.[28]

The Presbyterian Church of the USA

The Presbyterian Church of the USA (PCUSA) is another foreign partner of the Synod of Livingstonia. This church assists the synod's College of Theology at Ekwendeni(now Ekwendeni Campus of the University of Livingstonia) with funds and educational materials such as computers and books. It also provides scholarships for secondary and post-secondary education and assists the University of Livingstonia in general with funding. It also funds the Synod's Water and Sanitation Programme and provides general support for the synod. Apart from monetary and material support, PCUSA also sends missionary personnel with different expertise to contribute to the work of the Synod of Livingstonia. Some current PCUSA missionaries in the Synod of Livingstonia include couples James and Jodi McGill and Tyler and Rochelle Holm.[29] James McGill coordinates the clean water and sanitation work of the Synod of Livingstonia while Jodi McGill is the synod's coordinator for primary health care, working with a congregation-based malaria prevention program, HIV/AIDS prevention and care, and other public health programs. She also works as a clinical instructor at the Ekwendeni College of Nursing.[30] Tyler Holm teaches theology at the University of Livingstonia while Rochelle Holm manages the Mzuzu University Water and Sanitation Centres.[31]

From this church the Synod of Livingstonia still has some more partners with individual presbyteries and congregations. Among the presbyteries and congregations that are partners with the Synod of Livingstonia are Meyers Park Presbyterian Church, Eastern Oklahoma Presbytery, Shepherd of the Hills Presbyterian Church and Mountain View Presbyterian Church.

---

28. See "Life and Mission Agency Committee Report," 13 Jan 2015.
29. Presbyterian Church (USA), "Presbyterian Mission," https://www.presbyterianmission.org/ministries/global/malawi/, accessed 17 July 2019.
30. Presbyterian Church (USA), "Presbyterian Mission."
31. Presbyterian Church (USA), "Presbyterian Mission."

Myers Park Presbyterian Church

The Myers Park Presbyterian Church has what it calls "partner countries." In all, Myers Park Presbyterian Church has five partner countries: the DR Congo, Cuba, El Salvador, Uganda, and Malawi. In Malawi the church's partner is the Synod of Livingstonia. The Synod of Livingstonia benefits from this partnership through assistance in the following areas: crisis nursery, community-based child care centres, hospitals, schools and clean water programmes.

Shepherd of the Hills Presbyterian Church

Through its mission outreach, Shepherd of the Hills Presbyterian Church has sponsored over 150 children through the World Vision Hope Child Programme, and it has also assisted in the building and funding of an AIDS block at Embangweni Mission Hospital. Apart from these mission actions, the Shepherd of the Hills Presbyterian Church has established a twinning relationship with Manyamula Congregation of Engalaweni Presbytery through which the local congregation has benefited in the funding of a building project for its manse, the building of a grain bank for lean periods and the installation of a solar school block lighting system.[32]

Mountain View Presbyterian Church

The relationship between Mountain View Presbyterian Church of the USA and Engalaweni Congregation of the CCAP Synod of Livingstonia in Mzimba has seen delegates of the two congregations visiting each other in order to strengthen their bond of friendship. This church helps its Malawian partner in the areas of school improvements and funding micro-businesses.[33]

Eastern Oklahoma Presbytery

Eastern Oklahoma Presbytery is one of the most vibrant partners of the Synod of Livingstonia. Apart from the financial support this church gives to the Synod of Livingstonia, it has initiated the twinning of several congregations, so much so that there are now many congregations in the Synod of

---

32. Shepherd of the Hills Presbyterian Church, "Africa Missions," http://www.shpc.org/africa-missions/, accessed 11 Apr 2015.

33. Mountain View Presbyterian Church, "Missions," http://www.mymvpc.com/home/missions, accessed 10 Mar 2015.

Livingstonia that have twinning partners in Eastern Oklahoma Presbytery in the USA.[34]

The GZB (Gereformeerde Zendingsbond)

Another important partner that assists the Synod of Livingstonia is the GZB, known in English as the Reformed Mission League. In the Dutch language it is *Gereformeerde Zendingsbond* but is popularly known by its acronym GZB.[35] This organization supports the Synod of Livingstonia directly alongside its commitment to the General Assembly and other synods.

Conclusion

The Synod of Livingstonia has so many partners, and it is not strange to imagine that the synod benefits a lot from these partnerships in terms of personnel, money and other resources since the partners come from countries that are not as poor as Malawi is economically. It is therefore obvious that it is the Synod of Livingstonia that benefits more from these partnerships though, to a lesser extent, the foreign partners also benefit in terms of international friendships and an opportunity to learn about the Christian faith from partners in circumstances of less abundance.

Blantyre Synod and Its Foreign Partners

Just like the Synod of Livingstonia, Blantyre Synod has several partners from foreign countries from whom it benefits a lot in terms of Christian sharing.

The Church of Scotland

For Blantyre Synod the parent church is and has always been the established Church of Scotland.[36] From 1876, when Blantyre Mission was founded, to 1959 when the Blantyre Mission Council was dissolved, the synod was solely under the supervision of the Church of Scotland, which sent missionaries and money and continues to do so even now. The Church of Scotland lists Blantyre Synod as one of its partner churches, and there are many

---

34. Eastern Oklahoma Presbytery, "Livingstonia," http://eokpresbytery.org/blog/?s=livingstonia, accessed 11 Apr 2015.

35. Synod of Livingstonia, "Minutes of Thirty-Third Synod Assembly," min. 50/12, 1(d).

36. See Ross, "Partnership in Mission and Postcolonial Politics," 12–130.

congregational twinning initiatives between the two churches. Apart from the regular personnel that come to Blantyre Synod from Scotland and the general support that the Church of Scotland renders to Blantyre Synod, there are several areas in which the Church of Scotland is continuously helping the work of Blantyre Synod. Some of these areas include the support for HIV prevention and awareness-raising within marriage, support for the Blantyre Synod Health and Development Commission, support to Mulanje Mission Hospital and enhanced couple counselling in an age of HIV and AIDS. Another component of this partnership is the Faithshare programme where exchange visits between the two churches do take place regularly.

The controversial issue of homosexuality proves to be slippery ground for the relationship between the two churches as well. In September 2011, St Michael's and All Angels congregation of Blantyre Synod ended their partnership with Queen's Cross Church in Aberdeen, Scotland because the Scottish congregation had ordained a gay pastor, Scot Rennie.[37] In view of such developments, when the Rev Diane Hobson visited Malawi in February 2012, she promised on behalf of the Church of Scotland that no gay missionaries would be sent to Malawi.[38] This means that there is mutual respect between the two partners despite their differences in responding to some contemporary issues such as gay rights.

The Presbyterian Church of Victoria (Australia)

Blantyre Synod is also in a partnership agreement with the Presbyterian Church of Victoria, Australia, through the Australian Presbyterian World Mission. This partnership involves the members of Blantyre Synod agreeing to pray for the spread of the gospel in Australia and to keep their Australian friends informed about the work of the gospel in Malawi through articles and literature.[39] On the part of the Presbyterian Church of Australia, there is commitment to sending visiting lecturers to provide ministry training at the Blantyre Synod's Theological Resource Centre or other places within the jurisdiction of Blantyre Synod and to assist in funding the renovation

---

37. Nation Online, "Scots Promise No Gay Missionaries to Malawi," *The Nation*, http://mwnation.com/scots-promise-no-gay-missionaries-to-malawi/, accessed 23 Feb 2015.

38. Nation Online, "Scots Promise No Gay Missionaries to Malawi."

39. Australian Presbyterian Women, "Partner Churches," http://www.apwm.org.au/partner-churches/malawi/, accessed 5 Apr 2015.

and running costs of the Theological Resource Centre. The Presbyterian Church of Australia has assisted Blantyre Synod in the establishment of the Orbus Centre for the Care of Orphans and Vulnerable Children, which is currently under the direction of Blantyre Synod but with some input from Australia.[40] This centre is located at Ngumbe in Traditional Authority Machinjiri's area in Blantyre District, and it was opened on 31 July 2010. The centre's programmes and activities are under the oversight of the Blantyre Synods' Health and Development Commission and the Synod's Education Department.[41]

Through this partnership the Presbyterian Church of Australia also assists Blantyre Synod schools and, in particular, the Presbyterian Ladies College in Melbourne has entered into a special relationship with Neno Girls Mission School.[42] The Presbyterian Ladies College is a Christian independent girls' school founded in 1875, and it is affiliated to the Presbyterian Church in Victoria.[43] Students of this college, particularly those in the Student Leadership Team and on the Social Work Committee, raise thousands of dollars for their school's support of Neno Girls Secondary School of CCAP Blantyre Synod.[44]

Presbyterian Church of the USA

With regard to the Presbyterian Church of the USA, Blantyre Synod's partnership is with the Pittsburgh Presbytery. This partnership was conceived in 1990, and from 1991 there have been exchange visits of over five hundred persons between the two partners, and they continue to take place. These visits involve relationship building, education events, pastoral exchange,

---

40. Australian Presbyterian Women, "Malawi, Country Information," http://www.apwm.org.au/wp-content/uploads/2014/08/Malawi-Country-Information-Sheet-2014.pdf, accessed 5 Apr 2015.

41. Orbus Africa, "Orbus Projects," http://www.orbusministries.org/projects.html, accessed 4 May 2015.

42. Presbyterian Ladies College, "Personal Development," http://www.plc.vic.edu.au/learning-plc_personal-development.aspx, accessed 16 Mar 2015.

43. Presbyterian Ladies College, "PLC's History," https://www.plc.vic.edu.au/about/our-school/plcs-history, accessed 16 Mar 2015.

44. Presbyterian Ladies College, "Personal Development," http://www.plc.vic.edu.au/learning-plc_personal-development.aspx, accessed 16 Mar 2015.

evangelism rallies, medical mission work and building construction.[45] According to Dr Silas Ncozana, former Blantyre Synod general secretary and one of the founders of the relationship:

> The purpose of the partnership between Pittsburgh Presbytery and the Synod of Blantyre CCAP, Malawi is to move us toward the fulfilment of Christ's prayer for unity among his disciples; that all are invited into His Kingdom, that the world may accept the gospel and have faith; that God's love may abound; that the Church may grow and be mutually encouraged in faith.[46]

On the part of PCUSA, the mission statement of the Malawi partnership of Pittsburgh Presbytery reads: "Our mission as the Malawi Mission Partnership Committee of Pittsburgh Presbytery (PCUSA) is to carry out God's plan for this world through mutual encouragement in our faith and life journey in partnership with the Synod of Blantyre of the Church of Central Africa (CCAP) in Malawi, Africa."[47] In 2012 the Pittsburgh Presbytery–Blantyre Synod partnership was joined by the Presbyterian Church of South Sudan, making a three-way church partnership. In January 2013, a team of representatives from Pittsburgh joined their Blantyre Synod colleagues to attend a General Assembly meeting of the Presbyterian Church of South Sudan.[48]

As can be seen, the partnership between the Blantyre Synod and Pittsburgh Presbytery has been there for some time, and it can be argued that Blantyre Synod has over the years benefited greatly from this relationship both in terms of material blessings and the opportunity for exposure as the members go to Pittsburgh in the USA for their exchange visits.

---

45. Pittsburgh Presbytery, "International Partnership," http://pghpip.org/about/about.shtml, accessed 6 Apr 2015.

46. Ncozana, "New Dawn for Partnership in Mission."

47. Pittsburgh Presbytery, "International Partnership of Pittsburgh Presbytery," https://pghpip.org/about/about.shtml, accessed 6 Apr 2015.

48. The Pittsburgh Presbytery, "A Letter from the General Minister to Pittsburgh Presbytery," http://www.pghpresbytery.org/news/sheldon_shares/2013/ss_010313.htm, accessed 13 Apr 2015.

Presbyterian Church in Canada

The Presbyterian Church in Canada, through its Presbyterian World Service and Development (PWS&D) arm, is carrying out a lot of programmes in Malawi through its partnership with Blantyre Synod. For example, the Mulanje Mission Hospital Orphan Care Programme compliments hospital services to orphans and to guardians on health care.[49] Through PWS&D, the Presbyterian Church in Canada has also involved itself in the Blantyre Synod's Church and Society Programme's civic and voter education by engaging in logistical exercises. In 2010, PWS&D supported the distribution of educational materials sourced from the Malawi Electoral Commission and the Public Affairs Committee. It also facilitated awareness meetings with local leaders and church committee members.[50]

In the area of education, the Presbyterian Church in Canada has helped with sanitation infrastructure development at Neno Girls Secondary School and also provided bursaries and scholarships to needy students. PWS&D has also helped in funding the Titukule Ana Programme for orphans. Through this activity many orphans have acquired vocational skills and some have managed to attend secondary education with support from this programme.[51]

PWS&D, in partnership with Blantyre Synod, has also been involved in relief work, especially in providing food items to families affected by drought. In 2010, with support from Blantyre Synod Health and Development Commission, PWS&D initiated a food assistance project in the Balaka area, which experienced drought during the 2009–2010 rainy season. The project also supported the targeted beneficiaries with training and seedlings to promote the adoption of cassava production as a drought resistant crop in the area.[52]

Within Blantyre District there is the Lirangwe Food Security Project which the PWS&D is funding through Blantyre Synod Health and Development Commission.[53] This project aims at diversifying and increasing

---

49. See Mulanje Mission Hospital, "Mulanje Mission Hospital in 2013," http://www.mmh.mw/wp-content/uploads/2012/03/MMH-ppt-updated-August-2013.pdf, accessed 17 Jul 2019.
50. PWS&D, "Malawi", https://presbyterian.ca/pwsd/malawi/, accessed 17 Jul 2019.
51. "Life and Mission Agency Committee Report," 13.1.80.
52. "Life and Mission Agency Committee Report," 13.1.76.
53. "Life and Mission Agency Committee Report," 13.1.76.

sustainable staple crop production in nine villages, targeting five hundred food insecure households.[54] In this project, conservation farming techniques are being introduced and promoted as a central focus of the project through a community based approach. The emphasis is on locally available resources in order to ensure sustainable results.[55]

PWS&D is also involved in the activities of empowering people with disabilities. It is doing this through the Tidzalerana Club where people with disabilities and their families come together to support each other and in the process some people are able to start engaging in income generating activities.[56]

Apart from the various projects mentioned above in which the Presbyterian Church in Canada through its PWS&D is proving its commitment to its partnership with Blantyre Synod, there are also contributions of personnel from the Canadian church to Blantyre Synod. For example, between 2007 and 2013 some Canadians served in several capacities with Blantyre Synod. In 2007, the Rev Glenn Inglis embarked on serving as Executive Director of the Blantyre Synod Health and Development Commission. His position was renewed in August 2010 so that he could serve up to the end of 2012. On the other hand, Ms Linda Inglis served in a volunteer missionary capacity as the Ecumenical Officer for Blantyre Synod. The Rev Dr Todd Statham was appointed to serve as a lecturer in Church History and Theology at Zomba Theological College between 2011 and 2013 as a missionary of Blantyre Synod. In the same vein, the Rev Michael and Ms Debra Burns were also appointed to serve in Blantyre Synod between 1 January 2011 and 31 December 2013. Michael served as associate minister at St James Church in the City of Blantyre.[57]

On this note we conclude some of the instances of the partnership between Blantyre Synod and the Presbyterian Church in Canada.

---

54. "Life and Mission Agency Committee Report," 13.1.76.
55. "Life and Mission Agency Committee Report," 13.1.76.
56. "Life and Mission Agency Committee Report," 13.1.81.
57. "Life and Mission Agency Committee Report," 13.1.11.

Scotland Malawi Partnership

Blantyre Synod's website specifically mentions the Scotland Malawi Partnership as one of its official partners.[58] Through this partnership there have been visits to Scotland from Blantyre Synod and projects funded in Malawi through the Scottish people's initiative. For example, Child Survival in Malawi (Scotland) is a Scottish charity supporting small community-based development initiatives in Malawi. In August 2009, two women from Blantyre Synod, who were involved in the Child Survival in Malawi projects, visited Scotland under the auspices of the Church of Scotland's Faithshare programme and facilitated by the Malawi-Scotland Partnership. These women were Grace Kulupando and Violet Chavura.[59]

While the Scotland Malawi Partnership embraces a lot of things between the two countries as signed in their 2005 agreement, it is important to note that the genesis of this partnership is the relationship of the Presbyterian churches in the two countries which go all the way back to the founding of the Livingstonia and Blantyre Missions which also have their roots in the activities of the missionary explorer Dr David Livingstone.[60]

The GZB (Gereformeerde Zendingsbond)

Last but not least among the official partners of Blantyre Synod is the Mission Board of the Protestant Churches in the Netherlands (GZB). According to Rev Lieuwe Schaafsma, GZB is mainly involved in three things in its partnership with Blantyre Synod: [1] Theological Education by Extension in Malawi (TEEM); [2] Orphan Care Programmes; and [3] Zomba Theological College.[61] Rev Schaafsma was himself the Director of TEEM for some time and between 2001 and 2009 he served in Blantyre Synod as an associate pastor at St Michael's and All Angels Church. GZB also funds the Ndirande Orphanage in Blantyre and contributes to the budget for Zomba Theological College.[62]

---

58. See CCAP Blantyre Synod, "Current Partnerships," http://www.ccapblantyresynod.org/current-partnerships.html, accessed 23 Jun 2015.

59. Pattison, "Member Focus: Child Survival in Malawi," 9.

60. Ross, *Malawi and Scotland*, 12–29, 30–47.

61. CCAP Blantyre Synod, "News," http://www.ccapblantyresynod.org/news.html, accessed 20 Mar 2015.

62. CCAP Blantyre Synod, "News."

After leaving Malawi, Rev Schaafsma visited the country again in 2012 when he led a group of young people from the Netherlands to Malawi. The young people, who all came from the Protestant church in the Netherlands (PKN), helped with some volunteer work in Blantyre Synod at Tidzalerana Shelter for the disabled in Ndirande and also at Mulanje Mission Hospital, all under the auspices of GZB.[63]

Another notable missionary from GZB in Blantyre Synod is the Rev Steven Paas, who made the initial contact with the synod in 1997 and ever since has been a regular visitor even after his period of missionary work expired. Apart from working as a minister in Blantyre Synod, Rev Paas also served as lecturer at Zomba Theological College. He is well known in academic circles for his contributions in compiling language dictionaries (*Chichewa/Chinyanja to English and English to Chichewa/Chinyanja*), historical research and the writing and spreading of various Christian literature.[64]

Conclusion

The partners of Blantyre Synod can be said to be making a huge impact on the work of the synod as it is evident that most of the relief and development programmes that Blantyre Synod has are being funded in one way or another by these partners. This is, therefore, another instance in which the foreign partnerships of the CCAP synods prove to be more beneficial to the African churches.

Nkhoma Synod and Its Foreign Partners

As is the case with the synods of Livingstonia and Blantyre with their former "mother," the Church of Scotland, Nkhoma Synod, too, has a very special relationship with the Dutch Reformed Church in South Africa, being the church whose missionary personnel established Nkhoma Mission which

---

63. CCAP Blantyre Synod, "News."

64. Some of Rev Steven Paas's publications include the following: *Ministers and Elders: The Birth of Presbyterianism* (Zomba: Kachere, 2007); *The Faith Moves South: A History of the Church in Africa* (Zomba: Kachere, 2006); *Dictionary: Mtanthauziramau; English Chichewa/ Chichewa English* (Nuremberg: VTR Publications, 2012); *Christian Zionism Examined: A Review of Ideas on Israel, the Church and the Kingdom* (Nuremberg: VTR Publications, 2012); *Digging out the Ancestral Church: Researching and Communicating Church History* (Blantyre: CLAIM-Kachere, 2002).

has evolved into the present Nkhoma Synod of the CCAP. Apart from this partnership, the synod has other partners from diverse places as we shall see below.

Dutch Reformed Churches in South Africa

The relationship between Nkhoma Synod and that of the Dutch Reformed Church in South Africa has been an evolving one. From the dawn of Malawian leadership of Nkhoma Synod to the present day, there have been changes in the relationship between Nkhoma Synod and the Dutch Reformed Church in South Africa in order to respond to the ever-changing circumstances in which this relationship operates. The current document that guides the relationship between Nkhoma Synod and the South African Reformed Churches is the Partnership Agreement of 2003. This partnership agreement is unique in that the South African partner is actually the Commission for Witness in South Africa, which is a representation of the family of the Dutch Reformed Churches in the Western and South Cape – namely, the Dutch Reformed Church in South Africa (DRCSA); the Uniting Reformed Church in Southern Africa (URCSA), Cape Synod; and Reformed Church in Africa, Sunthonshan Congregation. This partnership agreement is considered a continuation as well as further development and maturing of the relationships preceding this one with the Dutch Reformed Church in South Africa, whose missionary activity gave birth to Nkhoma Synod.

The genesis of this relationship in the post-missionary period was the Act of Agreement that was entered into in 1962 when Nkhoma Synod came under Malawian leadership. Consequently, indigenous Malawian leaders assumed full responsibility over all the work and all departments and property that were previously under the supervision of the General Administrative Committee (GAC), which comprised both indigenous Malawians and South African missionary personnel.[65] In the course of time, this Act of Agreement experienced several revisions which culminated in the Deed of Agreement of 1992. It is this 1992 Deed of Agreement that eventually gave way to the new Partnership Agreement in 2003 which is still active up to now.[66] In this Partnership Agreement there are specific obligations for the partners as

---

65. Brown, "Development in Self Understanding of the CCAP Nkhoma Synod," 20.
66. Rev Dr Winston R. Kawale, email communication, 22 April 2015.

explained below. Nkhoma Synod's obligations in this Partnership Agreement are to:

1. Receive prayer requests and pray for such needs of the Partner.[67]
2. Send Nkhoma Synod prayer requests to the Partners.[68]
3. Propose and discuss possible new projects with the Partner(s) and submit detailed project proposals for consideration by the Partner(s).[69]
4. Seek technical advice from the Partner on some projects to be carried out.[70]
5. Send budgeted financial and material requests for various projects in the fields of ministry, evangelism, social service and witness.[71]
6. Submit requests for personnel to serve in various fields.[72]
7. Provide a job description for the required personnel.[73]
8. Indicate which qualifications such personnel should preferably have.[74]
9. If necessary interview prospective candidates for a particular post.[75]
10. Determine the period of service of the candidate in consultation with the Partner.[76]
11. If, for whatever reason, it is deemed necessary for the services of a personnel member to be terminated earlier, the Synod shall decide upon this after due consultation with the Partner. The personnel concerned shall be given three months' notice of the termination of his/her service.[77]

---

67. Partnership Agreement, 8.1.1.
68. Partnership Agreement, 8.1.2.
69. Partnership Agreement, 8.1.3.
70. Partnership Agreement, 8.1.4.
71. Partnership Agreement, 8.1.5.
72. Partnership Agreement, 8.1.6.
73. Partnership Agreement, 8.1.7.
74. Partnership Agreement, 8.1.8.
75. Partnership Agreement, 8.1.9.
76. Partnership Agreement, 8.1.10.
77. Partnership Agreement, 8.1.11.

12. Evaluate and report annually concerning the work and performance of the personnel to the sending Partner.[78]
13. Take decisions concerning change of work or transfer of personnel after due consultation with the Partner and with the concurrence of the personnel member.[79]
14. Be accountable to the financial assistance provided by the Partners.[80]
15. Use all finances solely for the purposes they are intended for, with proper accountability and transparency. For this purpose, specific accounts will be identified for specific projects or Departments into which funds from Partners as well as contributions from donors may be deposited.[81]
16. Provide accommodation and basic furniture for the personnel from the partner churches.[82]

On the other hand, the obligations of the Commission for Witness, being the partner in South Africa, are to:

1. Receive prayer requests and pray for the needs in Nkhoma Synod.[83]
2. Receive and consider the financial, material and personnel requests from Nkhoma Synod.[84]
3. Provide technical advice and financial and material assistance to Nkhoma Synod.[85]
4. Send all the monies to Nkhoma Synod (cf. PA.8.1.14 and PA.8.1.15).[86]
5. Provide personnel requested and agreed upon for specific tasks.[87]
6. Be responsible for the payment of the salaries, travel expenses,

---

78. Partnership Agreement, 8.1.12.
79. Partnership Agreement, 8.1.13.
80. Partnership Agreement, 8.1.14.
81. Partnership Agreement, 8.1.15.
82. Partnership Agreement, 8.1.16.
83. Partnership Agreement, 8.2.1
84. Partnership Agreement, 8.2.2
85. Partnership Agreement, 8.2.3
86. Partnership Agreement, 8.2.4
87. Partnership Agreement, 8.2.5

pension, medical fund contributions, and any other allowances for the personnel.[88]
7. Provide funding for the maintenance of the accommodation provided by Nkhoma Synod.[89]
8. Provide personnel who are full members of their church or, in the case of prospective personnel from another denomination, first obtain the approval of Nkhoma Synod before sending such a person.[90]
9. Participate with Nkhoma Synod in providing counselling, spiritual care and moral support for its personnel.[91]
10. Receive annual reports from Nkhoma Synod on the performance of each personnel member.[92]
11. Wherever necessary, supply motor vehicles to Nkhoma Synod for use in particular project(s). These motor vehicles shall be registered under Nkhoma Synod (cf. PA.8.2.2).[93]
12. In consultation with Nkhoma Synod take such steps as may be necessary regarding the performance of personnel in terms of the accountability being expected of them.[94]
13. In consultation with Nkhoma Synod deal with such personal and official matters concerning members of the personnel as may be necessary.[95]
14. In case where personnel have to be evacuated from Malawi in an emergency situation, such as major medical problem, the sending partner shall be responsible for the evacuation expenses.[96]

While it can be argued that the evolution of the relationship between Nkhoma Synod of the CCAP and the Dutch Reformed Church in South Africa has done away with the "mother-daughter" relationship between the

---

88. Partnership Agreement, 8.2.6
89. Partnership Agreement, 8.2.7
90. Partnership Agreement, 8.2.8
91. Partnership Agreement, 8.2.9
92. Partnership Agreement, 8.2.10
93. Partnership Agreement, 8.2.11
94. Partnership Agreement, 8.2.12
95. Partnership Agreement, 8.2.13
96. Partnership Agreement, 8.2.14

two churches to that of equal partners, there is still some trace of dependence on the part of Nkhoma Synod, which makes it more of a receiver in this partnership, especially in relation to the issues of money and personnel from South Africa.

The Church of Scotland

Nkhoma Synod is also in partnership with the Church of Scotland, which actually is in partnership with all the three Malawian Synods of the CCAP as well as the General Assembly itself. This partnership mostly involves the work of Nkhoma Mission Hospital and the Faithshare programme between the two churches where personnel from the Church of Scotland and Nkhoma Synod share visits between Scotland and Malawi.[97]

The Presbyterian Church in Taiwan (PCT)

Another foreign partner which Nkhoma Synod had was the Presbyterian Church in Taiwan (PCT). This partnership was formalized in the year 2004 at the 49th General Assembly of the Presbyterian Church in Taiwan which took place from 13 to 16 April 2004.[98] During this General Assembly, Nkhoma Synod sent six delegates to the Taiwanese Church. This delegation included the Rev Stonham Sande Mwale, the synod's moderator, and the Rev Dr Winston R. Kawale, the synod's general secretary. The two signed the Partner Church Agreement with the Presbyterian Church in Taiwan on behalf of Nkhoma Synod during this visit.[99] Prior to this formal agreement with the General Assembly of the Presbyterian Church in Taiwan, Nkhoma Synod was already involved in a relationship with the Ta-an Presbyterian Church in Seven Stars Presbytery within the City of Taipei.[100]

Sadly, this partnership with the Presbyterian Church in Taiwan is no longer there as it died following the termination of diplomatic ties between the Government of Malawi and the Taiwanese Government. The Malawian Government in 2007 decided to establish ties with mainland China in line

---

97. Church of Scotland, "Our Partner Churches, http://www.churchofscotland.org.uk/serve/mission_worldwide/our-partner-churches/africa/malawi, accessed 14 Apr 2015.

98. Letter from William J. K. Lo (PCT General Secretary) to Partner Churches and Related Organisations, Friends around the Globe and PCT Related Missionary Personnel, April 2004, http://english.pct.org.tw/others/20040400.htm, accessed 29 Apr 2015.

99. Letter from William J. K. Lo (PCT General Secretary).

100. "Taiwan Presbyterians Open Mission Centre in Malawi."

with the international policy of "One China," which makes the Communist People's Republic of China eclipse Taiwan. Consequently, all the projects the Taiwanese were doing with Nkhoma Synod, such as mobile clinics in different congregations and a computer college in Lilongwe, came to a halt.[101] This is one incident in which international politics had a direct impact on the life of the church with regard to foreign relations.

The Reformed Church in America

Nkhoma Synod shares its Dutch Reformed roots with the Reformed Church in America (RCA), which also traces its history back to the Dutch Reformed Church in the Netherlands.[102] It is therefore not surprising for the two churches to be in a partnership agreement. Through this agreement, RCA sends its volunteers to Nkhoma Synod, and they assist the synod in various projects.[103] For example, through this partnership work has been done at Malingunde Women's Centre with regard to roof and interior repairing of the premises there, and there are also ongoing programmes funded by the RCA, such as the Malawi Children's Feeding Programme which tries to reverse malnutrition among children under five years of age.[104] Nkhoma Synod has also benefited from its partnership with the Reformed Church in America in the area of building a vocational school for AIDS orphans, training hospital staff, repairing electronics and tailoring hospital uniforms.[105]

Word and Deed Ministries

This is a Christian Ministry organization that partners with churches in the developing world on a variety of projects including child sponsorship, Christian Education, orphan care, disaster relief and vocational training.[106] The organization mobilizes and educates churches of Northern America through updates in the form of presentations, quarterly magazines, church

---

101. Rev Winston R. Kawale, email communication, 30 April 2015.
102. See DeJong, *Dutch Reformed Church in the American Colonies*.
103. Reformed Church in America, "RCA Global Mission," https://www.rca.org/rca-global-mission, accessed 28 Apr 2015.
104. Reformed Church in America, "Children's Feeding Program," https://www.rca.org/childrens-feeding-program, accessed 28 Apr 2015.
105. Reformed Church in America, "Children's Feeding Program."
106. Word and Deed, "Malawi," http://wordanddeed.org/about-us, accessed 29 Apr 2015.

bulletins, emails and website articles in order to raise awareness of the plight of the needy. Apart from its own partnership with Nkhoma Synod of the CCAP, Word and Deed Ministries has also linked the synod with the Free Reformed Churches of North America.[107]

The GZB (Gereformeerde Zendingsbond)

As with the other two Malawian synods of Livingstonia and Blantyre, and the General Assembly itself, Nkhoma Synod, too, is in partnership with the GZB of the Netherlands, which also supports the synod with funding and personnel.[108]

First Presbyterian Church of Quincy, Massachusetts

The First Presbyterian Church of Quincy, Massachusetts, becomes the latest partner of Nkhoma Synod of the CCAP following the signing of a partnership pact between the two churches that took place at Kaning'a CCAP in Lilongwe on 14 August 2016. This partnership aims primarily at supporting the Josophat Mwale Theological Institute (JMTI) of Nkhoma Synod through the American partner.[109]

Harare Synod and Its Foreign Partners

Among the five synods of the CCAP General Assembly, the Harare Synod seems to have the least number of foreign partners. In the course of this study only two were identified: Madison Avenue Presbyterian Church (MAPC) in the USA and the Presbyterian Church of Australia. However, on its website the synod only shows MAPC as its partner.[110]

Madison Avenue Presbyterian Church (MAPC)

The most important foreign partner the Harare Synod currently has is the Madison Avenue Presbyterian Church (MAPC).[111] This relationship began

---

107. See Free Reformed Churches of North America, *Acts of Synod 2011*, 21–22, 34, 171–173 and Free Reformed Churches of North America, *Acts of Synod 2012*, 138.

108. See GZB, "Mission," www.gzb.nl, accessed 29 Apr 2015.

109. See Mulenga, "Nkhoma, American Church Sign Pact," 9.

110. CCAP Harare Synod, "Harare Synod," https://www.ccaphresynod.com/hararesynodandmapc.htm, accessed 4 Apr 2015.

111. CCAP Harare Synod, "Harare Synod."

in 2007, and it has been signed or ratified twice.¹¹² The 2010 document which contains the current partnership agreement between the two churches is titled "Covenant of Partnership," and its purpose is stated as to "aim to strengthen each other's ministries and discipleship while developing a shared ministry between us."¹¹³

In this partnership, it was initially agreed that the partnership activities would include annual exchange visits between the members of the two churches, including praying for one another. MAPC was also expected to provide organizational and technical support for ministry in Harare Synod while Harare Synod was expected to send a pastor in residence to MAPC in the fall of each year. It was also planned that the youth of the two churches would be exchanging penpal letters. As the partnership progressed even the youth had a chance to exchange visits, thereby becoming exposed to the different contexts in which the two churches operate.¹¹⁴

Presbyterian Church of Australia

Through the work of its agency, Presbyterian Aid (PresAid), the Presbyterian Church of Australia renders assistance to the CCAP Harare Synod in various ways especially in the areas of relief, infrastructure development and theological education.¹¹⁵

The Harare Synod is yet to establish its own theological college for the training of its pastors. Consequently, its pastors are trained at Zomba Theological College in Malawi and at Chasefu Theological College in Zambia. The Presbyterian Church of Australia helps the Harare Synod by supporting its theological students through the theological education support it gives to Chasefu Theological College as well as direct support to the students themselves.¹¹⁶

---

112. Madison Avenue Presbyterian Church, "Zimbabwe Partnership," http://www.mapc.com/outreach/global-outreach/zimbabwe-partnership/, accessed 4 Apr 2015.

113. Madison Avenue Presbyterian Church, "Partnership Agreement," http://mapc.com.test.bandwidthproductions.com/files/pages/outreach/PartnershipAgreement.pdf, accessed 10 Apr 2015.

114. Madison Avenue Presbyterian Church, "Partnership Agreement."

115. Presbyterian Aid Australia, "The Story So Far," https://presaid.org.au/index.php/the-story-so-far, accessed 16 Apr 2015.

116. Presbyterian Aid Australia, "The Story So Far."

The Synod of Zambia and Its Foreign Partners

The Synod of Zambia identifies the following as its partners: the Presbyterian Church in USA, the Presbyterian Church in Ireland, the Presbyterian Church in Australia and a charity organization by the name of Romans 1:11 Trust.[117]

The Presbyterian Church of the USA (PCUSA)

In its relationship with the Presbyterian Church of the USA, the Synod of Zambia benefits from expert personnel secondment and aid for its various projects. The Presbyterian Church of the USA fulfils her duty to her partner church through its international development arm, the Presbyterian Mission Agency. Through this agency, PCUSA has a number of missionaries in Zambia who are serving in the areas of theological education, evangelism, health, agriculture and women and children ministries.[118]

The Presbyterian Church of Australia

The Presbyterian Church of Australia fulfils its partnership obligations to the CCAP Synod of Zambia through the work of Presbyterian Aid (PresAid). This agency helps the Synod of Zambia in many ways such as assisting the Zambian church with infrastructure development, budgetary support for the running of the synod and theological education support, especially through the assistance rendered to Chasefu Theological College in meeting the college's infrastructure and students' sponsorship needs. Among the students who are sponsored at this institution are Zimbabwean student ministers from the Harare Synod of the CCAP.[119]

The Presbyterian Church in Ireland

The CCAP Synod of Zambia is also a beneficiary of the assistance from the Presbyterian Church in Ireland, which also happens to be a partner of all three CCAP synods in Malawi – namely, Livingstonia, Blantyre and Nkhoma.

---

117. CCAP Zambia Synod, "History," http://www.ccapzambia.org/history.html, accessed 10 Mar 2015.

118. Presbyterian Church USA, "Zambia," https://www.presbyterianmission.org/ministries/global/zambia/, accessed 20 Mar 2015.

119. Presbyterian Aid Australia, "The Story So Far," http://presaid.org.au/index.php/the-story-so-far, accessed 16 Apr 2015.

The Synod of Zambia's Irish connections started back in the 1960s as the Synod of Livingstonia built the Lundazi Mission in Eastern Zambia in 1962 with assistance from the Presbyterian Church in Ireland.[120] This was before the Synod of Zambia was established, but since then the relationship between the CCAP Synod of Zambia and the Presbyterian Church in Ireland has continued.[121]

The Romans 1:11 Trust

Another interesting partner of the CCAP Synod of Zambia is a charity organization by the name of Romans 1:11 Trust. This charity's name came into existence inspired by the words found in Romans 1:11, which the Apostle Paul wrote to the Romans: "I long to see you, that I may impart to you some spiritual gift to strengthen you, that is, that we may be mutually encouraged by each other" (ESV). The Romans 1:11 Trust is a charity registered in the UK and currently doing most of its work in Uganda and Zambia.[122] Our interest in this book is the trust's work in Zambia as a partner of the CCAP Synod of Zambia. This trust, among other activities, facilitates exchange visits between Zambian churches and UK churches. The trust assists its Zambian partner in building projects, education sponsorship and general social assistance to the needy.

The Romans 1:11 Trust assisted Rev Kondwani Nkhoma, the first female pastor in the CCAP Synod of Zambia, in building her a retirement home. Another female pastor, Rev Susan Tembo, is having her daughter sponsored in her clinical medicine course in Lusaka by the same organization.[123] The many activities that the Romans 1:11 Trust is doing, both in Zambia and Uganda, are recorded in the trust's related online newsletter titled *Mutually Encouraged*.[124]

---

120. Presbyterian Church in Ireland, "Global Mission," https://www.presbyterianireland.org/Mission/Mission-Partners/Church-of-Central-Africa-Presbyterian.aspx, accessed 3 Apr 2015.

121. Presbyterian Church in Ireland, "Global Mission."

122. Romans 1:11 Trust, "Zambia," http://www.romans111.org.uk, accessed 4 Apr 2015.

123. Romans 1:11 Trust, "Zambia."

124. Romans 1:11 Trust, "Zambia."

Conclusion

The CCAP Synod of Zambia is the youngest of the five synods in the CCAP General Assembly, but it, too, has managed to have a good number of foreign partners who are making an impact on the life of the synod in its work of spreading the gospel and ministering to whole persons.

Foreign Relations and the Unity of the CCAP Synods

A cursory glance at the various partnerships that the CCAP synods have with foreign churches and organizations shows that these partnerships are formed independent of the other synods in the General Assembly. It is interesting to note that certain churches in the Western world have different partnership agreements with different synods of the CCAP. One church can actually have independent partnership agreements with two or more CCAP synods. Apart from their relationships with the different synods, some foreign partners add the General Assembly as a distinct partner on top of the individual synods.[125]

Since the different CCAP synods benefit a lot in terms of money, personnel and other resources through these partnerships, it follows that the synods would want to have as many partners as possible in order to maximize their benefits. While there has never been any recorded case of rivalry among the synods due to foreign relations or partnerships, it can be argued that the continued separate relationships, independent of one another, cannot at the same time be promoting unity among the synods.

An Evaluation of the CCAP Synods' Foreign Relations

The relationships that the synods of the CCAP have with their foreign partners are not unique with this federative denomination. Other churches in many parts of the world have similar partnerships. It is therefore not surprising to find that there are similarities in these partnerships.

In the first place, there are basically two types of partnerships: permanent partnerships and temporary ones. Permanent partnerships in the case of

---

125. Best examples in this regard are the Church of Scotland and the GZB.

the CCAP are mostly with those churches that were in the past considered "mother" churches of the synods, for example, the Church of Scotland in the case of Blantyre Synod. Today the concept of "mother-daughter" relationship is being discarded in favour of the modern understanding of the kind of relationship that exists between a missionary-sending church and a mission turned into a local autonomous church, hence the emphasis on the word "partnership" since the two are now considered equal partners. In the second category we have churches and organizations that form partnerships that exist for a specific period of time, after which the partnership is either reviewed and renewed or concluded. In either case, there are two issues to consider: The first issue is whether the partnership is relational or contractual. The second issue considers the question of whether the partnership is for the betterment or development of the partner with lesser resources.

In the first question, there is a tendency to associate the thinking of resource-rich partners from the Western world as viewing their partnership with the other churches as mostly based on a contractual kind of understanding while the non-Western world partners tend to view the partnership as a relational one. In any case, the partnerships that the CCAP synods are participating in make them more contractual than relational, especially when one looks at the partnership agreements that are signed by representatives of the parties as formal legal documents. In the second issue, the current study has established that the activities of the partnerships between the CCAP synods and their foreign partners are actually more for development as they are mostly aimed at empowering the resource-poor partner instead of just relieving the partner from temporary predicaments as is the understanding in the concept of "betterment."

Mutuality and Equality

The emphasis of these partnerships is mutuality and equality though practically it is not always easy to have partners who come from two different parts of the world to be equal in everything, especially when we consider that the two worlds in question are poles apart in terms of economic and material differences. This reality makes some observers doubt if the Western churches really benefit anything from these partnerships. It has been observed that the partners from resource-rich countries do not benefit from these partnerships in terms of money and expert personnel but through experiencing the unity of the body of Christ that transcends cultural, racial and national boundaries.[126] In so doing, they grow from cultural isolation to an understanding of how people of other parts of the world live their Christian faith. The partner church from a resource-rich country also expands the ecumenical and missionary horizons of its local churches, enabling them to assume responsibility one for another and in the process learning reciprocally from each other's faith.[127]

On the other hand, the partners that come from resource-poor countries (in our context, the CCAP synods and their General Assembly) benefit from these partnerships in terms of capacity building and economic empowerment. With regard to capacity building, there are a lot of activities that need to be carried out in the various CCAP synods that need trained and expert personnel. Since churches are not good competitors on the job market for highly qualified ambitious individuals, the coming in of expatriate personnel from partner churches helps the CCAP synods enhance their capacity in various departments. With regard to economic empowerment, the CCAP churches receive grants and budgetary support from their partners abroad. When it comes to exchange visits between partner churches and organizations, the CCAP church members benefit through exposure as they travel to different countries where their partner churches are located.

Criticism against Partnerships

As with all manner of things, church partnerships are not immune to criticism. The stronger partners are sometimes accused of paternalism. According to Gailyn van Rheenen, paternalism occurs when missionaries and their sending churches and agencies consciously or unconsciously assume that they possess superior knowledge, experience and skills and, consequently, exert control over local Christians and their leaders. This control is almost always exerted through financial arrangements and the implicit authority of money.[128] This kind of scenario has the potential to produce the dominance of a sending culture over the mission process.[129] In that case the partnership

---

126. Global Ministries, *Global Church Partnership Handbook*, 2.
127. Global Ministries, 3.
128. Van Rheenen, "Money and Missions (Revisited)."
129. Van Rheenen.

would not qualify as a true Christian partnership. Luis Bush describes a partnership as "an association of two or more Christian autonomous bodies who have formed a trusting relationship, and fulfil agreed-upon expectations by sharing complementary strengths and resources, to reach their mutual goal."[130] According to Samuel Chiang, there are seven principles of effective partnership: (1) agreement on doctrine and ethical behaviour; (2) agreement to share common goals; (3) development of an attitude of equality; (4) avoidance of dominance of one another; (5) ability to communicate openly; (6) demonstration of trust and accountability; and (7) the ability to pray together.[131]

With regard to the various partnerships discussed in this chapter between CCAP synods in Central Africa and their foreign partners from the rest of the world, it can be stated that so far there are no tendencies of paternalism on the part of the foreign partners, at least not openly. This may be because the CCAP synods are no longer younger churches dominated by their leaders; they are complex organizations that have bureaucratized to such an extent that individual whims, if any, play a very insignificant role.

In most cases it is the question of money and how it is used that mar partnerships. Van Rheenen has come up with several ways of gauging the rightful use of money in the context of church partnerships.[132] To begin with he mentions monitoring whether huge amounts of money are used only for the sake of maintaining local churches instead of planting and opening new ones. Where no new churches are opening, it is assumed that resources are only being used to perpetuate or maintain what is there without any growth taking place. In the case of the CCAP, the ever-increasing numbers of Christians and new congregations and presbyteries that are being established are an indication of the growth of the churches and thus the rightful use of money from both local resources and partner organizations, at least from a missiological point of view.

With regard to support from partners, it is necessary to check whether money creates an unhealthy dependence or if it encourages national church initiative. Relating this to the CCAP synods, it is evident that the synods are

---

130. Bush and Lutz, *Partnering in Ministry*, 46.
131. Chiang, "Partnership at the Crossroads," 284–289.
132. Van Rheenen, *Missions*, 202.

in many ways able to make their own decisions, and even though they still need money from their partners, they are not irredeemably dependent upon this kind of outside support to the extent of not initiating new things that they consider important in relation to the mission of the church in their areas of jurisdiction. The three Malawian synods of Livingstonia, Blantyre and Nkhoma are always coming up with new initiatives in various sectors such as health and education. With regard to education, all three Malawian synods keep on establishing new schools in both primary and secondary sections. Of late, they are either establishing or expanding their universities. Currently the Synod of Livingstonia has just started developing a third campus for the University of Livingstonia at Lusangazi in the outskirts of Mzuzu City where it wants to develop a faculty of animal science.[133] Nkhoma Synod is taking strides in developing the Nkhoma University in its two campuses of Nkhoma and Lilongwe while Blantyre Synod has just established its own university.[134] The Synod of Zambia, too, has its own initiative in combining theological education with agricultural development.[135] All these initiatives are not coming from partner churches but from the synods themselves, which means that the synods are not in partnerships that dictate what they should be doing.

It becomes a snare in some churches when the leadership of a local church which is in a partnership agreement with a foreign partner from a resource-rich country takes advantage of the partnership to close themselves from the scrutiny of fellow leaders. This calls for a national leadership that is ethically, morally and spiritually responsible to other national church leaders who understand their culture as they deal with partner churches. In this case, the leadership can easily be monitored so that should there be any anomaly the whole church leadership should be empowered to correct the wrong thing. Within the CCAP synods, the top leadership is openly

---

133. Ronald Chibwe, in discussion with the author, Mzuzu, 11 April 2015.

134. Tikondane Vega, "University of CCAP Blantyre Synod to Open in Malawi This Year," *Nyasa Times*, https://www.nyasatimes.com/university-of-ccap-blantyre-synod-to-open-in-malawi-this-year-rev-maulana/, accessed 23 Apr 2015.

135. Nancy Collins, "Mission Connections," https://www.presbyterianmission.org/ministries/missionconnections/nancy-collins/, accessed 25 Apr 2015. See also CCAP Synod of Zambia, "Chunga Chicken Farm," http://www.ccapzambia.org/chunga-chicken-farm.html, accessed 24 Apr 2015.

accountable to the rest of the leadership of the church. This means that even when temptations are there to abuse positions the system easily catches up with the culprits. In the course of this study, some leaders of the synods were heavily censured on the way they were handling donor money. Consequently, some lost their positions or were unceremoniously removed by their synods' governing bodies.

The Position of a Missionary in a Resource-Poor Partner Church

The other tricky issue with regard to partnerships is the position of missionaries in the local church that is in partnership with a foreign missionary sending church. These missionaries are supposed to be ethically, morally and spiritually responsible to teammates on the field, to national church leaders and to the church leaders of their sending denomination or agency.[136] In the case of the CCAP, especially in the three Malawian synods that were founded by overseas missionaries, it was at first normal for the missionaries to want to solve problems for the local churches in a paternalistic way, treating them as children needing direction, provision and supervision.[137] Some Malawian clergy rebelled against this way of doing things as they felt oppressed by missionary paternalism.[138]

After the transfer of church leadership from missionaries to indigenous leaders, the missionaries have continued to be present in the CCAP albeit in a different manner as they are now not only accountable to their sending churches or missionary organizations but also to the local church leadership. Besides, it is the local church that ensures that the missionaries are working in accordance with the needs and leadership direction of the local church.

Since support cannot be permanent in any church partnership, the partner that benefits in terms of money and resources is expected to grow and develop its own capacity so that it is eventually supported by its own people in future. The CCAP synods here seem to be children of their time in regard to their expectation of continued support from partner churches. While it is

---

136. See Van Rheenen, "Money and Missions (Revisited)."
137. Edouard Lassegue, quoted in Compassion Team, "Strong Partnership Is about Relationships."
138. See Mwasi, *Essential and Paramount Reasons for Working Independently*, 16–17.

true that the CCAP congregants contribute substantial amounts of money for the running of their synods, that money is not enough when it comes to funding programmes and projects, hence the need to continue expecting financial assistance from the partners.

Regarding the lifestyles of the leaders of the churches, it is sometimes tempting to lead a life that is not in line with the local economy but with the level of the members of the supporting partners. To what extent are CCAP pastors living according to the standards of their supporting partners? I argue that the average CCAP clergy does not live a flamboyant lifestyle that raises the eyebrows of the Malawian populace. Granted, there are disparities in the lifestyles of the different pastors of the church, but these differences do not come in because of money from partner churches, except in very rare cases where certain individual pastors have benefited because of individual connections and personal friendships outside formal church partnership arrangements. There are no observations so far that some pastors are leading a life that is akin to the societies of their partner churches rather than the local societies wherein they are ministering. It has to be mentioned, though, that apart from differences in education and family background, the status of clergy families also differs due to the ability of the local congregations they are serving in supporting their pastor with material blessings. Usually the disparities are between urban congregations and rural congregations, hence the reluctance sometimes from certain clergy to transfer from an urban congregation to a rural one when told to do so by their synods.[139]

In the same vein, there may be disparities between local Christians and the missionaries from partner churches that support the local church financially. Where the disparities are pronounced, some Christians may not feel comfortable to fellowship in the homes of missionaries who seem to live in a different world. In the past, the missionaries had all the benefits of the advanced material and technological culture of their home societies, and the first generation of the CCAP clergy did not find it embarrassing to pose for photographs with their missionary colleagues without wearing shoes while in

---

139. I have witnessed discord in some synods after a pastor refused to go to a rural parish where the synod had decided to transfer him or her from an urban one. In certain instances, such pastors have been disciplined by their synods. Some have even led breakaway churches with their sympathizers.

jackets and ties.¹⁴⁰ Nowadays, due to the influence of globalization and the modernization and westernization of many African societies, there are very few things that missionaries have that would look out of this world. Within the CCAP, many missionaries from the partner churches live lifestyles that are not very different from the average middle class Central African. There are, therefore, fewer differences in the urban churches between the lives of the missionaries and the average church members. This does not mean that there are more poor people in the rural areas than in urban areas but that there are more people who are financially powerful in urban areas than in rural areas. In this case, even for the missionary, an urban congregation would be sociologically more acceptable than a rural one where differences between the missionary and local Christians would be more pronounced and therefore less comforting unless one takes pride in being the odd one out in terms of material culture.

In a situation where clear-cut procedures for partnership agreements are not there, it is possible to have one leader being supported more than other leaders, thereby creating jealousy on the part of those who feel left out. In the CCAP synods, with synodical procedures that are beyond individual manipulation, it is actually the synod that determines who is qualified or not when it comes to benefits that come with various partnerships. In the example of Faithshare visits, say with the Church of Scotland, the synods decide who should go to Scotland for the exchange programme. In this case, a minister who is serving a rural congregation and away from the day-to-day business of the synod can be selected for the programme.

Who Controls Whom?

The final thing to consider with regard to partnerships in the CCAP is whether the support the synods and the General Assembly receive creates hierarchies so that churches and institutions are controlled by the West rather than by local leadership. On the part of the partnerships that are there between the CCAP and its foreign partners, there is no direct control from the West. This does not mean that there are no instances where the Western

---

140. See McCracken, *Politics and Christianity in Malawi 1875–1940*. The cover picture depicts the first indigenous clergy of Livingstonia on their ordination with bare feet though wearing formal attire flanked by their missionary colleagues.

partners want to influence some changes by way of suggestion, especially considering that they do make some financial contributions towards the operations of the synods. For example, Myers Park Presbyterian Church recommended to the Synod of Livingstonia the need to abolish payment vouchers/receipts in order to cut expenses. The general secretary reported this recommendation to the Executive Committee of the synod, but the Executive Committee, while appreciating the recommendation, decided that it would look into it in the future.[141] One thing this incident proves is that the CCAP is not under pressure to conform to the wishes of its partners who have a stronger economic muscle.

Conclusion

This chapter has looked at the foreign relations that the CCAP synods have, especially through partnership agreements. What has been established is that even though the synods graduated from the status of "daughter churches" of the churches that sent missionaries that established the missions that evolved into the CCAP, they are still very much related to these churches. In this regard, the partnerships they have with the former "mother churches" are permanent partnerships which have no intention of going away in the foreseeable future. One can therefore argue that the partnerships with former "mother churches" were automatic in that, in any case, the relationship had to continue despite the changes that have taken place over the decades. The former relationships of sending churches and missions have evolved into some kind of permanent partnership via the once tolerated but now rejected "mother-daughter" relationship.

It has also been seen that these permanent relationships that have evolved from the mother-daughter relationships do not hinder the CCAP synods from seeking new partnerships with other churches and organizations. Neither do they hinder other Western churches that hitherto had no any relationships with the CCAP from initiating new partnerships with the Central African Church. I argue that this is one instance of proving that the former daughter churches are becoming mature in that they can initiate further relationships without asking for the permission of or even informing

---

141. Synod of Livingstonia, "Minutes of Thirty-Third Synod Assembly," min. 59/12.

the former mother churches, which at one time in history had all the powers to dictate what the daughter churches could or could not do – even their stay in the CCAP union was dependent on the goodwill of the mother churches.[142]

It can also be argued from the discussion in this chapter that the CCAP synods are not really underdogs when it comes to West-South relations in the body of Christ. Granted, the CCAP synods are not as rich as their Western partners, and their contributions in the partnerships are not evaluated in monetary or material terms, but they are able to raise their voice and prove to be equal partners.

Negatively, it has been observed that the more partnerships continue to be established, the more the CCAP will continue to expect aid from resource-rich partners. While this is no longer a problem at the congregational level, since many congregations are happily fending for themselves, at the presbytery, synod and General Assembly levels the church is not ready to be completely independent of donor money or support from partners.[143] The implication for this in the wider society is that the churches may not be able to urge their national governments to stop depending on donor aid when they themselves are doing the same, and they do not appear to be planning for any economic independence soon.

I, therefore, argue that if the synods still look up to their partners for financial aid and material support, they cannot at the same time be thinking seriously about a closer unity of the CCAP. This means that while foreign relations are assisting the CCAP to carry out its many developmental programmes, they are at the same time hindering the full maturity of the CCAP into a true African church in Central Africa, fully united under one leadership that transcends federal unity.

---

142. See Pauw, "Mission and Church in Malawi," 346–347.

143. What is actually happening is that new presbyteries that are being formed are being added to the list of beneficiaries of donor aid from partner churches and other well-wishers. In one of the meetings of the General Administration Committee of the Synod of Livingstonia there was a specific request that Lilongwe Presbytery, which is in the Central Region, should also be covered by donor aid coming to the synod as is the case with other presbyteries and the request was accepted. See Synod of Livingstonia, "Minutes of the General Administration Committee Meeting," min. 32/11.

CHAPTER 7

Unity beyond Border Disputes

Introduction

This chapter explores the current relationship of the five synods of the CCAP in what can be termed a "post-border dispute" period, especially considering the stands taken by the Livingstonia and Nkhoma synods of not recognizing boundaries between them, thereby apparently lessening the tension in the CCAP General Assembly. Many observers, however, are of the view that the border issue is not over but that the two synods have swept the dirt under the carpet, pretending that their declaration of "no more borders" has solved the problem, when in actual fact it is a recipe for socio-theological pitfalls in the sense that matters of ethnicity, and the catholicity of the church, will always have a bearing on the church's witness to the kingdom of God. Finally, the chapter presents an ecclesiological evaluation of some proposals being made for the sake of the future of the CCAP.

Oneness of the Synods without Borders

The formation of the CCAP epitomized missionary cooperation in Malawi, at least among those of the Reformed and Presbyterian tradition. It was hoped that the united church would open its arms and embrace new members that would want to join it, and that expectation has always been there in the history of the CCAP.[1] However, the CCAP has remained a product of the efforts of the Scottish and Dutch Presbyterian/Reformed missions

---

1. Pauw, "Mission and Church in Malawi," 265.

only, without being joined by any other church from other quarters as it was initially hoped. This meant that the union had to continue with the three original members and later the five synods when Nkhoma and Livingstonia gave birth to the synods of Harare and Zambia, respectively. One can therefore only imagine what the CCAP would have been had it been joined by other denominations from a different missionary background.[2]

It can be observed that the five synods are very close to each other in terms of theological and historical roots. As it has been demonstrated earlier on in this study, the history and theology of all the CCAP synods can be traced back to the ministry of the Genevan Reformer John Calvin in the sixteenth century. From the beginning and to a large extent even up to now, the CCAP synods devised and followed a method of keeping their oneness intact by respecting one another's sphere of influence in the belief that they were one denomination under the umbrella of the General Assembly. For a synod to go and work into another synod's territory was considered an anomaly and as an unnecessary duplication of the work of spreading the same gospel that the other synod was preaching in the area. This was the origin of the concept of comity, which was originally started by the founding missionaries of the synods and was continued by the local leadership of the synods and the General Assembly when the missionaries handed over the leadership of the church to the locals. The only development that has disturbed this state of affairs is the boundary dispute between the synods of Livingstonia and Nkhoma in Malawi, especially now that the two synods have agreed not to consider or respect boundaries between them. Added to this is the presence of multiple congregations of all three Malawian synods in South Africa. The question one would ask at this stage is: Are the synods still one as far as denominational identity is concerned since they are now competing among themselves? At least that is the situation between Livingstonia and

---

2. In the 1960s there was a renewed discussion for the possibility of coming up with a united denomination from different backgrounds. This initiative included the Anglicans and the Churches of Christ as well as the three Malawian CCAP Synods, and Bishop Stephen Neil of the united Church of South India once chaired the deliberations of the Church Union Committee's consultations at Chilema. This initiative did not work partly because the CCAP synods themselves could not agree to step into more visible unity because of their own differences. This hindered the progress for further accommodation from other denominations. For a thorough and testimonial treatment of this initiative see Jackson, *Send Us Friends*, 318–329.

Nkhoma in Malawi. Besides, the three Malawian synods operate side by side in South Africa using the name of the CCAP while recognizing their differences according to synodical affiliation in Malawi.

All this shows that the oneness of the synods is only in terms of the basics of their theology, historical roots and rudimentary cooperation in the General Assembly. The way the synods are treated and the way they operate make them denominations in their own right. One can therefore argue that the oneness of the CCAP as a denomination can only be in the effective organization of the General Assembly and the ability of the synods to keep away from their sisters' territories when it comes to establishing churches in those territories, realizing that their sister's efforts are their own as they are all one. While this issue currently seems to affect only the synods of Livingstonia and Nkhoma, in future it is likely to escalate because the context in which the synods operate is always changing. For example, the synods of Livingstonia, Nkhoma and Blantyre are not confined to their areas of influence in Malawi. Livingstonia has churches side by side with Harare Synod in Bulawayo and Harare in Zimbabwe, as well as her presence in South Africa. Even though it was decided at the General Assembly meeting of 2007 that the Malawian synods should pull out of Zimbabwe and South Africa and hand over their congregations to churches of the Reformed and Presbyterian tradition, nothing has happened to that effect.

It can therefore be concluded that as long as the synods continue to pursue their own synodical agenda, including ignoring their own boundaries, we cannot talk of a unified denomination. However, even if the synods were to surrender their churches and pull out from their encroached positions, there would not be much change in the life of the denomination when the umbrella body is clearly weaker than the synods.

Consolidating Synodical Independence

The history of the CCAP from the 1970s to date can be described as a history of intended greater unity with the opposite practical results. Each and every General Assembly meeting has witnessed a call to greater unity among the CCAP synods, and the 2002 constitution went even further to outline areas of cooperation and closer unity. However, what is transpiring on the ground, even after the 2002 constitution, is the fact that the synods are becoming more and more autonomous, hence consolidating their independence despite the common use of the name CCAP for all of them. This trend is reflected in the synods' ministries, especially where the synods have congregations side by side with their sister synods, as is the case in South Africa and Zimbabwe.

Foreign Expansion

The CCAP synods have over the years expanded to foreign countries. The initial expansion was when the CCAP synods of Livingstonia and Nkhoma (while they were still missions) established congregations in Zambia, Zimbabwe and Mozambique. Nkhoma Mission's responsibility over the Mozambican congregations ceased prior to her joining the CCAP family. However, her responsibility over the Zimbabwean churches continued up to the time the HarareSynod was established. The Synod of Livingstonia's responsibility over some of the Zambian congregations also continued until the formation of the Synod of Zambia. As has been seen in these two countries, the churches there grew to such an extent that the two new synods of Harare and Zambia were born, making the CCAP to have five synods.

This initial expansion was followed later by the opening of new churches in South Africa. This initiative has seen the Synod of Livingstonia establishing several congregations in South Africa, which form the Johannesburg Presbytery. Previously the Johannesburg Presbytery included the Synod of Livingstonia congregations of Bulawayo and Harare in Zimbabwe, but, of late, the Zimbabwean congregations have also established their own presbytery in order to reduce transport costs to and from Johannesburg.[3] The South African congregations of the Synod of Livingstonia's Johannesburg Presbytery include the following: Johannesburg North, Johannesburg Central, Johannesburg South and Cape Town.[4] The Synod of Livingstonia has in recent years also spread to neighbouring Tanzania. The churches in Tanzania are under Ngerenge-Mbeya Presbytery and Chitipa Presbytery.[5]

---

3. Rev S. Kadogana, in discussion with the author, Mzuzu, 21 April 2016.

4. CCAP Synod of Livingstonia, "Presbyteries," https://www.ccapsolinia.org/presbyteries/, accessed 10 Apr 2015.

5. Rev M. G. K. Mzembe, in discussion with the author, Khondowe, 31 July 2015. Also Rev Frank S. Kadogana, phone interview, 9 September 2015.

Some observers point out that the CCAP congregations in South Africa and Tanzania should change their names because "Central Africa" does not exist in South Africa and Tanzania. I consider this to be food for thought that if the CCAP really wants to sustainably expand beyond Central Africa, then it should consider finding a relevant name for the sake of its non-Central African congregations.[6] Interestingly, even a breakaway sect from the CCAP synods in Johannesburg called itself Church of Central Africa Presbyterian in Johannesburg.[7]

While the Synod of Livingstonia has specific presbyteries for the churches under its jurisdiction outside Malawi, Blantyre Synod's style is to have the foreign congregations placed under the presbyteries that are in Malawi. For example, the congregations in Johannesburg are under the oversight of Blantyre City Presbytery.[8] It therefore follows that whenever there is need for a pastor in South Africa, the church in Malawi sends one.[9] Nkhoma Synod, too, has her own congregations in South Africa. The Johannesburg congregation of Nkhoma Synod is actually registered as a non-profit company, with its classification as international church and related activities. Nkhoma Synod's congregation is under Mvera Presbytery. The idea of having Nkhoma Synod's South African congregation placed under Mvera Presbytery was for the recognition of the importance of Mvera in the history of Nkhoma Synod since that is where the first DRC mission was established.[10]

The synods of Harare and Zambia have yet to open churches in South Africa or in any other neighbouring country. One explanation for the two synods not having churches in South Africa would be that they are still small compared to the Malawian synods, and, therefore, they would not be in a position to expand outside their own countries of origin at this stage.

---

6. Peter Chipanga, "CCAP Blantyre Synod Embraces Cape Town," *The Nation* (20 July 2017), https://mwnation.com/ccap-blantyre-synod-embraces-cape-town/, accessed 17 Jul 2019.

7. See Nyasa Times Reporter, "Independent CCAP Established in J'Burg: Simwinga says Church Not Affiliated to any Malawian Synods, *Nyasa Times* (27 January 2016), https://www.nyasatimes.com/independent-ccap-established-in-jburg-simwinga-says-church-not-affiliated-to-any-malawi-synods/, accessed 17 Jul 2019.

8. Rev Innocent Chikopa, electronic correspondence, 2 June 2015.

9. Currently the pastor is Rev Kutani who is responsible for Turfontein, Boksburg and Sasolburg prayer houses under the Berea CCAP congregation.

10. Rev Dr Winston R. Kawale, in discussion with the author, 9 July 2015.

The second explanation, at least in the case of Harare Synod, is that it is largely a church of Malawian immigrants in Zimbabwe, and it would not be easy for them to go and open another church of immigrants in South Africa.[11] As for the Synod of Zambia, there is a possibility for them also to establish a church in South Africa, following their own immigrants there if the Malawian scenario is anything to go by. This must be seen in view of the fact that South Africa is the biggest economy in the SADC region and one of the most prosperous countries in Africa, making it a destination for many who are in search of greener pastures from the SADC region and beyond.[12]

The proliferation of different brands of the CCAP in South Africa, all coming from Malawian synods, was a cause for embarrassment to some in the General Assembly and it was decided that efforts should be made to have the CCAP congregations in South Africa united into one CCAP without the encumbrances of Malawian synods' names. However, when a General Assembly delegation visited the South African congregations, it was told in no uncertain terms that they had no business trying to unite the different synods' congregations in South Africa when they have not been successful in doing the same in Malawi.[13] Apart from this initiative, the General Assembly also resolved at its 21st meeting that the CCAP congregations in South Africa be transferred from the hands of the synods of Livingstonia, Blantyre and Nkhoma to South African churches of the Presbyterian/Reformed family.[14] The resolution has never been carried out, and it has never been followed. Since the year 2007, when this resolution was made, up to the present time, the three Malawian CCAP synods of Livingstonia, Blantyre and Nkhoma are still operating their congregations in South Africa unhindered and unperturbed by this General Assembly resolution.

A closer look at this General Assembly resolution reveals that there are actually four conditions that need to be met for it to be successfully carried out. The first condition is the willingness of the congregants to be transferred to the South African churches. It was not considered at that time, and it has not been considered up to now, if the members of the various CCAP

---

11. See Juma, "Immigration and Its Effects on Our Church."
12. See Saurombe, "Role of South Africa in SADC Regional Integration."
13. Rev Dr Winston R. Kawale, in discussion with the author, 8 May 2014.
14. CCAP General Assembly, Press Release, 25 January 2007.

congregations in South Africa would be willing to be detached from their home synods in order to be under the pastoral oversight of South African Reformed/Presbyterian denominations in obedience to a General Assembly resolution. While opinion is likely to be divided in any congregation, I argue that the majority of the congregants would not want to join South African churches because they are socially and culturally comfortable in their Malawian synods' congregations.[15] Besides, if joining a South African Presbyterian/Reformed church was an easier option for the Malawian immigrants, why did they not join those churches in the first place? It has to be pointed out that church affiliation is more than merely an administrative issue. It is spiritual, cultural, emotional, social and otherwise, hence it is not a simple thing to make a decision in a lofty committee and assume that the congregants in the various congregations will find it easier to adhere to that decision.[16]

Second, the other issue to consider was the willingness of the South African churches themselves to take over pastoral oversight of the Malawian immigrant congregations. How would they integrate these whole congregations of Malawian immigrants into their system without creating tensions in their churches? Whatever advantages there would be for the South African churches, implementing this decision would not be an easy thing for them considering matters of the sociology of religion.[17] Some CCAP clergy are of the view that the South African churches would easily accept the responsibility.[18] Interestingly, in the case of Nkhoma Synod, the Dutch Reformed Church has at one time assisted the Nkhoma Synod pastors in South Africa by providing money for the renewal of their expired work permits in South Africa.[19] This enabled the Nkhoma Synod pastors to continue leading Nkhoma Synod churches in South Africa under the auspices of the Dutch Reformed Church in South Africa but it was not suggested by the

---

15. This does not mean that segregation is a good thing in the church, but it is to underscore the fact that Christians in many cases behave according to social realities and not in view of the ideal when it comes to their church life.

16. For a brief but lucid discussion of the correlates of religious affiliation see Robertson, *Sociology*, 420–421.

17. Robertson, *Sociology*, 420.

18. Rev Dr Winston R. Kawale, in discussion with the author, 9 July 2015.

19. Rev Dr Winston R. Kawale, in discussion with the author, 9 July 2015.

South African "mother" church that it should take over the responsibility of caring for the Nkhoma congregations in South Africa.

The third condition to be met is the readiness of the synods to execute such a resolution. Despite the resolution being carried in the General Assembly meeting, how prepared and ready were the synods to do such a thing? The silence on this issue since the resolution was passed in 2007 is clear evidence that it was never in the interest of the synods to attempt such a thing, despite the General Assembly's recommendation or resolution in the heat of debates concerning the synods' differences. Ironically, the General Assembly even came up with dates for this process, as seen in the following passage from its press release: "The General Assembly resolved to set up a committee to oversee the implementation of the process of pulling back, a process which should be done by 30 June 2007. Synods are encouraged to begin the process of consultation, sensitisation and handover at earliest convenience."[20] Over a decade after the decision, the synods are yet to find it convenient to start the "process of consultation, sensitisation and handover."[21] Consequently, it is business as usual in the South African congregations, with pastors going and coming back.

Lastly, the other issue to consider is the capacity of the General Assembly to fulfil such a daunting task within a given period of time, exercising authority over the synods by way of supervision and dealing punitively with defaulting synods. So far, nothing has been done on this issue, and it seems the issue has died a natural death after no synod or General Assembly members mentioned it again in their subsequent meetings. In any case, the period between 2007 and 2013 was one of the most trying periods in the history of the General Assembly as the organization became almost dead due to the disagreements emanating from the Livingstonia and Nkhoma synods' boundary dispute. Consequently, the CCAP synods continue to operate their foreign congregations unhindered, emphasizing their synodical differences even in foreign lands. This is another instance in demonstrating that the synods are actually independent denominations despite their use of the CCAP name as if they are one denomination.

---

20. CCAP General Assembly, Press Release, 25 January 2007.
21. CCAP General Assembly, Press Release, 25 January 2007.

Loose Cooperation and Synodical Sisterhood

Despite all their differences and seemingly lack of cooperation, the CCAP synods still cooperate and regard one another as sister synods under the union. It is this fact that allows the General Assembly to continue working and sustaining CCAP unity though in itself it is not a force to reckon with. My observation is that the General Assembly is and can only be what the synods allow it to be. Since the General Assembly's very mandate comes from the good will of the synods, it will continue to disappoint those that expect much from it in relation to providing unified leadership to the five synods of the CCAP.

So far, we have seen that the current arrangement of the CCAP synods does not favour a General Assembly that is stronger than the synods. In any case, you cannot have people coming from their own synods strengthening the General Assembly when their own welfare is in the hands of their respective synods and not in the General Assembly. The sisterhood of the synods therefore continues without making it stronger and without even trying to make the General Assembly stronger.

The observation, therefore, is that the synods are in some kind of a loose cooperation as their cooperation does not go the whole way to behaving like one denomination, but they do recognize their sisterhood in the General Assembly. That is why, even though in some places they are competing for members, when a member of a congregation transfers from a congregation of one synod to another, they are warmly welcomed in the new synod's congregation, and issues concerning differences or rivalry among the synods are not raised. I have witnessed this in many Sunday worship services in Mzuzu City where the new members of congregations, usually referred to as visitors when coming from the Central Region of Malawi, explain that they were either members of Nkhoma Synod or Synod of Livingstonia in the Central Region, and they are welcomed just like anyone else irrespective of which congregation or presbytery or synod they are coming from. The situation is the same when they go to Blantyre Synod.

Such observations make some commentators to conclude that the differences and rivalries among CCAP synods are merely administrative since the grassroots congregations have no problems with synodical differences, as what matters to them is that they belong to the CCAP. The only exceptions to this observation are those congregations that are in controversial places where belonging to a particular synod sends a message to those that belong to a different one.

The Synods as Different Denominations

So far, this book has shown that the CCAP synods share the same theological and historical roots back to John Calvin in Geneva, which should make it easier for them to be fully united under one denomination whose structure goes beyond the federal structure of the current CCAP General Assembly. However, the synods are very different from each other due to the influence of the churches that established the mission stations that developed into the synods as we know them. Moreover, the synods do not want to give up their differences, a thing which their foreign partners seem to cherish.

It has to be remembered, though, that since Harare Synod developed from Nkhoma Synod and the Synod of Zambia developed from the Synod of Livingstonia, there are more similarities between Nkhoma and Harare on the one hand and between Livingstonia and Zambia on the other. However, despite the closeness in the synods that are more related to each other, the current status of the synods shows that they are all independent denominations, and their day-to-day business is conducted without much ado about the position of the other synods or that of the General Assembly.[22] In any case, apart from the steering committee, the General Assembly only meets once every four years and sometimes even less frequently when the synods fail to organize themselves for a General Assembly meeting for some reason, as was the case between 2007 and 2013. This means that the cooperation described above works among the CCAP synods in the same way it works for other churches with which the CCAP cooperates. For example, someone transferring from the CCAP Synod of Livingstonia going to Blantyre Synod

---

22. At the time of gathering information for this study only the Synod of Zambia mentioned the General Assembly on its website and acknowledged the fact that the synod is under the General Assembly. See CCAP Zambia Synod, "Organizational Chart," www.ccapzambia.org/organisational-chart.html, 4 Apr 2015.

is treated in the same way as someone transferring from, say, the Zambezi Evangelical Church to any of the CCAP synods.[23]

This observation proves that, apart from the common use of the name CCAP, the synods are indeed different denominations, which makes the CCAP under the umbrella of the General Assembly not a denomination at all. It is this meta-denominational characteristic of the General Assembly that causes the current study to deny the oneness of the five synods under one denomination. The observation that the CCAP is a mere federation of independent denominations, therefore, makes much sense. It is in view of this observation that one begins to understand the neglect of the General Assembly premises by the synods as well as the lack of vibrancy in the organization at that higher level because the organization is practically meta-denominational in nature.

It is this realization – that the organization is actually meta-denominational – that has created two schools of thought with regard to peoples' search for a solution to the problems currently rocking the CCAP. The first school of thought is of the view that the synods are already far advanced in working on their own, so much so that the best course would be to let them continue without imposing unnecessary restrictions on them for the sake of the unity of the General Assembly. Practically, this view supports the abolition of synodical boundaries so that the independent synods can continue to operate freely and open new churches wherever they want, even in competition with sister synods. Such a scenario would give CCAP Christians of a particular locality the chance to choose their synod of choice among the five synods of the General Assembly, depending on the presence of the synods in the area. The relationship of the synods in this case would continue to be a loose one without efforts to increase the efficiency of the General Assembly since the goal is not to empower the General Assembly for the sake of the unity of the synods as one denomination. On the contrary, it is to perpetuate and enhance synodical independence and autonomy, thereby respecting the synods as independent organizations, which they have always been.

---

23. The synods have lists of churches with which they cooperate, and my observation is that these churches are on the same level with sister synods when it comes to their former members in the CCAP congregations.

While the oneness of the synods under the General Assembly has always been seen as a mark of unity in the CCAP, the perpetuation of synodical boundaries among the synods has had its own negatives. For example, the differences in the political regions in Malawi are magnified by differences in language and culture. The fact that the CCAP synods roughly correspond to these differences has always made the synods in Malawi to be identified by the differences as observed in the regions. The danger of clinging to synodical boundaries, therefore, has been that the synods would continue to be associated with certain ethnic groups and their particular cultures and languages.[24] On the other hand, those that are championing for the continued independence of the synods argue that when synods embark on evangelism and discipleship irrespective of their boundaries, people will eventually stop associating the synods with particular ethnic groups. This would be enhancing the catholicity of the church since the church is not supposed to be identified with a particular ethnic and/or linguistic group. The General Assembly would therefore be an assembly of people from different cultural, ethnic and linguistic backgrounds across all the synods without any synod being identified with earthly designations of culture, ethnicity and language.

More Unity of the Synods Reconsidered

Views that lament the CCAP's departure from unity advocate for a stronger CCAP under the revamped General Assembly. How this would actually work is not fully explained by the advocates of this view, but the general thinking, after observing that there can be no true unity while the synods retain a lot of power, is that the synods should be dissolved so that the presbyteries can be empowered.[25] Thereafter, the General Assembly would be the assembly of the representatives of the presbyteries rather than of the synods.[26] But what proponents of this view do not say is what would happen to the synods' headquarters when the synods are dissolved. Would they be turned into presbytery headquarters of the presbytery in which geographical vicinity

---

24. See Abale-Phiri, "Interculturalisation as Transforming Praxis," 144.
25. See Nkhonjera, "Church of Central Africa Presbyterian," 80.
26. Nkhonjera, 82.

they are currently situated? Who would be empowered to do such a thing since the General Assembly does not have the capacity to do it? Will the synods and their leadership accept fading into insignificance for the sake of a stronger CCAP under the General Assembly? These are some of the questions to ponder when considering a new post-boundary dispute CCAP, and it seems the answers to these questions are currently not available.

In his online news article, Victor Kaonga muses, by way of suggestion, that perhaps it is time there was a "United Presbyterian Church (UPC)" in order to deal with the problem of unity in the CCAP.[27] What Victor Kaonga does not explain is whether the United Presbyterian Church he is proposing should rise from the ashes of the old CCAP or should be a breakaway church that purports to uphold what the CCAP stands for, though it is failing to succeed in that position. I think Mr Kaonga's point is the second one since in the same breath he mentions the establishment of the Presbyterian Church of Malawi (PCM) which was formed in 1998 due to the resistance of the then CCAP leadership to embrace innovations in the church as introduced by the charismatic movement.[28] When the Presbyterian Church of Malawi was born in 1998, some people were of the view that it was going to replace the CCAP or cause a serious division in the denomination. However, what eventually happened was that the PCM only proved to be a split-off from the CCAP, and over the years it has not been able to exert much influence in the country. As a result, the change the original PCM members were agitating for in the CCAP did not take place. The CCAP has continued up till now, and it has over the years made some changes to suit those influenced by the charismatic renewal, but it has not fundamentally changed. It is, however, a force to reckon with in Malawi more than the PCM, which is yet to make its presence felt in many areas. One therefore wonders if the formation of the UPC, as Mr Kaonga proposes, would achieve anything apart from merely causing another split-off denomination from the CCAP in the way it happened with the PCM and other churches that have broken away from the

---

27. Victor Kaonga, "CCAP Crisis: Time for United Presbyterian Church," *Nyasa Times*, Straight Talk, "Comment No. 44," https://www.nyasatimes.com/ccap-crisis-time-for-united-presbyterian-church/, 1 of 6 6/8/2015 4:23 PM.

28. See Munyenyembe, *Christianity and Socio-Cultural Issues*, 46–47. Also M'banga, "Emergence of Independent Churches."

CCAP over the course of history due to what their founders perceived to be negative elements in the federative denomination.

Incidentally, it has to be mentioned that in the history of the CCAP the nomenclature of United Presbyterian Church (UPC or UP) is not a new thing as it is part and parcel of the roots of the Synod of Livingstonia back in Scotland. To a certain extent, these roots also touch on the history of Blantyre Synod by virtue of its being a mission of the Church of Scotland. The name United Presbyterian Church has appeared and still appears in many countries today, but at this stage in this book we are concerned with the United Presbyterian Church of Scotland (UP) which existed between 1847 and 1900.[29] This church was formed in 1847 when the United Secession Church and the Relief Church merged to form one denomination. In the year 1900, this church merged with the Free Church of Scotland to form the United Free Church of Scotland (UFC). In 1929 the United Free Church of Scotland united with the Church of Scotland.

Interestingly, before the United Presbyterian Church merged with the Free Church of Scotland in 1900, the Free Church had already established the Livingstonia Mission in Malawi as of 1875. However, more interestingly, the leader of the Free Church of Scotland's Livingstonia Mission was none other than the celebrated missionary Dr Robert Laws, who happened to be a church minister originally not of the Free Church of Scotland but of the United Presbyterian Church (UP). It can therefore be argued that the two denominations were united in the person of Dr Robert Laws before they merged into one church in 1900, forming the United Free Church of Scotland. It is this merger of the United Free Church of Scotland with the Church of Scotland that connects the UP with Blantyre Synod.

What this means is that the name UPC or UP, and what it stands for as per Mr Victor Kaonga's suggestion, are things that are already in the "blood" of the CCAP through historical circumstances. Therefore, as one commentator argued against Victor Kaonga's proposal concerning the establishment of the United Presbyterian Church, the solution to the problems rocking the CCAP is not in a name, no matter how uniting that name may sound, because even the name CCAP itself was meant to unite rather than

---

29. See McKerrow, *History of the Foreign Missions*, and Robson, *Missions of the United Presbyterian Church*. Also "United Presbyterian Church of Scotland."

divide.[30] Mr Kaonga's proposal, though with good intentions, fails to offer something that can really transform the CCAP in its unity because neither new names nor breakaways have proved to be a solution to the problems such as the CCAP is currently facing. This means that with or without Mr Victor Kaonga's proposal there are still only two options for the CCAP at this crossroads: (1) Either let the synods continue to exist as independently as possible as separate denominations with the General Assembly working as a loose umbrella body in which the synods recognize and celebrate their theological and historical togetherness no matter how lackadaisically; or (2) Let the synods pave the way for stronger presbyteries that would be united under a stronger CCAP General Assembly. The succeeding sections discuss these two options in detail.

The First Option: More Independence of the Synods with No Boundaries

The question is how can one of the two proposals work in practical terms? Given the present scenario in the CCAP, the first option is easier for the synods than the second one because, in a way, the synods are already trying to achieve the first option, though not all synods are in support of it. On the part of the Synod of Livingstonia, the philosophy of "live and let live" is already in operation with their Nkhoma Synod colleagues in Malawi; and also with both Nkhoma and Blantyre synods, by default, in South Africa; and with the Harare Synod in Zimbabwe. The issue becomes complicated when Blantyre Synod is brought into the Malawian equation because the Synod of Livingstonia so far has not provided any justification whatsoever to go into Blantyre Synod's territory and start planting congregations there. Whether the Synod of Livingstonia had other motives for going into Nkhoma Synod's territory or not, what is known officially is their own testimony that they are now in Nkhoma Synod's territory because Nkhoma Synod would not withdraw from Livingstonia's territory into which it had encroached for more than half a century.[31] Whether Livingstonia's move is justified or not in this regard is not the issue at present. The issue is that if synodical boundaries

---

30. See Kaonga, "CCAP Crisis."

31. Synod of Livingstonia, "Solution to the Border Dispute between Nkhoma and Livingstonia Synods."

are supposed to continue being respected among the synods, then both the Synod of Livingstonia and Nkhoma Synod are wrong because they have violated a fundamental principle of CCAP oneness as hitherto understood.

This status, though contrary to the spirit of the General Assembly's current constitution, gives the synods of Livingstonia and Nkhoma the freedom to continue planting churches into each other's territory and thereby promoting the philosophy of "live and let live." This means that in as far as the synods of Livingstonia and Nkhoma are concerned, the first option for the future of the CCAP is already being practised as these two synods are existing side by side, with no respect for boundaries between them, as denominations that are different but also one in name under the weak unity that is the CCAP General Assembly. The same scenario is happening in South Africa where the two synods have churches under the name of the CCAP with no reference to any territorial boundaries with regard to their influence in that country. Blantyre Synod is a participant in as far as the South African scenario is concerned while in Malawi it is enjoying a neutral position, albeit with some apprehension due to the behaviour of the two sister synods of Livingstonia and Nkhoma. While Blantyre Synod has some problems with Nkhoma Synod in some of their shared boundaries, the issue between the two is not as pronounced as is the case with the Livingstonia and Nkhoma boundary dispute.[32]

In any case, if the first option of CCAP unity is to be sustained, it means that all the boundaries separating the different synods' territories will have to be abolished. Consequently, Nkhoma and Livingstonia synods will have a justification for planting new congregations in the formerly exclusive territory of Blantyre Synod. On the other hand, Blantyre Synod would also be free to go and establish churches in the Central and Northern Regions of Malawi, which are traditionally known as Nkhoma and Livingstonia synods' spheres, respectively. The same would apply to the synods of Harare and Zambia; they, too, would be free to plant their own brand of CCAP Christianity wherever they wanted, be it in Malawi, Zambia or Zimbabwe, irrespective of the presence of one or more of their own sister synods' congregations in the area. That would be the final nail in the coffin of the missionary and

---

32. Cf. Zgambo, "Conflict within the Church," 225.

synodical comity that has characterized Presbyterian cooperation in this part of the world from the nineteenth-century missionary era.

The Second Option: A Stronger General Assembly and Presbyteries with No Synods

Theoretically, the second option promises to be a better option for the future of the CCAP. In the first place, it is an option that guarantees the unity of the CCAP under a stronger General Assembly. Second, since the proposed major presbyteries will not correspond to regional boundaries and ethnic groups, it is likely to cure the problem of regionalism in the CCAP. However, as already hinted at, who will see to it that synods have completely died in order for the presbyteries and the General Assembly to take full control of the CCAP? This means that while this second option promises better things than the first, it is the most difficult to accomplish given the situation as it is in the CCAP synods at present. The process of de-registering the synods and distributing their property to the presbyteries and the General Assembly would be a mammoth task even if the will to do it were there.

So far, the general observation is that no synod is willing to dissolve for the sake of a more united CCAP denomination with a stronger and more efficient General Assembly. The positions of the synods of Livingstonia and Nkhoma are that the boundaries of the synodical territories should be abolished once and for all so that the synods are not restricted by boundary agreements when they desire to go and establish their branches wherever they want. Cautiously, it is being emphasized that this arrangement should currently apply only to the synods of Livingstonia and Nkhoma since Blantyre, Harare and Zambia are not directly involved in the Livingstonia/Nkhoma dispute.

However, as we have seen before, this is a tricky issue because it would not make sense to have a constitution of the CCAP General Assembly that treats the synods differently on the issue of boundaries because of two synods that have decided not to respect the boundaries between them. Moreover, one would question why the boundaries should matter only in Malawi and not in other countries where CCAP synods are establishing congregations side by side. A good example here is South Africa, where, as we have already seen, we have congregations belonging to Livingstonia, Blantyre and Nkhoma synods with no mention of the issue of synodical boundaries there.

An Ecclesiological Evaluation of the Two Options

While the synods' observance of boundaries seems not to be a good thing, it has one advantage of making sure that people do not congregate based on regional, ethnic, cultural or linguistic grounds. For example, a member of the Synod of Livingstonia who goes into Blantyre Synod's territory automatically becomes a member of Blantyre Synod if he continues with his CCAP affiliation. In his new congregation he is likely to notice that there are people from many corners of Malawi with different linguistic and ethnic backgrounds. By joining this group, the new member's experience of being a Christian is enriched. However, if there can be a Synod of Livingstonia congregation in the vicinity such a member would be tempted to join the Synod of Livingstonia's congregation rather than the Blantyre Synod's one. While that would be quite convenient to the member in question, it would not be a good thing for the church as a whole. First, by always associating with people from one's own region, people tend to become naive, short-sighted and prejudiced, which are things that are against the spirit of Christianity. Besides, by sticking to one's own people group in terms of region, ethnicity or language, a Christian community tends to live in isolation, reminiscent of Jewish ghettos in medieval Europe. I argue, notwithstanding sociological pressure, that such a scenario is against the catholicity of the church, since earthly designations divide the body of Christ. Not going for this option would be safer in the sense that congregations would avoid the risk of being associated with regionalism, tribalism and any other form of segregation that is not acceptable in the body of Christ.[33] It is unfortunate that the CCAP synods in Malawi found themselves in this situation by default. The good missionary idea of respecting one another's sphere of influence (comity), while preaching what was believed to be the same gospel message as understood from the point of view of Reformed Theology, eventually made the synods to be associated with the people and regions of their missionary influence.[34] It is for this reason that a synod can easily operate in its traditional area, but when it goes into another synod's territory, the issue of a particular ethnic group invading another group's territory is mentioned.

---

33. Cf. Phiri, "CCAP Border Dispute a Danger to the Nation."
34. See Pretorius, "Story of the Dutch Reformed Church," 16.

This notwithstanding, when people of other regions are in a region not considered their own, they are easily served by that region's synod, but it becomes intolerable for that synod to serve them when they are in their region of origin because it is a synod associated with another group of people. This is the mentality that needs to die if the synods are to pass the test of the catholicity of the church. It is this observation that makes the establishment of a stronger General Assembly with presbyteries excluding synods a better option because in that case issues of territorial control in connection to ethnic, cultural and linguistic designations would be minimized.

Conclusion

In this chapter, I have tried to look at the different proposals that are being suggested as a way forward for the CCAP in this post-boundary dispute era. This has been done from the point of view of ecclesiology in order to show that the issues that affect the church administratively have repercussions in other dimensions of the church's life as it continues with its kingdom witness. The discussion in this chapter is another instance to show that the synods are separate denominations that cooperate loosely within the CCAP General Assembly, whose future and welfare does not look very bright at the moment. It has been observed that the unity of the CCAP can continue with a weaker General Assembly while enhancing the independence of the synods or by strengthening the General Assembly while dissolving the synods and empowering the presbyteries. What is coming out quite clearly is that the CCAP is at a crossroads and a decision is supposed to be made by the current leadership to map the way forward for the future of the CCAP, otherwise the current setup of the General Assembly and its synods appears to have outlived its usefulness in the history of this federative denomination.

When the early missionaries came to establish the church in Central Africa, their desire was to see the kingdom of God taking root in this part of the world. Their emphasis of Christianity and commerce has been criticized by some as being shaped by their own outlook. Nevertheless, theirs was a true endeavour for the promotion of the kingdom of God, especially with regard to its concept of being the redemptive reign of Christ in people's lives.[35]

---

35. Shaw, *Kingdom of God in Africa*, 16.

The early missionaries did their part, and sometimes they had to make a lot of sacrifices for the sake of the kingdom of God. In certain circumstances, even some of the churches to which some of the missionaries belonged had to be dissolved or were swallowed up by other churches in trying to unify the Christian cause for the sake of the kingdom of God, which has priority over denominations. It, therefore, becomes imperative for the current generation of CCAP leadership to consider their own contribution to the witness of the kingdom of God in their generation beyond commitments to mere names or physical and administrative structures.

CHAPTER 8

Concluding Thoughts

As we come to the end of the discussion on the history of the CCAP as a federative denomination, several issues stand out. The formation of the CCAP in 1924 was more like the appearance of the first shoots of leaves from the ground when a seed has just germinated and is beginning to grow. It is obvious that when we consider other things the life of the new seedling, in as far as its history is concerned, goes beyond what is seen as a new plant shooting from out of the ground. It is for this reason that this study decided to go deeper in appreciating the history of the CCAP by going back several steps in the history of Reformed Theology and Presbyterianism in order to show the oneness of the missions that formed the CCAP from the cradle of their theology and history. The argument in this regard is that despite whatever has happened in the evolution of the CCAP, it is a given fact that the synods of the CCAP can trace their theology and history back to John Calvin in Geneva. This should encourage the CCAP synods to consider their oneness seriously as the church struggles to remain united in view of the independent status of its synods and its experience of unprecedented developments in the course of its history.

This study has also shown that the CCAP is a child of revivals as the missions that gave birth to the denomination were actually influenced by the spirit of revival. As such, the CCAP ought to continue in the spirit of revival by being ever open to spiritual renewal that has the power to rejuvenate the church and empower it for further devolvement in the course of its history. I argue, in this regard, that the CCAP synods are one even in the spirit of revival and can therefore deal with their negative differences that try to snuff revivalism by perpetuating traditionalism.

In the formation of the CCAP, there was much cooperation among the missionaries. Even the pioneer missionary parties themselves were highly cooperative in their endeavour to plant the church in this part of the world. This also shows that the synods have always been one in cooperation and not in competition with one another, at least in their earlier history. However, things began to change with the actual process of the formation of the CCAP as the different attitudes of missionary personnel from the three original missions began to manifest. The result of such differences was that the formation of the CCAP endured many compromises for the sake of the success of unity. The problem with the compromises that were made for the sake of this ecumenical project was that many things were not ironed out during the formative years of this federative denomination. Besides, the emerging African leadership did not play a significant role in the formation of the union, yet they were the ones to be entrusted with its future life.

As a result of the unfinished business of the establishment of the CCAP, and subsequent developments in the course of the history of the denomination, the unity of the church that was originally conceived did not really take place. Consequently, the three original synods in Malawi have remained independent of one another, just as would have been the case if they were different denominations altogether. The same trend continued when the CCAP congregations in Zimbabwe and Zambia attained the status of synods, thereby making the CCAP an umbrella body of five distinct denominations under the names of the synods.

In view of these observations, it follows that whatever unity the future of the CCAP holds, it must, first of all, be acknowledged that there is actually no one CCAP denomination but five denominations. It must also be realized that despite whatever has been said before, the CCAP has actually never been a denomination but a kind of meta-denominational organization. From this premise, it can be considered whether a closer unity and oneness of the CCAP as a denomination is what the leadership wants.

The efforts of the CCAP to move forward in its unity have often been hampered by references to a history that cannot be fully apprehended, as it was beyond the grasp of African leadership to take full control of the CCAP while the missionaries who were the initiators of the project belonged to their own camp in the church, as it were. The onus is therefore on the current leadership to reorientate the "denomination" since current developments show that it has reached a stage where a drastic landmark decision in its history is supposed to be made. I argue that this denominational reorientation can only be successful if the leaders of the synods are concerned more with the future of the CCAP and its contribution to the witness for the kingdom of God rather than with the glorious past of the missionary era from whence the synods are coming. This is not to suggest that history should not matter but rather that one should learn from the mistakes of history while daring to be original in the present circumstances. If the current generation of CCAP synod leaders fails to do this, they can be assured that the future generations will have nothing substantial to write about or recall from it. The responsibility placed upon the shoulders of the leaders of the CCAP calls for great sacrifices in a bid to make this church organization an authentic witness to the kingdom of God in the present generation.

Bibliography

Some Oral Informants

Asidi, Rev Jafali. Blantyre Synod Minister. Mzuzu, 20 May 2014.
Chakhaza, Mr Hanock. Administrator, St Michael's' and All Angels Congregation. Blantyre, 14 February 2014.
Chikopa, Rev Innocent. Blantyre Synod Minister. Blantyre, 23 October 2014.
Chingota, Rev Dr F. L. Blantyre Synod Minister, Ex-general Assembly Moderator, PAC Chairman. Zomba, 15 February 2014.
Chipofya, Rev D. Moderator, Synod of Livingstonia. 12 March 2015.
Chisambi, Mr Thomas. Tourist Guide, Livingstonia Mission. 30 July 2015.
Chisi, Rev Mrs M. Synod of Livingstonia Minister. 10 April 2013.
Kadogana, Rev F. Synod of Livingstonia Minister. 2 October 2013.
Kamanga, Rev J. Synod of Livingstonia Minister. 10 April 2013.
Kamnyamata, Mr Greshan. Lecturer and Acting Dean of Education. Nkhoma University, 21 February 2014.
Kawale, Mr Nathaniel. Retired Church Elder, Nkhoma Synod. Nkhoma, 20 February 2014.
Kawale, Rev Dr Winston R. Nkhoma Synod Minister, Former Secretary General and Mzuzu University Lecturer. Mzuzu, 8 May 2014.
Likhoozi, Rev Matalius. Nkhoma Synod Minister and Nkhoma University Lecturer. Nkhoma, 20 February 2014.
M'bawa, Rev C. Blantyre Synod Minister and General Assembly Secretary General. Blantyre, 15 November 2014.
Mbolembole, Rev Masauko. Blantyre Synod Minister. Blantyre, 14 February 2014.
Mgawi, Rev Dr K. Nkhoma Synod Minister and First Secretary General. Nkhoma, 21 February 2014.
Mlowoka, Rev Mrs G. Synod of Livingstonia Minister. Ekwendeni, 11 April 2013.
Mwale, Rev Kapombe C. Synod of Livingstonia Minister. Mzuzu, 12 May 2013.

Mzembe, Rev M. G. K. Retired Synod of Livingstonia Minister and Stone House Manager. Khondowe, 29 July 2015.
Nyasulu, Rev Dr T. P. K. Synod of Livingstonia Minister, Education Secretary and General Assembly Moderator. Mzuzu, 20 November 2014.
Nyirenda, Mr Dennis. Stone House Librarian and Archivist, Livingstonia Mission. Khondowe, 30 July 2015.
Nyirenda, Rev K. R. M. Synod of Livingstonia Minister and Former General Assembly Deputy Secretary General 1. Mzuzu, 12 December2014.
Nyondo, Rev Dr L. N. Synod of Livingstonia Minister and Secretary General. Mzuzu, 5 September 2014.
Williams, Mr Matt. Lecturer, Faculty of Theology, University of Livingstonia, and PCI Missionary. Mzuzu, 12 May 2014.

Primary Sources

Blantyre Synod. "Blantyre Synod Response." Unpublished document on the Livingstonia-Nkhoma Border Dispute.
———. "Blantyre Synod Statement on the Present State of Unrest 1958." In *Christianity in Malawi: A Source Book*, edited by Kenneth R. Ross, 217–222. Gweru: Mambo Press, 1996.
———. *Katekisimu*. Blantyre: CLAIM, n.d.
———. "Malongosoledwe a Mapemphero." (Order of Worship Service.)
———. "Organisation and Procedure in the Blantyre Synod." Synod's operational booklet.
CCAP General Assembly. "Memorandum of Understanding on the Plan of Action for the Synods of Blantyre, Livingstonia and Nkhoma." 28 March 2006.
———. "Minutes of General Assembly Standing Committee Meeting Held at CCAP Secretariat, Lilongwe." 16 September 2006."
———. Press Release. 25 January 2007.
"The CCAP General Assembly Constitutional Schedule." Explanations on the General Assembly's Constitution.
CCAP General Synod. "Minutes of the Forum of the Standing Committee on Dwangwa Dispute." CHAM Secretariat Conference Room, Lilongwe, 27 September 1996.
———. "Some Worrisome Trends Which Undermine the Nurturing of Our Young Democracy." Pastoral letter of the CCAP General Synod, 2001.
CCAP. "Extracts of Minutes of Synod 1924–1945."
———. "Minutes of Eighth Synod." Nkhoma, 25–29 April 1956, min. 36.
———. "Minutes of First Meeting of Synod." 17–22 September 1924.

———. "Minutes of Second Meeting of Synod." 13–15 October 1926.

———. "Minutes of Sixteenth General Synod." Ekwendeni, 5–10 August 1987.

———. "Minutes of Sixth Synod." 7–15 October 1948.

———. "Minutes of Synod." 1932, min. 36.

———. "Minutes of Synod." 1936, min. 28(4).

———. "Minutes of the General Synod." Chongoni, 9–13 November 1994.

———. "Minutes of the General Synod." 24–27 August, 1982.

———. *Minutes of the General Synod Held at Chongoni from 16th to 17th August 1977.* Nkhoma: Nkhoma Press, 1977.

———. "Minutes of the Ninth Synod (Special)." Livingstonia, 18–21 April 1958, min. 25.

Chase, Deborah A. (PCUSA). Text of speech at CCAP General Assembly, 2002.

———. "An Apology and Plea for Unity." 5 May 2006.

Chibambo, Yesaya. "Letter to Livingstonia Mission Council 1921." In *Christianity in Malawi: A Source Book*, edited by Kenneth R. Ross, 155–159. Gweru: Mambo Press, 1996.

Chingota, Felix. "Commission of Inquiry Report." Email to all CCAP Synods and the General Assembly, 24 July 2006.

———. "Lost Opportunities." Speech delivered at the Bi-annual Meeting of Synod of Livingstonia, 23–28 September 2006.

Chiotha, Mrs L. "Commission of Inquiry on Border Dispute." Email to Synod of Livingstonia, 10 May 2006.

Chitsulo, S. G. "Prophetic Message for Reconciliation between Nkhoma and Livingstonia Synods." 2 January 2007. Unpublished letter.

Church of Scotland. *Assembly Reports*. FMC Report, East Africa Section, 1881.

Commission of Inquiry on the Border Dispute between Livingstonia and Nkhoma Synods. "Itinerary for Consultations at Livingstonia Synod: Saturday 20 to Sunday 21 May 2006." Letter to General Secretary of the Synod of Livingstonia.

———. "Work Plan: 06 May–18 June 2006."

"The Constitution of the Church of Central Africa Presbyterian 1956." Passed by the meeting of the Eighth Synod, Nkhoma, 25–29 April 1956. Amended by the meeting of the Ninth (Special) Synod, Livingstonia, 18–21 April 1958.

"The Constitution of the Church of Central Africa Presbyterian General Assembly." Adopted at Lilongwe, 8 December 2002.

"The Constitution of the Synod of Blantyre of the Church of Central Africa Presbyterian (CCAP)." N.d.

"The Constitution of the Synod of Livingstonia of the Church of Central Africa Presbyterian." Adopted in August 1959 and amended in September 1959.

"The Constitution of the Synod of Salisbury of the Church of Central Africa Presbyterian (CCAP)." N.d.

Council of Reformed Churches in Central Africa (CCAP Nkhoma Synod, CCAP Harare Synod, RC Zambia, ARC Zimbabwe, IRM Sinodo De Mphatso). *Buku la Katekisima*. Nkhoma: Nkhoma Press, 1965.

"Deed of Agreement between the Dutch Reformed Church in South Africa and Nkhoma Synod of the Church of Central Africa Presbyterian in Malawi." 1971.

Domingo, Charles. Letter correspondence to Joseph Booth, 19 September 1911. In *Christianity in Malawi: A Source Book*, edited by Kenneth Ross, 131–143. Gweru: Mambo Press, 1996.

Falconer, Norma (Church of Scotland). "The Struggle for Unity in the CCAP." Email to CCAP General Assembly, CCAP Synods of Blantyre, Livingstonia and Nkhoma and All Partner Churches of the CCAP, 14 February 2006.

Free Reformed Churches of North America. *Acts of Synod 2011*. Mitchell: Free Reformed Publications, 2011.

———. *Acts of Synod 2012*. Mitchell: Free Reformed Publications, 2012.

Friends of the Livingstonia Synod–Zomba. "Relationship between Livingstonia and Nkhoma Synod." Letter to the General Secretary of the Synod of Livingstonia, 2 May 2005.

Kainja, G. D. "Memorandum of Understanding on the Border Dispute between Nkhoma Synod and Livingstonia Synod." Legal document binding Livingstonia and Nkhoma Synods to abide by the findings of the Commission of Enquiry on the Boundary Dispute.

Kalengo, G. H. T., and T. S. E. Katsukuluta, eds. *CCAP Nkhoma: Synod, Buku la Chilangizo*. Nkhoma: Nkhoma Synod, 2009.

"Life and Mission Agency Committee Report to the 137th General Assembly of the Presbyterian Church in Canada." 2011.

Mangisa, Reynold. "Questions of Conscience on Livingstonia-Nkhoma Relations." Letter to the General Secretary of the Synod of Livingstonia, 14 February 2007.

"Memorandum of Understanding on the Border Dispute between Nkhoma Synod and Livingstonia Synod." 2006.

"Minute of Meeting of Commissioners from the Dutch Reformed Mission and Livingstonia Mission to Deal with the Transfer of the Missions of Kasungu and Tamanda from the Livingstonia Mission to the Dutch Reformed Church Mission." Kasungu, 8 October 1923".

"Minutes of the General Assembly Standing Committee held at St Peter's Church on 17–18 July 1996."

"Minutes of the General Assembly Sub-committee on Dwangwa held on 9–10 September 1995."

"Minutes of the Second Meeting of the Committee Responsible for the English Services Held at Lingadzi CCAP." 24 July 1980.

Mpasazi Presbytery. "On Nkhoma Synod's Continued Presence and Desire for Co-existence in Livingstonia Territory." Letter to the Synod of Livingstonia, 6 October 2006.

Munthali, Maurice C. E. "Border Dispute." Memo to ministers and heads of departments of the Synod of Livingstonia, 16 May 2005.

Mvula, H. K. "There Is a Crisis in the CCAP Church." Letter to the Moderator of the Synod of Livingstonia, copied to the Acting General Secretary and Moderator Elect, 3 May 2005.

Nkhoma, Howard Matiya. "Christ's Generosity through the Livingstonia Mission: 1875–2005: A Night Song from the Plateau of Livingstonia on the Encroachment of Nkhoma Synod into Livingstonia Mission Area." 25 May 2005.

———. (General Secretary, Synod of Livingstonia). Email correspondence to all partner churches, Mzuzu, 29 January 2007.

Nkhoma Synod. "Choosing the Right Leaders." Pastoral letter, 2009.

———. "Exercising Our Faith through Prayer in Our Time, In Our Nation." Pastoral letter, 2012.

———. "Extracts of the Minutes of the Meeting of the Moderamen held at Nkhoma on the 4th September 1984."

———. "Extracts of the Minutes of the Meeting of the Moderamen held at Nkhoma on the 1st October 1984."

———. "Minutes of the Meeting of Moderamen." Lilongwe, 29 October 1982.

———. "Minutes of the Meeting of Moderamen." Lilongwe, 2 May 1983.

———. "Minutes of the Meeting of Moderamen." Nkhoma, 6 June 1983.

———. "Reconsidering the Future of Our Country, Malawi: Genuine Change Required." Pastoral letter, 2003.

———. "Renewal and Regeneration of Our Nation: A Call for Church Responsibility." Pastoral letter, 2014.

———. "The Constitution of the Nkhoma Synod of the Church of Central Africa Presbyterian (CCAP) as amended in 1968."

———. "Translation of Extracts of the Minutes of the Meeting of the Moderamen Held at Namoni Katengeza Lay Training Centre on the 15th April 1985."

———. "Translation of Extracts of the Minutes of the Meeting of the Moderamen Held at Nkhoma on the 7th May 1984."

———. "Translation of Extracts of the Minutes of the Meeting of the Moderamen Held at Nkhoma on the 8th of June 1984."

———. "Translation of Extracts of the Minutes of the Meeting of the Moderamen Held at Nkhoma on the 3rd April 1985."

———. "Translation of Extracts of the Minutes of the Meeting of the Moderamen Held at Lilongwe CCAP on the 1st May 1985."

———. "Translation of Extracts of the Minutes of the Meeting of the Moderamen Held at Lilongwe CCAP on the 13th May 1985."

———. "Translation of Extracts of the Minutes of the Meeting of the Moderamen Held at Lilongwe CCAP on the 4th September 1985."

———. "Translation of Extracts of the Minutes of the Meeting of the Moderamen Held at Lilongwe CCAP on the 16th September 1985."

———. "Translation of Extracts of the Minutes of the Synodical Committee Meeting, Held at Namoni Katengeza Lay Training Centre on the 9th April 1985."

———. "Translation of Minutes of Joint Financial Committee, 24 March 1981."

———. "Translation of Minutes of Moderamen." 3 April 1984.

———. "Translation of Minutes of Moderamen." 10 March 1980.

———. "Translation of Minutes of Moderamen." 15 March 1979.

———. "Translation of Minutes of Moderamen." 1 May 1981.

———. "Translation of Minutes of Moderamen." 2 May 1981.

———. "Translation of Minutes of Moderamen." 2 September 1980.

———. "Translation of Minutes of Moderamen." 3 September 1979.

———. "Translation of Minutes of Moderamen." 5 August 1980.

———. "Translation of Minutes of Moderamen." 5 March 1976.

———. "Translation of Minutes of Moderamen." 8 March 1977.

———. "Translation of Minutes of Synodical Committee Meeting." 10 April 1981.

———. "Translation of Minutes of Synodical Committee Meeting." 11 April 1981.

———. "Translation of Minutes of Synodical Committee Meeting." 23 April 1979.

———. "Translation of Minutes of the Emergency Meeting of Synodical Committee at Lilongwe CCAP on 16 August 1983."

———. "Translation of the Minutes of the Meeting of the JFC Held at Chongoni on the 1 May 1987."

Nkhoma Synod (Sinodi ya Nkhoma). *Zolamulira, Zopangana ndi Zolangiza*. Buku 1. Nkhoma: Nkhoma Synod of the CCAP, 2004/2008.

———. *Zolamulira, Zopangana ndi Zolangiza*. Buku 2. Nkhoma: Nkhoma Synod of the CCAP, 2001.

Parrat, John. Letter correspondence to Rev Human, 25 February 1977.

Partnership Agreement between Nkhoma Synod and the Commission for Witness, 2003.

Presbyterian Church of Ireland. *2013 General Assembly Annual Reports.*.

Sangaya, J. D. "Life and Work of Blantyre Synod." Appendix IV to the CCAP's *Minutes of the General Synod Held at Chongoni from 16th to 17th August 1977*. Nkhoma: Nkhoma Press, 1977

Sneddon, Sandy (Associate Secretary, Church of Scotland World Mission Council). Letter correspondence to Rev Dr Winston Kawale (General Secretary, Nkhoma Synod), 14 August 2007.

Sturrock, John. Email to Felix Chingota, 12 July 2006.

Synod of Livingstonia. *Agenda for the Third Committee Meeting for the Task Force of the Operation beyond the Borders*. William Koyi Conference Hall, Mzuzu, 10 May 2006.

———. "A Press Statement on the Border Issue between the CCAP Synods of Livingstonia and Nkhoma." 22 October 2008.

———. "Findings on CCAP Nkhoma Synod: Churches Established in the Territory of Livingstonia Synod." 2005.

———. "Issues of Concern in Regard to General Assembly's Request That We Sit as Active Delegates and Take Up the Moderatorship." Caucus document for the General Assembly meeting, 24 January 2007.

———. "Life and Work." Report presented to the 20th CCAP General Assembly Meeting, Blantyre, 20–23 January 2007."

———. *Mdauko, Mendeskero na Milimo ya Umanyano wa Wanakazi* [A Handbook of the History, Procedure and Activities of the Women's Guild]. Mzuzu: Synod of Livingstonia Literature Department, n.d.

———. *Minister's Handbook on Church Government, Practice and Procedure*. Mzuzu: CCAP Livingstonia Synod, 1997.

———. "Minutes of the General Administration Committee Meeting." Ekwendeni Mission Station, 26–30 August 2011.

———. "Minutes of the Operation beyond Borders Taskforce Committee." William Koyi Conference Centre, 21 March 2006.

———. "Minutes of the Synod Meeting." Ekwendeni Mission Station, 5–10 September 2002.

———. "Minutes of Thirty-Second Synod Assembly." Mzimba Station, 28 August–2 September 2010.

———. "Minutes of Thirty-Third Synod Assembly." Karonga Teachers Training College, 10–17 August 2012.

———. "Minutes of Twenty-Eighth Synod Meeting." Karonga Teachers Training College, 12–17 November 2002.

———. "Minutes of Twenty-Fifth Synod Meeting." Ekwendeni Station, 3–8 November 1999.

———. "Minutes of Twenty-Fourth Synod Meeting." 1996.

———. "Observations and Key Issues Raised." 2006.

———. "Re: CILIC's Offer to Mediate the Border Dispute." Email to Mrs E. Chanika, 26 April 2005.

———. "Re: Malani Msowoya's Commentary on the Border Dispute." Email to MBC Director General, 25 April 2005

———. "Solution to the Border Dispute between Nkhoma and Livingstonia Synods." Press release issued at the Thirtieth Synod Assembly held at Bandawe Mission Station, 22–27 September 2006.

———. "Tentative Programme for the Official Launch of the Lilongwe Congregation on Sunday, 17 September 2006."

Synod of Livingstonia Members. "Concern over the Opening of CCAP Synod of Livingstonia Churches inside Nkhoma Synod Jurisdiction." Letter to the Moderator of the Synod of Livingstonia, 26 April 2006.

United Free Church of Scotland. *Reports to the General Assembly of the United Free Church of Scotland*. Edinburgh: UFCS, 1926.

Other Sources

Abale-Phiri, Hastings Matemba. "Interculturalisation as Transforming Praxis: The Case of the Church of Central Africa Presbyterian Blantyre Synod Urban Ministry." DTh (Missiology), University of Stellenbosch, 2011.

African Elections Database. "14 June 1993 Referendum." *African Elections Database*, http://africanelections.tripod.com/mw.html#1993_Referendum. Accessed 27 June 2019.

Allen, William. *The History of Revivals of Religion*. http://www.revival-library.org/index.php/catalogues-menu/general-histories/history-of-revivals-of-religion. Accessed 1 May 2013.

Association of Christian Educators in Malawi (ACEM). "Mother Bodies." www.acemmalawi.wordpress.com/.

Australian Presbyterian Women. "Malawi, Country Information." http://www.apwm.org.au/wp-content/uploads/2014/08/Malawi-Country-Information-Sheet-2014.pdf. Accessed 5 April 2015.

———. "Partner Churches." http://www.apwm.org.au/partner-churches/malawi/. Accessed 5 April 2015.

Banda, Grace Patience. "A Study of Assessment of Women's Rights in Nkhoma Synod: A Case Study of Three CCAP Congregations in Lilongwe City." BA (Theology and Religious Studies), Mzuzu University, 2010.

Banda, Griffie G. Victor. "The Role of Men's Guild in Relation to Women's Guild in Nkhoma Synod of the Church of Central Africa Presbyterian: A Case Study of Lilongwe and Mlanda Presbyteries." BA (Theology and Religious Studies), Mzuzu University, 2010.

Bibliography

Barry, William. "John Calvin." *The Catholic Encyclopedia*. Vol. 3. New York: Robert Appleton, 1908. Accessed 20 February 2013. http://www.newadvent.org/cathen/03195b.htm.

Baur, John. *Two Thousand Years of Christianity in Africa: An African History 62–1992*. Nairobi: Paulines, 1994.

Beeke, Joel R. "The Dutch Second Reformation (*Nadere Reformatie*)." Accessed 20 May 2013. http://www.abrakel.com/2009 /11/dutch-second-reformation-dr-joel-r_06.html.

Boeder, Robert B. *Alfred Sharpe of Nyasaland: Builder of Empire*. Blantyre: Society of Malawi, 1980.

Bolink, P. *Towards Church Union in Zambia*. Franker: T. Weber, 1967.

Botha, F. J. Mkhristu ndi Ndale za Dziko. Nkhoma: Nkhoma Press, 1963.

Bradley, J. E., and R. A. Muller. *Church History: An Introduction to Research, Reference Works, and Methods*. Grand Rapids: Eerdmans, 1995.

Brock, Sheila M. "James Stewart and Lovedale: A Reappraisal of Missionary Attitudes and African Response in Eastern Cape, South Africa, 1870–1905." PhD (Divinity), University of Edinburgh, 1974.

Brown, Craig, "Anglican Minister to Take Free Church Congregation." *The Scotsman*, http://www.scotsman.com/news/scotland/top-stories/anglican-minister-to-take-free-church-congregation-1-2910003. Accessed 20 April 2015.

Brown, Walter Lawrence. "The Development in Self Understanding of the CCAP Nkhoma Synod as Church during the First Forty Years of Autonomy: An Ecclesiological Study." PhD (Theology), University of Stellenbosch, 2004.

Bush, Luis, and L. Lutz. *Partnering in Ministry: The Direction of World Evangelism*. Downers Grove: InterVarsity Press, 1990.

Bwalya, Kelly. *The Life of Dr Wyson Moses Kauzobafa Jele*. Mzuzu: Mzuni Press, 2014.

Calvin, John. *Commentary on the Book of Psalms, Vol 12*. In *Calvin's Commentaries*, translated by James Anderson. 22 vols. Grand Rapids: Baker, 1993.

———. "Commentary on Matthew 24:14." In *Harmony of the Gospels*, Vol. 3, 112–234. Edinburgh: Oliver & Boyd, 1960.

———. *Institutes of the Christian Religion*, 1560. Translated and annotated by Ford Lewis Battles. London: Collins Flame Classics, 1975.

Carey, William. *An Enquiry into the Obligations of Christians to Use Means for the Conversion of the Heathens*. Leicester: Ann Ireland, 1792.

Caseby, Ronald. *Going with God: The Biography of Reverend Alexander Caseby from 1898 until 1991*. Sussex: Book Guild, 1993.

CCAP Blantyre Synod. "Chilema Ecumenical Centre." http://www.ccapblantyresynod.org/chilema-ecumenical-center.html. Accessed 23 June 2015.
———. "Current Partnerships." http://www.ccapblantyresynod.org/current-partnerships.html. Accessed 23 June 2015.
———. "News." http://www.ccapblantyresynod.org/news.html. Accessed 20 March 2015.
CCAP Harare Synod. "Harare Synod." https://www.ccaphresynod.com/hararesynodandmapc.htm. Accessed 4 April 2015.
———. "Nyabira School." www.ccaphresynod.com/ourschool.htm. Accessed 11 August 2015.
CCAP Synod of Zambia. "Chunga Chicken Farm." http://www.ccapzambia.org/chunga-chicken-farm.html. Accessed 24 April 2015.
———. "Community Schools." www.ccapzambia.org/community-schools.html. Accessed 11 August 2015.
———. "History." http://www.ccapzambia.org/history.html. Accessed 10 March 2015.
———. "Organizational Chart." www.ccapzambia.org/organisational-chart.html. Accessed 4 June 2015.
———. "Partners." http://www.ccapzambia.org. Accessed 17 April 2015.
Chakanza, J. C., and Kenneth R. Ross. *Religion in Malawi: An Annotated Bibliography*. Blantyre: CLAIM-Kachere, 1998.
Chambers, D. "The Church of Scotland's Nineteenth Century Foreign Missions Scheme: Evangelical or Moderate Revival?" *Journal of Religious History* 9, no. 2 (December 1976): 115–138.
Chapalapata, McDonald. "BT Synod Votes Out Mangisa, Chimenya." *Sunday Times*, 27 February 2011.
Chiang, Samuel E. "Partnership at the Crossroads: Red, Yellow or Green Light?" *Evangelical Missions Quarterly* (July 1992): 284–289.
Chifungo, Phoebe Faith. "Women in the CCAP Nkhoma Synod: A Practical Theological Study of Their Leadership Roles." PhD (Practical Theology), University of Stellenbosch, 2014.
Chikakuda, W. E. "Karl Barth's Concept of the Church for the World." DTh, Stellenbosch, 1994.
Chikopa, Innocent Brave. "The Rise and Decline of Zomba Theological College as a Uniting Factor for the CCAP General Assembly and as an Ecumenical Institution." BA (Theology and Religious Studies), Mzuzu University, 2010.
Chilenje, Victor. "A History of the Church of Central Africa Presbyterian (CCAP) in Zambia 1880s–1998." BA (Theology), Justo Mwale Theological College, 1998.

———. "The Origin and Development of the Church of Central Africa Presbyterian (CCAP) in Zambia 1882–2004." PhD, University of Stellenbosch, 2007.

Chimpweya, James. "Mangisa Speaks on Case." *Nation on Sunday*, 13 February 2011.

———. "Reverend Nyasulu Is General Assembly Moderator." *The Nation*, 29 December 29.

———. "Saint Michael's Clocks 120." *Nation on Sunday*, 27 March 2011.

Chipanga, Peter. "CCAP Blantyre Synod Embraces Cape Town." *The Nation* (20 July 2017). https://mwnation.com/ccap-blantyre-synod-embraces-cape-town/. Accessed 17 July 2019.

Chirnside, A. *The Blantyre Missionaries: Discreditable Disclosure*. London: Ridgeway, 1880.

Chirwa, Panji V. "The Impact of Sunday School on Children in Presbyterian Churches: A Case Study of Selected Congregations in the CCAP Synod of Livingstonia." BA (Theology), Mzuzu University, 2012.

Chisamba, Edward. "Nkhoma, Livingstonia Spare Rev Lunan the Blushes." *Malawi News*, 28 March–3 April 2009.

Chuba, B. S. *A History of Early Christian Mission and Church Unity in Zambia*. Ndola: Missions Press, 2005.

Church of Scotland. *East African Mission, Life and Work in British Central Africa* (August–December 1897).

———. *East African Mission, Life and Work in British Central Africa* (December 1893).

———. *East African Mission, Life and Work in British Central Africa* (May 1891).

———. "Our Partner Churches." http://www.churchofscotland.org.uk/serve/mission_worldwide/our-partner-churches/africa/malawi. Accessed 14 April 2015.

Clowney, E. P. "Presbyterianism." In *New Dictionary of Theology*, edited by Sinclair B. Ferguson, 531–539. Downers Grove: InterVarsity Press, 1988.

Coertzen, P. *Church and Order: A Reformed Perspective*. Leuven: Peeters, 1998.

Cole-King, P. A. "Lilongwe." *Nuusbrief uit Malawi*, January 1974.

Collins, Nancy. "Malawi: A Report on the Recent CCAP General Assembly." www.pcimissionoverseas.org/news/item/635/malawi-a-report-on-the-recent-ccap-general-assembly/. Accessed 18 December 2013.

———. "Mission Connections." https://www.presbyterianmission.org/ministries/missionconnections/nancy-collins/. Accessed 25 April 2015.

Colvin, Tom. *A Record of Fathers and Founders of Blantyre Synod*. Edinburgh: Blantyre, 1976.

Compassion Team. "A Strong Partnership Is about Relationships." *Compassion Blog*. Compassion International, February 2012. http://blog.compassion.

com/a-strong-partnership-is-about-relationships /#ixzz3 Xr48yB5Q. Accessed 10 April 2015.

Cooper, Harris. *Synthesizing Research: A Guide for Literature Reviews*. London/ New Delhi: Sage, 1998.

Cox, J. T. *Practice and Procedure in the Church of Scotland*. Edinburgh: William Blackwood & Sons, 1948.

Craswell, Gail. *Writing for Academic Success*. Los Angeles: Sage, 2005.

Cronjé, J. M. *Born to Witness*. Pretoria: NG Sendingpers, 1982.

Daneel, M. S. *Mbiri ya CCAP Sinodi ya Harare 1912–1982*. Harare: Church of Central Africa Presbyterian, 1982.

Dawson, R. B. *Livingstone: The Hero of Africa*. London: Seeley, 1874.

DeJong, Gerald F. *The Dutch Reformed Church in the American Colonies*. Grand Rapids: Eerdmans, 1978.

Denlinger, Aaron. "How the Scots Changed the World." https://www.ligonier.org/learn/articles/how-scots-changed-the world. Accessed 30 May 2019.

Demarest, B. "Heresy." In *New Dictionary of Theology*, edited by Sinclair B. Ferguson and David F. Wright, 291–293. Downers Grove: InterVarsity Press, 1988.

Dowley, Tim, ed. *The History of Christianity*. Oxford: Lion, 1990.

Dowsett, Rose. "The Evangelisation of the World in this Generation: Vignettes from Scottish Evangelicals Response, 1890–2009." In *Roots and Fruits: Retrieving Scotland's Missionary Story*, edited by Kenneth R. Ross, 70–83. Oxford: Regnum, 2014.

Eastern Oklahoma Presbytery. "Livingstonia." http://eokpresbytery.org/blog/?s=livingstonia. Accessed 11 April 2015.

Elmslie, W. A. *Among the Wild Ngoni*. Edinburgh: Oliphant Ferrier, 1899.

Fiedler, Klaus. "The Charismatic and Pentecostal Movements in Malawi in Cultural Perspective." *Religion in Malawi* 9 (November 1999): 28–38.

———. *The Making of a Maverick Missionary: Joseph Booth in Australia*. Zomba: Kachere, 2008.

———. *Missions as the Theology of the Church*. Mzuzu: Mzuni Press, 2012.

———. "The Process of Religious Diversification in Malawi: A Reflection on Method and a First Attempt at a Synthesis." *Religion in Malawi* 11 (November 2004): 18–24.

———. *The Story of Faith Missions: From Hudson Taylor to Present Day Africa*. Oxford: Lynx/Regnum, 1994.

———. *Teaching Church History in Malawi*. Zomba: Kachere, 2005.

Fiedler, Rachel NyaGondwe. "The Challenge of Theological Education for Women in Malawi." Supplement, *Studia Historiae Ecclesiasticae* 35 (December 2009): 119–134.

Finlayson, Alexander. *Unity and Diversity: The Founders of the Free Church of Scotland.* Fearn: Christian Focus, 2010.

Finney, C. G. *Lectures on Revivals of Religion.* Cambridge, MA: Belknap Press, 1960.

Focus on Malawi. "The Raven Trust: Supporting the Development of Eye Care." http://www.theraventrust.org/about/. Accessed 10 April 2015.

Fraser, Agnes R. *Donald Fraser of Livingstonia.* London: Hodder & Stoughton, 1934.

Fraser, Donald. *The Future of Africa.* London: Church Missionary Society, 1911.

———. *Winning a Primitive People.* London: Seeley Service, 1914.

Fuller, L. K. *Going to the Nations: An Introduction to Cross-Cultural Missions.* Jos: Nigeria Evangelical Missionary Institute, 1993.

Gereformeerde Zendingsbond (GZB). "Mission." www.gzb.nl. Accessed 29 April 2015.

Global Ministries. *A Global Church Partnership Handbook: Guidelines for Disciples Regions/Areas/Districts and UCC Conferences/Associations in the Pursuit of Vital Reciprocal Relationships with International Partners through Global Ministries.* Revised 2009. http://d3n8a8pro7vhmx.cloudfront.net/globalministries/legacy_url/534/Revised-GCP-Handbook-for-web.pdf?1419962364. Accessed 2 August 2015.

Gondwe, Esela. "The Continuity and Change of the Umanyano Women's Guild of the Livingstonia Synod." BA (Humanities), University of Malawi, 2006.

Gondwe, Hawkins Chepah Tom. "The Possible Influence of Crucial Pauline Texts on the Role of Women in the Nkhoma Synod the Central African Presbyterian Church." MA (Biblical Studies), University of South Africa, 2009.

Grigg, John A. *The Lives of David Brainerd: The Making of an American Evangelical Icon.* Oxford: Oxford University Press, 2009.

Gunde, Samuel. "A Church Historical Enquiry Regarding Growth of Membership in the Church of Central Africa, Presbyterian – Harare Synod (1912–2012)." MA (Theology), University of Stellenbosch, 2013.

Hallencreutz, C. F. *Religion and Research: An Introductory Guide for Students.* Gweru: Mambo Press, 1987.

Hammond, Peter. "Andrew Murray and the 1860 Revival." LinkedIn SlideShare, 14 May 2012. http://www.slideshare.net/frontfel/andrew-murray-and-the-1860-revival.html. Accessed 23 May 2013.

———. "The Family, Faith and Upbringing of David Livingstone." Slide Share, https://www.slideshare.net/frontfel/the-family-faith-and-upbringing-of-david-livingstone. Accessed 30 May 2013.

Hara, Handwell Yotamu. *Reformed Soteriology and the Malawian Context.* Zomba: Kachere, 2008.

Hetherwick, Alexander. *The Romance of Blantyre: How Livingstone's Dream Came True*. London: James Clarke, 1921.

Hodges, Melvin L. *On the Mission Field: The Indigenous Church*. Chicago: Moody Press, 1953.

Hofmeyr, J. W. "Challenges for Writing Church History in Africa in a Global Age: A Zambian Perspective." *Skrif en Kerk, Jrg* 1 (1998): 37–45.

Holder, R. Ward. "John Calvin." *Internet Encyclopedia of Philosophy*. https://www.iep.utm.edu/calvin/. Accessed 25 February 2013.

Hunter, Robert. *History of the Free Church of Scotland in India and Africa*. 1873. Reprint, London: Forgotten Books, 2013.

Jack, James William. *Daybreak in Livingstonia*. Edinburgh: Oliphant, Anderson & Ferrier, 1901.

Jackson, Bill. "Breaking Down the Wall: The Diary of a Participant in the Emergency of 1959." *Bulletin of the Scottish Institute of Missionary Studies* 10 (1994).

———. *Send Us Friends*. Belfast: Bill Jackson, 1996.

Jere, Peter Mbiko. "Livingstonia Going Too Far." *The Nation*, 25 February, 2009.

Johnson, Robert. "What Is Reformed Theology?" *Institute for Reformed Theology*. http://reformedtheology.org/SiteFiles /WhatIsRT.html. Accessed 5 March 2013.

Jorgensen, Dannys L. *Participant Observation: A Methodology of Human Studies*. London/Delhi: Sage, 1999.

Juma, Joseph. "Immigration and Its Effects on Our Church." *RecFocus* 3, no. 1 (March 2003): 1–3.

Jumbe, Master. "When the Church Becomes Tasteless." *Nation on Sunday*, 4 April 2010.

Kadogana, Frank. "How Church Discipline Exercised in CCAP Synod of Livingstonia: A Case Study of Mazembe CCAP Congregation in Nkhata-Bay District." BA (Theology), Mzuzu University, 2012.

———. "The Origin and Growth of Karonga CCAP Mission in Karonga and Chitipa from 1900 to 2013." MA (Theology and Religious Studies), Mzuzu University, 2015.

Kamanga, Joseph. "A History of Nkhamenya Presbytery of the Synod of Livingstonia of the CCAP (1986–2013)." BA, University of Livingstonia, 2014.

Kamuyanja, Foster. "The Impact of Church of Central Africa Presbyterian Youth Urban Ministry in Nkhoma Synod (CCAPYUM): A Case Study of Selected Churches within Lilongwe Presbytery." BA (Theology and Religious Studies), Mzuzu University, 2012.

Kaonga, Samson Salmon. "A History of the Birth and Growth of Livingstonia Synod's Congregation in Kasungu District in the Context of the Border

Dispute with Nkhoma Synod (2005-2012)." BA (Theology), Mzuzu University, 2012.

Kaonga, Victor. "CCAP Crisis: Time for United Presbyterian Church." *Nyasa Times*, Straight Talk, "Comment No. 44." http://www.nyasatimes.com/2015/04/28/ccap-crisis-time-for-united-presbyterian-church/1 of 6 6/8/2015 4:23 PM.

Kapira, Robinson M. B. "A History of Wenya Presbytery in the Church of Central Africa Presbyterian (CCAP) Synod of Livingstonia." BA (Education), Mzuzu University, 2013.

Karamaga, André. *Problems and Promises of Africa*. Nairobi: All Africa Conference of Churches, 1993.

Kasakula, George. "Mangisa's Position Untenable." *Weekend Nation*, 20 November 2010.

———. "Synods Mere Clubs." My Diary. *Weekend Nation*, 20–21 September 2008.

Kasakura, Archibald. "Synods Giving Up on Border Row: Leaders Admit Uniting Nkhoma and Livingstonia Not a Stroll in the Park." *Malawi News*, 24–30 December 2011.

Kawamba, Brighton. *The Blantyre Spiritual Awakening and Its Music*. Mzuzu: Luviri Press, 2018.

Kawale, W. R. "A Biblical Analysis of the Impact of the Border Wrangle on CCAP." Seminar paper, Mzuzu University, 2017.

Keyes, Larry. "OC International in an Indian Partnership." In *Kingdom Partnerships for Synergy in Missions*, edited by William D. Taylor, 229–235. Pasadena: William Carey Library, 1994.

Khonje, Boston. "A Historical Study of the Establishment and Contribution of the Student Christian Organisation of Malawi (SCOM) to the Malawian Society (1961-2012)." MA (Theology and Religious Studies), Mzuzu University, 2013.

Langworthy, Harry. *"Africa for the African": The Life of Joseph Booth*. Blantyre: CLAIM-Kachere, 1996.

Latourette, Kenneth Scott. *A History of Christianity*. Vol. 1. Peabody: Prince Press, 2007.

———. *A History of the Expansion of Christianity*. Vol. 3. Grand Rapids: Zondervan, 1976.

Laws, Robert. *Reminiscences of Livingstonia*. Edinburgh: Oliver & Boyd, 1934.

Lee, H. B. "Calvin's Sudden Conversion (Subita Conversio) and Its Historical Meaning." *Acta Theologica Supplementum* 5 (2004): 103–116.

Lee, Nigel. *Calvin on the Sciences*. Cambridge: Sovereign Grace Union, 1969.

Lester, James D. *Writing Research Papers: A Complete Guide*. New York: Pearson Education, 2010.

Letham, R. W. A. "Reformed Theology." In *New Dictionary of Theology*, edited by Sinclair B. Ferguson, 569–572. Downers Grove: InterVarsity Press, 1988.

Linden, Ian, and Jane Linden. *Catholics, Peasants and Chewa Resistance in Nyasaland (1889–1939)*. London: Richard & Clay, 1974.

Liponda, Lucy. "Muluzi Sponsored Clergy Lose Polls." *Malawi Digest*. 24 August 2009.

Livingstone, David. *Missionary Travels and Researches in Africa*. London: John Murray, 1875.

Livingstone, W. P. *Laws of Livingstonia: A Narrative of Missionary Adventure and Achievement*. London: Hodder & Stoughton, 1923.

London Missionary Society. *Transactions of the Missionary Society* 1 (1795–1802).

Lo, William J. K. (PCT General Secretary). Letter correspondence to Partner Churches and Related Organisation, Friends around the Globe and PCT Related Missionary Personnel. http://english.pct.org.tw/others /20040400.htm. Accessed 29 April 2015.

Luce, Arthur Aston. "The Kikuyu Scheme of Federation." *The Irish Church Quarterly* 8, no. 31 (July 1915): 186–199.

MacDonald, Duff. *Africana: Or the Heart of Heathen Africa*. Edinburgh: Blackwood, 1893.

Mackichan, Dugald. *The Missionary Ideal in the Scottish Churches*. London: Hodder & Stoughton, 1927.

Madison Avenue Presbyterian Church. "Partnership Agreement." http://mapc.com.test.bandwidthproductions.com/files/pages/outreach/PartnershipAgreement.pdf. Accessed 10 April 2015.

———. "Zimbabwe Partnership." http://www.mapc.com/outreach/global-outreach/zimbabwe-partnership/. Accessed 4 April 2015.

Malawi News. "Commerce for Liberation as Livingstone Saw It." 28 March–3 April 2009.

Matemba, Arthurny A. "The Significance of Church Elders in Nkhoma Synod of the CCAP: A Case Study of Mchinji Presbytery." BA (Theology), Mzuzu University, 2012.

Matonga, Golden. "Livingstonia Synod Snubs Dialogue Initiative." *The Guardian*, 7 December–8 December 2011.

Mburu, Thuo, "Revival and Mission Movements: Bedfellows or Marriage Partners? – Part 1." https://svm2.net/abandonedtimes/revival-and-mission-movements-bed-fellows-or-marriage-partners---part-1/. Accessed 20 May 2013.

McCracken, John. "Andrew Ross and the Radical Strand in Scotland's Missionary Tradition." In *Roots and Fruits: Retrieving Scotland's Missionary Story*, edited by Kenneth R. Ross, 84–90. Oxford: Regnum, 2014.

———. *Politics and Christianity in Malawi 1875–1940: The Impact of the Livingstonia Mission in the Northern Province*. Blantyre: CLAIM-Kachere, 2000.

McHugh, J. "Presbyterianism." In *The Catholic Encyclopaedia*. New York: Robert Appleton Co. http://www.newadvent.org/cathen/12392b.htm. Accessed 1 April 2013.

McIntosh, H. *Robert Laws: Servant of Africa*. Cadberry: Handsel, 1993.

McIntosh, J. R. "The Disruption." *Christian Library*. www.christianlibrary.org/download/file/fid/19887. Accessed 26 June 2019.

McKerrow, John. *History of the Foreign Missions of the Secession and United Presbyterian Church*. Edinburgh: A. Elliot, 1867.

McNeill, Patrick. *Research Methods*. London: Routledge, 1990.

McPherson, Alexander, ed. *Westminster Confession of Faith*. Glasgow: Free Presbyterian Publication, 1994.

McPherson, F. *North of Zambezi: A Modern Missionary Memoir*. Edinburgh: Handset Press, 1998.

Mgawi, K. J. *Mbiri ya CCAP Nkhoma Sinodi Kuyambira Mchaka cha 1962 Mpaka 2012: 50 Mzaka za Madalitso*. Nkhoma: CCAP Nkhoma Synod, 2012.

———. *Mbiri ya Mpingo ndi Mudzi wa Nkhoma, 1896 mpaka 1996*. Nkhoma: Nkhoma Press, 1996.

Mkandawire, A. C. *Yuraia Chatonda Chirwa: The Faithful Servant*. Mzuzu: Dudu Nsomba, 2003.

Mkandawire, Mjura. *The Founders of Livingstonia*. Khondowe: Mjura Mkandawire, n.d.

Mlenga, Joyce Dainess. "Women in Holy Ministry in the Church of Central Africa Presbyterian Synod of Livingstonia: A Study of Perceptions." PhD module (Theology and Religious Studies), Mzuzu University, 2008

Mlenga, Moses. *History of Livingstonia Mission: 50 Years of Post-Missionary Leadership (1958–2008)*. Zomba: Kachere, 2012.

Mlowoka, Gloria. "An Investigation into the Establishment and Impact of Ekwendeni College of Theology of the University of Livingstonia in the CCAP Synod of Livingstonia." BA (Theology and Religious Studies), University of Livingstonia, 2014.

Mmana, Deogratias. "BT Synod to Hold Prayers over Mangisa Court Case." *Weekend Nation*, 25 December 2010.

———. "Church Organisation Supports Pastoral Letter." *Weekend Nation*, 20 November 2010.

———. "Mangisa Replaces Kadawati on the Late Ethel Mutharika's Mausoleum Committee." *Weekend Nation*, 4 December 2010.

Moir, Fred L. M. *After Livingstone: An African Trade Romance*. Blantyre: Rotary Club of Blantyre, 1986.

Moore, Nick. *How to Do Research: The Complete Guide to Designing and Managing Research Projects*. London: Library Association Publishing, 2000.

Morning Post (London). "The Kikuyu Controversy: Archbishop of Canterbury's Judgment." 26 April 1915.

Morrison, J. H. *Forty Years in Darkest Africa: The Story of Dr Laws of Livingstonia*. Edinburgh: Foreign Mission Committee of the United Free Church of Scotland, 1917.

Mountain View Presbyterian Church. "Missions." http://www.mymvpc.com/home/missions. Accessed 10 March 2015.

Mpaka, Charles, and Lawrence Chauluka. "150 Years with Livingstone." *Malawi News*, 28 March–3 April 2009.

Mpaka, Charles. "David the Livingstone." *Malawi News*, 28 March–3 April 2009.

———. "The First of Kamuzu Banda's Thousand Steps." *Malawi News*, 28 March–3 April 2009.

Mpaso, Paida. "The Big Interview: Mercy Chilapula." *The Nation*, 27 October 2014. www.mwnation.com/mercy-chilapula. Accessed 1 June 2014.

Mpehera, Everson. "An Investigation on the Factors that Prompt People to Move from the Mainline Churches to Charismatic Churches: A Case Study of Christ Citadel International Church and Msangu CCAP of Area 23 in Lilongwe-Malawi." BA (Theology and Religious Studies), Mzuzu University, 2012.

———. "The Making of the Total Person." *Malawi News*, 28 March–3 April 2009.

Msiska, Stephen Kauta. *Golden Buttons: Christianity and Traditional Religion among the Tumbuka*. Blantyre: CLAIM-Kachere, 1998.

Mugambi, J. N. K., and Laurenti Magesa. *The Church in African Christianity*. Nairobi: Initiatives, 1990.

Muheya, Green. "Blantyre Synod Elects Female Moderator, New SG." *Nyasa Times*, 22 August, 2011. https://www.nyasatimes.com/blantyre-synod-elects-female-moderator-new-sg/.

Mulanje Mission Hospital. "Mulanje Mission Hospital in 2013." http://www.mmh.mw/wp-content/uploads/2012/03/MMH-ppt-updated-August-2013.pdf. Accessed 17 July 2019.

Mzungu, Watipaso. "CCAP General Assembly Calls for Peaceful Elections." http://mwnation.com/ccap-general-assembly-calls-for-peaceful-elections/. Accessed 26 February 2014.

Ncozana, Silas. "New Dawn for Partnership in Mission: An African Perspective." http://pghpip.org/about/mp_brochure_2012.pdf. Accessed 6 April 2015.

Ndekha, Louis. "Chinula, Charles Chidongo." *Dictionary of African Christian Biography (DACB)*. www.dacb.org/stories/malawi/chinula_charles.html. Accessed 14 June 2014.

Muheya, Green. "Blantyre Synod Elects Female Moderator, New SG." *Nyasa Times*, 22 August, 2011. https://www.nyasatimes.com/blantyre-synod-elects-female-moderator-new-sg/.

Mulenga, Mauris. "Nkhoma, American Church Sign Pact." *The Globe*, 19–25 August 2016.

Mumba, William K. L. "Democratization Process in Malawi 1992–1999: The Role and Attitude of the CCAP Synod of Livingstonia." BA (Theology), University of Malawi, 2000.

Munyenyembe, Rhodian G. *Christianity and Socio-Cultural Issues: The Charismatic Movement and the Contextualisation of the Gospel in Malawi*. Mzuzu: Mzuni Press, 2011

Munyimbili, Grayson. "A History of Women's Guild (Umanyano) in Ekwendeni CCAP Congregation." MA (Theology and Religious Studies), Mzuzu University, 2012.

Mushindo, P. B. *The Life of a Zambian Evangelist: The Reminiscences of Paul Bwembya Mushindo*. Lusaka: University of Zambia Institute for African Studies, 1993.

Musopole, Augustine. "Is CCAP a Failed Ecumenical Experiment?" *Transformed* 1, no. 1 (August-October 2009): 4–7.

Mwafulirwa, Brown Fiskani. "Examining the Contribution of the CCAP Synod of Livingstonia towards Environmental Sustainability: A Case of Kanyankhunde Congregation in Euthini Presbytery." BA (Theology), Mzuzu University, 2013.

Mwangomba, Chance. "The Life and Work of the Rev Wedson Paul Chibambo and Lucy Chibambo of the CCAP Synod of Livingstonia." BA (Theology and Religious Studies), University of Livingstonia, 2013.

Mwasi, Yesaya Zerenji. *Essential and Paramount Reasons for Working Independently*. Blantyre: CLAIM-Kachere, 1999.

Mwenya, Edward. "History of the United Church of Zambia from the Origins to 1988." MA (Theology), Faculty of Protestant Theology, Yaounde Cameroon, 1989.

Namangale, Frank. "CCAP Wants Govt to Open Up MBC." *The Nation*, 29 March 2014.

Nation Online. "Scots Promise No Gay Missionaries to Malawi." *The Nation*. http://mwnation.com/scots-promise-no-gay-missionaries-to-malawi/. Accessed 23 February 2015.

The Nation. "Livingstonia Synod Needs Discipline." 13 April 2013. www.mwnation.com. Accessed 17 April 2013.

Ncozana, Silas. "New Dawn for Partnership in Mission: An African Perspective." A Paper presented at a gathering celebrating the partnership between CCAP Blantyre Synod and Pittsburgh Presbytery, n.d.

———. *Sangaya: A Leader in the Synod of Blantyre of the Church of Central Africa Presbyterian*. Blantyre: CLAIM-Kachere, 1996.

———. *The Spirit Dimension in African Christianity: A Pastoral Study among the Tumbuka People of Northern Malawi*. Blantyre: CLAIM-Kachere, 2002.

Ndekha, Louis. "Chinula, Charles Chidongo." *Dictionary of African Christian Biography (DACB)*. www.dacb.org/stories/malawi/chinula_charles.html. Accessed 14 June 2014.

Neil, Stephen. *A History of Christian Missions*. Harmondsworth: Penguin, 1964.

New York Times. "No Kikuyu Heresy Trial." 10 February 1914.

Ng'onamo, Innocent. "The Influence of Girls' Traditional Initiation Rites on Christian Initiation Ceremonies at Mtunthama CCAP." MA module (Theology and Religious Studies), Mzuzu University, 2011.

Nkhonjera, Lapani. "The Church of Central Africa Presbyterian: Formation and Impact on Its Unity and Disunity." Bachelor of Divinity, Zomba Theological College, 2008.

Nhlane, Steven. "You Can't End War by Fighting." *Malawi News*, 4–10 October 2010.

Niesel, Wilhelm. *The Theology of Calvin*. London: Lutterworth Press, 1956.

Nkomazana, Fidelis. "Livingstone's Ideas of Christianity, Commerce and Civilization." *Pula: Botswana Journal of African Studies* 12, nos. 1/2 (1998): 44–57.

Nyambose, H. W. K. "The Establishment and Contribution of the Overtoun Institute in Northern Malawi and Beyond (1895–2010)." MA (Theology and Religious Studies), Mzuzu University, 2015.

Nyasa Times, "CCAP against Women Wearing Mini Skirts. *Nyasa Times*. http://www.nyasatimes.com/2013/05/20/ccap-against-women-wearing-miniskirts. Accessed 20 May 2013.

Nyasa Times Reporter. "Independent CCAP Established in J'Burg: Simwinga Aays Church Not Affiliated to Any Malawian Synods, *Nyasa Times* (27 January 2016). https://www.nyasatimes.com/independent-ccap-established-in-jburg-simwinga-says-church-not-affiliated-to-any-malawi-synods/. Accessed 17 July 2019.

Nyasulu, T. P. K. "Church Discipline in Early Livingstonia Mission." In *Mission in Malawi: Essays in Honour of Klaus Fiedler*, edited by Jonathan Nkhoma et al. Mzuzu: Mzuni Publishing, forthcoming.

Nyika, Felix. "Apostolic Office amongst Malawian Neo-Charismatic Churches: A Contextual, Biblical, Theological and Historical Appraisal." PhD (Theology and Religious Studies), Mzuzu University, 2015.

Nyirenda, Angela Kadzakumanja. "Women's Voice in Church of Central Africa Presbyterian (CCAP) in Malawi: A Critical Evaluation Especially with Nkhoma Synod." MA (Diakonia and Social Practice), Diakonhjemmet University College, 2013.

Nyirongo, Edwin. "Blantyre Synod Moves to Reconcile after Elections." *The Nation*, 26 August 2015.

———. "General Synod to Discipline Livingstonia." *The Nation*, 29 September 2006.

———. "Nyondo's Sedition Case Suspended." *The Nation*, 15 September 2010.

Nyondo, Madalitso. "Face to Face with Rev Nyondo." *Northern Life Magazine* 2, no. 2 (2014): 28.

Nzunda, Matembo, and Kenneth Ross. *Church, Law and Political Transition in Malawi*. Gweru: Mambo Press, 1995.

Oppenheim, A. M. *Questionnaire Design and Interviewing Approach*. London: Pinter Publishers, 1992.

Orbus Africa. "Orbus Projects." http://www.orbusministries.org/projects.html. Accessed 4 May 2015.

Paas, Steven. *Digging Out the Ancestral Church: Researching and Communicating Church History*. Blantyre: CLAIM-Kachere, 2002.

———. *Ministers and Elders: The Birth of Presbyterianism*. Zomba: Kachere, 2007.

———. *The Faith Moves South: A History of the Church in Africa*. With contributions by Klaus Fiedler. Zomba: Kachere, 2006.

Pachai, B. "Christianity and Commerce in Malawi: Some Pre-Colonial and Colonial Aspects." In *Malawi Past and Present: Selected Papers from the University of Malawi History Conference* 1967, edited by B. Pachai et al., 37–68. Blantyre: CLAIM, 1971.

———. *Malawi: The History of the Nation*. London: Longman, 1973.

Pachai, B. et al., eds. *Malawi Past and Present: Selected Papers from the University of Malawi History Conference 1967*. Blantyre: CLAIM, 1971.

Packer, J. I. "Theology of Revival." In *New Dictionary of Theology*, edited by Sinclair B. Ferguson, 588. Downers Grove: InterVarsity Press, 1988.

Parsons, Janet Wagner. "Scots and Afrikaners in Central Africa: Andrew Charles Murray and the Dutch Reformed Church Mission in Malawi." *The Society of Malawi Journal* 51, no. 1 (1998): 21–40.

Pattison, Sue. "Member Focus: Child Survival in Malawi." *Scotland Malawi Partnership Newsletter* 3, no. 1 (2015): 3.

Paul, Robert. "Reformed Churches and Evangelism: Historical Background." In *Major Themes in the Reformed Tradition*, edited by D. K. McKim, 354–560. Grand Rapids: Eerdmans, 1992.

Pauw, Christoff Martin. "Mission and Church in Malawi: The History of the Nkhoma Synod of the Church of Central Africa Presbyterian 1889–1962." Doctor of Theology, University of Stellenbosch, 1980.

Phiri, D. D. "CCAP Border Dispute a Danger to the Nation." *The Nation*, 23 November 2010.

———. *Chidongo Chinula*. London: Longman, 1975.

Phiri, Isabel Apawo. *Women, Presbyterianism and Patriarchy: Experiences of Chewa Women in Central Malawi*. Blantyre: CLAIM-Kachere, 2000.

Phiri, Sofi. "On Livingstonia Synod and DPP Running Mate." *The Nation*, 25 February 2009.

Pittsburgh Presbytery. "International Partnership of Pittsburgh Presbytery." https://pghpip.org/about/about.shtml. Accessed 6 Apr 2015.

———. "A Letter from the General Minister to Pittsburgh Presbytery." http://www.pghpresbytery.org/news/sheldon_shares/2013/ss_010313.htm. Accessed 13 Apr 2015.

———. "Malawi Partnership of Pittsburgh Presbytery." http://pghpip.org/about/mp_brochure_2012.pdf. Accessed 6 April 2015.

———. "News." http://www.pghpresbytery.org/news/sheldon_shares/2013/ss_010313.htm. Accessed 13 April 2015.

Presbyterian Aid Australia. "The Story So Far." http://presaid.org.au/index.php/the-story-so-far. Accessed 16 April 2015.

Presbyterian Church (USA). "Mission Connections." http://www.presbyterianmission.org/ministries/missionconnections. Accessed 20 March 2015.

———. "Presbyterian Mission." https://www.presbyterianmission.org/ministries/global/malawi/. Accessed 17 July 2019.

———. "Zambia." https://www.presbyterianmission.org/ministries/global/zambia/. Accessed 20 March 2015.

Presbyterian Church in Canada. "Life and Mission Agency Report." http://presbyterian.ca/wp-content/uploads/ga137_report_life_and_mission_agency.pdf. Accessed 20 April 2015.

———. "Malawi." http://presbyterian.ca/pwsd/malawi/. Accessed 11 April 2015.

———. "Mission." http://presbyterian.ca/pwsd/mission/. Accessed 11 April 2015.

Presbyterian Church in Ireland. "Zambia." http://www.presbyterianmission.org/ministries/global/zambia. Accessed 3 April 2015.

———. "Global Mission." https://www.presbyterianireland.org/Mission/Mission-Partners/Church-of-Central-Africa-Presbyterian.aspx. Accessed 3 April 2015.

Presbyterian Ladies College. "Personal Development." http://www.plc.vic.edu.au/learning-plc_personal-development.aspx. Accessed 16 March 2015.

———. "PLC's History." https://www.plc.vic.edu.au/about/our-school/plcs-history. Accessed 16 March 2015.

Presbyterian Women. "Overseas News." *Wider World*, March–May 2015.

Pretorius, J. L. "The Story of School Education in Malawi, 1875–1941." In *Malawi Past and Present*, edited by Gordon W. Smith et al., 69–79. Blantyre: CLAIM, 1971.

Pretorius, Peter. "An Introduction to the History of the Dutch Reformed Church Mission in Malawi, 1889–1910." In *The Early History of Malawi*, edited by B. Pachai, 122–134. London: Longman, 1971.

PWS&D. "Malawi." https://presbyterian.ca/pwsd/malawi/. Accessed 16 July 2019.

Rankin, James. *A Handbook of the Church of Scotland*. Oxford: Blackwood, 1879.

Raven Trust. "Focus on Malawi." http://focusonmalawi.blogspot.com. Accessed 7 December 2014.

Reid, I. E. "Myth and Reality of the Missionary Family: A Study of the Letters of Rev. J. R. (Jack) Martin and His Wife, Mary Evelyn (Mamie), Written from Livingstonia Mission, Malawi, 1921–28, with Particular Emphasis on the Position of Missionary Wives." Master of Theology, University of Edinburgh, 1999.

Reformed Church in America. "RCA Global Mission." www.rca.org/. Accessed 28 April 2015.

Retief, M. W. *William Murray of Nyasaland*. Lovedale: Lovedale Press, 1958.

Ritchie, Bruce. *The Scottish Church and Foreign Mission*. Kachere Text 65. Zomba: Kachere, 2011.

Robertson, Ian. *Sociology*. New York: Worth Publishers, 1983.

Robertson, William. *The Martyrs of Blantyre*. London: James Nisbet, 1903.

Robson, George. *Missions of the United Presbyterian Church: Described in a Series of Stories*. Edinburgh: Offices of the United Presbyterian Church, 1896.

Romans 1:11 Trust. "Zambia." http://www.romansoneeleventrust.org.uk/wp/. Accessed 4 April 2015.

Ross, Andrew C. *Blantyre Mission and the Making of Modern Malawi*. Blantyre: CLAIM-Kachere, 1996.

———. *Colonialism to Cabinet Crisis: A Political History of Malawi*. Zomba: Kachere Series, 2009.

———. "*Wokondedwa Wathu*: The Mzungu Who Mattered." *Religion in Malawi*, no. 8 (1998): 2–7.

Ross, Kenneth R., ed. *Christianity in Malawi: A Source Book*. Gweru: Mambo Press, 1996.

———. "Crisis and Identity: Presbyterian Ecclesiology in Southern Malawi, 1891–1993. *Missionalia* 25, no. 3 (November 1997): 385–398.

———, ed. *God, People and Power in Malawi: Democratization in Theological Perspective*. Blantyre: CLAIM-Kachere, 1996.

———. *Malawi and Scotland: Together in the Talking Place since 1859*. Mzuzu: Mzuni Press, 2013.

———, ed. *Roots and Fruits: Retrieving Scotland's Missionary Story*. Oxford: Regnum, 2014.

———. "Some Worrisome Trends: The Voice of the Churches in Malawi's Third Term Debate." *African Affairs* 103, no. 410 (January 2004): 91–107.

———. "The Transformation of Power in Malawi 1992–94: The Role of the Christian Churches." In *God, People and Power in Malawi: Democratization in Theological Perspective*, edited by Kenneth Ross, 15–40. Blantyre: CLAIM-Kachere, 1996.

Ross, Kenneth. "Vernacular Translation in Christian Mission: The Case of David Clement Scott and Blantyre Mission 1888–1898." In *Gospel Ferment in Malawi: Theological Essays*, edited by K. R. Ross, 107–126. Gweru: Mambo Press, 1995.

Roxborough, John. "The Legacy of Thomas Chalmers." *International Bulletin of Missionary Research* 23, no. 4 (October 1999): 173–176.

———. *Thomas Chalmers: Enthusiast for Mission: The Christian Good of Scotland and the Rise of the Missionary Movement*. (Rutherford Studies in Historical Theology). Carlisle: Paternoster, 1999.

Saurombe, Amos. "The Role of South Africa in SADC Regional Integration: The Making or Breaking of the Organization." *Journal of International Commercial Law and Technology* 5, no. 3 (2010): 124–131.

Schneider, Fred D. "Kikuyu and Ecclesia Anglicana." Fortieth anniversary issue, *Historical Magazine of the Protestant Episcopal Church* 41, no. 1 (March 1972): 37–65.

Schoffeleers, Mathew. *In Search of Truth and Justice: Confrontations between Church and State in Malawi 1960–1994*. Blantyre: CLAIM-Kachere, 1999.

Seaton, W. J. *The Five Points of Calvinism*. Edinburgh: Banner of Truth Trust, 1970.

Shaw, M. *The Kingdom of God in Africa: A Short History of African Christianity*. Katunayake, 2006.

Shepherd of the Hills Presbyterian Church. "Africa Missions." http://www.shpc.org/africa-missions/. Accessed 11 April 2015.

Sinclair, Margaret. *Salt and Light: The Letters of Jack and Mamie Martin in Malawi 1921–28*. Blantyre: CLAIM-Kachere, 2002.

Sindima, Harvey J. *The Legacy of Scottish Missionaries in Malawi*. Lewiston: Edwin Mellen Press, 1992.

Smith, Gordon W. et al., eds. *Malawi Past and Present*. Blantyre: CLAIM, 1971.
Smith, K. W. "Murray, Andrew Jr." *Dictionary of African Christian Biography (DACB)*. http://www. dacb.org/stories/southafrica/murray_andrew_jr.html. Accessed 20 May 2013.
Snelson, P. *Education Development in Northern Rhodesia 1883–1945*. Lusaka: Kenneth Kaunda Foundation, 1974.
Soko, Boston. "The Ngoni Response to Early Christian Missions: The Case of Loudon." In *Mission in Malawi: Essays in Honour of Klaus Fiedler*, edited by Jonathan Nkhoma et al. Mzuzu: Mzuni Publishing, forthcoming.
Somanje, Caroline. "Blantyre Synod Apologises: Retracts Mangisa's Statement on Pastoral Letter, Cleric under Probe." *The Nation*, 17 November 2010.
———. "Shake Up at BT CCAP Synod: Mangisa, Chimenya Forced to Step Down, Kadawati Barred from Second Term." *The Nation*, 2 December 2010.
———. "Twists and Turns on Religious Front in 2010." *The Nation*, December 2010.
Steele, David. *Infant Baptism*. Mzuzu: CCAP Synod of Livingstonia, n.d.
Statham, Todd, "Jonathan Sangaya 1907 to 1979 Church of Central Africa Presbyterian (CCAP) Malawi." Dictionary of African Christian Biography. http://www.dacb.org/stories/malawi/sangaya-jonathan.html.
Stefon, Matt. "Netherlands Reformed Church." *Encyclopaedia Britannca*. http://www.britannica.com/EBchecked/topic/410259/Netherlands-Reformed. Accesssed 28 March 2013.
Strauss, Anselm, and Juliet Corbin. *Basic Qualitative Research, Techniques and Procedures for Developing Ground Theory*. London: Sage, 1998.
Sundkler, Bengt. *Church of South India: Movement towards Union, 1900–1947*. London: Lutterworth Press, 1954.
Sundkler, Bengt, and Christopher Reed. *A History of the Church in Africa*. Cambridge: Cambridge University Press, 2000.
Synod of Livingstonia. "Presbyteries." www.caapsolinia.org/?page_id=63. Accessed 10 April 2015.
"Taiwan Presbyterians Open Mission Centre in Malawi." Reformiert Online: Reformed Online. http://www.reformiert-online.net/aktuell/details.php?id=1189&lg=eng. Accessed 29 April 2015.
Tengatenga, James. *The UMCA in Malawi: A History of the Anglican Church 1861–2010*. Zomba: Kachere, 2010.
Terry, John Mark. "Indigenous Churches." In *Evangelical Dictionary of World Missions*, edited by Walter E. Elwell, 483–484. Grand Rapids: Baker Books, 2000.
Theopedia. "Calvin." www.theopedia.com/John_Calvin. Accessed 11 March 2013.

Thompson, T. Jack. *Christianity in Northern Malawi: Donald Fraser's Missionary Methods and Ngoni Culture.* Leiden: Brill, 1995.

———. "Fraser, Donald." In *Biographical Dictionary of Christian Missions*, edited by Gerald H. Anderson, 224. New York: Macmillan Reference, 1998.

———, ed. *From Nyassa to Tanganyika: The Journal of James Stewart CE in Central Africa 1876–1879.* Blantyre: Central Africana, 1989.

———. *Ngoni, Xhosa and Scot.* Zomba: Kachere, 2007.

———. *Touching the Heart: Xhosa Missionaries to Malawi 1876–1888.* Pretoria: University of South Africa, 2000.

Travel Scotland. "The Great Disruption of 1843." http://www.scotland.org.uk/scotland-in-the-nineteenth-century/disruption?highlight=WyJncmVhdCIsIidncmVhdCIsIidncmVhdCcuIiwiZGlzcnVwdGlvbiIsImdyZWF0IGRp c3J1cHRpb24iXQ==. Accessed 29 May 2013.

Tucker, Ruth. *From Jerusalem to Irian Jaya.* Grand Rapids: Zondervan, 1983.

"United Presbyterian Church of Scotland." Genealogy of the Grant Family in Southern Ireland. http://www.grantonline.com/proctor-family-genealogy/places/united-presbyterian-church/united-presbyterian-church.htm. Accessed 23 June 2015.

Uprichard, R. E. H. *What Presbyterians Believe.* Ahoghill: The Oaks, 2011.

Ursinus, Zacharias, and Caspar Olevianus. *Heidelberg Catechism.* Blantyre: CLAIM-Kachere, 2003.

Van Rheenen, Gailyn. *Missions: Biblical Foundations and Contemporary Strategies.* Grand Rapids: Zondervan, 1996.

———. "Money and Missions (Revisited): Combating Paternalism." *Monthly Missiological Refection* 13. Missions Resource Network. https://www.mrnet.org/system/files/library/money_and_missions_revisited_combating_paternalism.pdf. Accessed 24 April 2015.

Van Wyk, Jurgens Johannes. *The Historical Development of the Offices according to the Presbyterian Tradition of Scotland.* Zomba: Kachere Series, 2004.

Vega, Tikondane. "University of Blantyre Synod to Open in Malawi This Year." *Nyasa Times*, 5 February 2015. www.nyasatimes.com /2015/02/05/university-of-blantyre-synod-to-open-in-malawi-this-year-rev-maulana/.

Verstraelen-Gilhuis, Gerdien. *From Dutch Mission Church to Reformed Church in Zambia: The Scope for African Leadership and Initiative in the History of a Zambian Mission Church.* Franeker, Netherlands: T. Wever, 1982.

Vorster, J. M. *An Introduction to Reformed Church Polity.* Pretoria: UP, n.d.

Wallace, R. S. "Calvin, John." In *New Dictionary of Theology*, edited by Sinclair B. Ferguson, 120–124. Downers Grove: InterVarsity Press, 1988.

Walls, Andrew. "Missionary Societies and the Fortunate Subversion of the Church." *Evangelical Quarterly* 88, no. 2 (1988): 141–155.

———. "Missions." In *Dictionary of Scottish Church History and Theology*, edited by N. Cameron, 567–594. Downers Grove: IVP, 1993.

———. "Three Hundred Years of Scottish Missions." In *Roots and Fruits: Retrieving Scotland's Missionary Story*, edited by Kenneth R. Ross, 4–37. Oxford: Regnum, 2014.

Warfield, B. B. *Calvin and Calvinism*. New York: Oxford University Press, 1931.

Warhurst, P. R. "Portugal's Bid for Southern Malawi, 1882–1891." In *Malawi Past and Present*, edited by B. Pachai et al., 20–36. Blantyre: CLAIM, 1971.

Webster, John C. B. "The Church of South India Golden Jubilee." *International Bulletin of Missionary Research* 22, no. 2 (April 1998): 50–54.

Weller, John, and Jane Linden. *Mainstream Christianity to 1980 in Malawi, Zambia and Zimbabwe*. Gweru: Mambo, 1984.

Wikipedia. "Dutch Reformed Church in South Africa." https://en.wikipedia.org/wiki/Dutch_Reformed_Church_in_South_Africa. Accessed 8 April 2013.

Williams, Garry. "John Calvin in the Valley of the Shadow of Death." Banner of Truth. http://www.banneroftruth.org/pages/articles/article_print.php?1642. Accessed 10 April 2013.

Williams, Isaac. Letter to Mr Bennie, no date, in *Lovedale News*, 25 October 1876.

Witte, John. "Calvin the Lawyer." In *Tributes to John Calvin on His 500th Birthday*, edited by David Hall and Martin Padgett, 1–23. Phillipsburg: P & R, 2010. http://ssrn.com/abstract=1863624. Accessed 8 April 2013.

Word and Deed. "Malawi." http://wordanddeed.org/about-us. Accessed 29 April 2015.

World Council of Churches. "Presbyterian Church of East Africa." http://www.oikoumene.org/en/member-churches/presbyterian-church-of-east-africa. Accessed 15 October 2013.

Wright, David F., and Gary D. Badcock, eds. *Disruption to Diversity: Edinburgh Divinity 1846–1996*. Edinburgh: T&T Clark, 1996.

Zeze, Willie Samuel Dalitso. "'Christ, the Head of the Church?': Authority, Leadership and Organizational Structure within the Nkhoma Synod of the Church of Central Africa Presbyterian." Doctor of Theology, University of Stellenbosch, 2012.

———. "Christianity: A State-Sponsored Religion in Malawi? A Critical Evaluation of the Relationship between the CCAP Nkhoma Synod and the MCP-led Government (1964–1994)." Accessed 18 June 2014. www.iclrs.org/content/events/28/751.pdf.

Zgambo, Humphreys F. C. "Conflict within the Church: A Theological Approach to Conflict Resolution with Special Reference to the Boundary Disputes between the Livingstonia and Nkhoma Synods in Malawi." MTh, University of Fort Hare, 2011.

Index of Subjects

A
abortion 121
Act of Agreement 208
Africanization
    of the church 67
African Mission Committee 50
African voice, lack of 89
Afrikaners 77
Anglo-Boer War 77, 113
Ansgarius 54
Apostolic Church 26
Apostolic Faith Mission 23
Arminians 10
Assemblies of God 23
Association of Christian Educators in
    Malawi (ACEM) 102
Australian Presbyterian World
    Mission 201

B
Bandawe headquarters 58, 72
Bandawe Mission 56, 141
Bandawe station 52, 57, 73, 74, 106
baptism, infant 7, 128
Barrier Act of 1926 93
Belgic Confession 18, 20
Blantyre District 204
Blantyre Mission 1, 16, 17, 19, 23,
    25, 35–37, 41, 44, 45, 47, 48,
    50–52, 55, 56, 62–73, 78, 84,
    89, 92, 132, 200, 206
Blantyre missionaries 64–66
Blantyre Mission Council 69, 200

Blantyre Presbytery 79, 80, 82, 91,
    126, 128, 129
Blantyre Scandal 67
Blantyre Synod 1, 16, 17, 21, 43,
    87, 94–96, 98, 99, 101, 102,
    107, 108, 112, 113, 116, 117,
    121, 122, 125, 142, 144, 145,
    150, 160, 161, 172, 174, 175,
    180, 183, 184, 200–207, 214,
    219, 222, 231, 233, 234, 237,
    242–246
Blantyre Synod Health and
    Development Commission
    201, 204
Blantyre Synod's Theological Resource
    Centre 201
Blantyre Synod University 103
border disputes 186, 229
Botswana 32
Bua River 133

C
Calvinism 5, 10, 18, 20, 30
Calvinists 10, 11
Calvinist Theology 5, 7, 8, 10, 18, 21
Canons of the Synod of Dort 20
Cape Colony 39
Cape DRC Synod 41, 77, 127, 208
Cape Maclear 51–53, 57, 58
Cape Maclear Mission 57
Cape Revival, 1860 22, 39, 41–43
Cape Town 51, 126
Cape Town congregation 232

281

Cashgate Scandal 119, 120, 185
catholicity, of the church 151, 153
Catholic University of Malawi 104
CCAP
 African leadership 250
 constitution 147
 different denominations 239
 establishment of 250
 federation 153
 first option, independent synods 243
 independence of 232
 independent denominations 238, 239
 practices 91
 second option, no synods 245
 South Africa 234
 theology 127
 unity of 111, 117, 125–129, 131, 137, 144, 150, 156, 165–167, 171, 176–178, 181, 183, 190, 218, 231, 237, 240, 241, 244, 245, 247, 249
 university 104
CCAP federation 81, 89, 94, 123
CCAP General Assembly 1, 2, 86, 94, 95, 104, 111, 112, 118, 119, 121, 123, 131, 138–141, 143, 145, 147–151, 155–158, 162, 163, 165, 171, 172, 175–177, 179, 184, 185, 203, 214, 218, 225, 227, 229–231, 234, 236–240, 245, 247
 budget 167
 commissioners 161, 162
 constitution 92, 147, 148, 156, 160–162, 164–166, 170, 185, 186, 231, 244
 disputes 174, 178
 efficiency 166, 173, 176, 181
 implementation of decisions 170
 inter-synodical dialogue 182
 inter-synodical disputes 173, 174, 181
 leadership 168, 170, 176, 180
 Malawian leadership 160
 meetings 160
 moderator 159
 personnel 170
 premises 168, 169
 recognition of 172
 resolution 234, 236
 stability 179
CCAP General Assembly Standing Committee 161, 163, 167
CCAP General Synod 88, 93, 94, 117, 126, 136, 137, 144, 156–159, 163–165, 185
CCAP Student Organisation (CCAPSO) 110
CCAP synods
 dissolution of 240
 Malawian 250
CCAP Youth Fellowships (CCAPYUFS) 111
CCAP Youth Urban Ministry(CCAPYUM) 111
Chamakala Agreement of 1967 136
Chamakala and Majiga Agreements 145
Chancellor College 99
charismatic denominations 95
charismatic movement 22, 110, 241
Charismatic Revival 22, 23
Chasefu station 88
Chasefu Theological College 215, 216
Chewa/Ngoni wars 135
Chewa people 135
Chibavi (congregation) 96
Chichewa (language) 98
Chigwirizano cha Amayi 87, 104
Chigwirizano cha Amuna 108
Chikuse Ngoni 54
Chilanga Mission 134
Child Survival in Malawi (Scotland) 206
Chilema Lay Training Centre 101

Index of Subjects

Chinyanja (Chichewa) Bible 85
Chinyanja (language) 98, 207
Chipata station 75
Chiradzulu 69
Chitambo station 88
Chitheba station 88
Chitipa Presbytery 232
Chitumbuka (language) 97
Christendom
   divisions 82
   European 26
Christian Health Association of
   Malawi (CHAM) 103, 137
Christianity, in Malawi 19
Christian Women's Guild 104
church, medieval 8
churches
   daughter 226
   indigenous 190
   Malawi 151, 194
   Malawian 179
   North American 213
   Reformed and Presbyterian 132
   Zambian 128
Churches of Christ 99
church growth, Malawi 69
church history, Malawi 23
church leadership, indigenous 223
Church of Central Africa 80
Church of Central Africa in Rhodesia
   (CCAR) 83
Church of Central Africa Presbyterian
   (CCAP) 80, 91
Church of Scotland 1, 13–16,
   26–31, 33, 45, 51, 79, 114,
   129, 138, 139, 172, 191–195,
   200, 207, 212, 219, 225
Church of Scotland Foreign Mission
   Committee 48, 63, 64, 66, 68
Church of Scotland World Mission
   178
Church of South India 83, 230
church-state relations 91, 112
civil jurisdiction 66

Claim of Right 15
clergy
   Malawian 223
   status of 224
College of Theology at Ekwendeni
   198
colonial period 112
colonists, Dutch 127
comity 1, 47, 84, 85, 230, 245, 246
   in Malawi 85
   practical 85
   Presbyterian 132
Commission for Witness 210
Commission of Inquiry 65–67, 69,
   138–141, 182
congregations
   foreign 236
   Malawian immigrant 235
   transfer of 139
conservatism 95
Consultative Board of Federated
   Missions (CBFM) 85
Covenant Theology 27
Cyclopaedic Dictionary of the
   Mang'anja Language 68

D

Dark Continent 33
David Gordon Memorial Hospital
   193, 197
Deed of Agreement 208
democracy, multiparty 117, 119, 122
Democratic Progressive Party (DPP)
   120, 121, 180
Die Volksvriend 40
Directory for Public Worship 27
disabilities 205
disjunction certificates 129
Disruption, the 14–16, 34, 35
diversity
   CCAP 94
   linguistic 152
Domasi 69
double predestination 27, 28

DRC Mission Council 133
Dutch East India Company 39
Dutch Reformed Church (DRC) 14, 17–19, 21, 25, 37–41, 51, 72, 213, 235
Dutch Reformed Church in South Africa (DRCSA) 1, 17, 19, 21, 23, 37, 38, 40, 42, 43, 72, 172, 207, 208, 211, 235
Dutch Reformed Church Mission (DRCM) 51, 71, 74, 77, 80–84, 88, 92, 98, 113, 128, 133, 134
Dwangwa-Bua 135
Dwangwa River 135, 136

E
Eastern Oklahoma Presbytery 191, 198, 199
ecumenism 47, 82, 83
education 59, 85, 102, 103, 204
  civic 172
  post-secondary 198
  primary 102, 103, 222
  secondary 102, 103, 204, 222
  tertiary 103, 104
  theological 98, 102, 108, 168, 215, 216, 222
  university 222
Ekwendeni 197
Ekwendeni College of Theology 100
Ekwendeni Hospital 197
Ekwendeni sub-station 53
Embangweni Mission Hospital 197, 199
Episcopal Conference of Malawi 102
Episcopal polity 20
Evangelical Association of Malawi 102
Evangelical Awakening 31
evangelicals 15
evangelists
  African 60, 68, 78
  Xhosa 54

F
Faculty of Theology at the University of Livingstonia 100
Faithshare programme 194, 201, 206, 212, 225
Federation of Rhodesia 113
First Presbyterian Church of Quincy 214
Focus on Malawi 195, 196
foreign partnerships
  benefits 219, 220
  Blantyre Synod 200
  CCAP 189–191, 218, 225
  CCAP General Assembly 177, 178
  contractual 219
  criticism 220
  financial assistance 224
  Harare Synod 214
  lifestyle of church leaders 224
  missionaries 223
  Nkhoma Synod 207
  permanent 218
  relational 219
  Synod of Livingtonia 191
  Synod of Zambia 216
  temporary 218
Form of the Presbyterial Church Government 27
Formula Consensus Helveticus 20
Forum for CCAP Unity (FCU) 182, 183
Four Square Gospel 23
France 5, 13
Free Church of Scotland 14, 16, 33–35, 48–50, 82, 172, 191–193, 242
Free Church of Scotland Foreign Mission Committee 72
freedom fighters 113
Free Reformed Churches of North America 214
French Confession 20
Friends of Livingstonia 181

G

General Assembly, unity of 182, 239
Geneva 5, 8, 12, 21
Gereformeerde Zendingsbond (GZB) 200, 206, 207, 214
Germany 5
Gowa Mission 99
Great Awakening 22, 23, 30, 31, 34, 41, 45
Gweru and Bulawayo Presbytery 87
Gweru Presbytery 87

H

Harare Highfield Presbytery 87
Harare Presbytery 86, 87
Harare Synod 1, 17, 19, 47, 86, 87, 93, 94, 99, 102, 108, 125, 132, 160, 161, 175, 184, 214–216, 230–233, 238, 243, 244
    Malawian immigrants 234
Heidelberg Catechism 18, 20
Henry Henderson Institute 71
heresies 153
Het Réveil 42
High Church Anglicanism 70
HIV/AIDS prevention 198, 201
Holiness Revival (Second Evangelical Awakening) 22, 23, 34, 40, 45
Holland 5, 9, 38
Holy Communion 96
Holy Spirit 7, 22
homosexuality 121, 180, 185, 193, 201
hospitals, Malawi 103

I

independence, fight for 113
India 33, 83
institutions, theological 99, 102, 107
intercessory prayer 172
interpretation, biblical 126
"Irresistible Grace" 11

J

Johannesburg Central congregation 232
Johannesburg North congregation 232
Johannesburg Presbytery 232
Johannesburg South congregation 232
Josophat Mwale Theological Institute (JMTI) 99, 100, 214
jurisdiction, constitutional 132

K

Kambiri Lodge 138
Kamoto station 88
Kanjoka 133
Kapeni 99
Kapirintiwa 133
Kararamuka 73
Karonga 143
Kasungu station 80
Kazembe station 88
Kenya 83
Khondowe sub-station 53, 58
Kikuyu 70
Kikuyu Conferences 83

L

labour, migrant 128
Lake Malawi 33, 49–51, 85
Lake Malawi Anglican University (LAMAU) 99
Lake Malawi mission station 49
Lake Nyasa 51, 52
language
    causing division 152, 153
    Tumbuka 152
Larger Catechism 12, 27
leaders, indigenous 98, 190
leadership
    African 250
    native 69
Lenten Pastoral Letter 117

Leonard Kamungu Theological
   College 99
liberalism
   Scottish 81
   theological 126
Life Ministry 23
Lilongwe 168
"Limited Atonement" 11
Lirangwe Food Security Project 204
liturgy 95, 165, 167
   CCAP 91, 94
living standards, missionaries 224
Livingstonia Mission 1, 16, 19, 23,
   25, 33–37, 41, 47–55, 57, 59,
   60–62, 64, 71–74, 76, 78, 82,
   88, 89, 92, 103, 114, 129,
   132–134, 191, 192, 206, 242
Livingstonia Presbytery 79, 80, 82,
   91, 126, 128, 129
Livingstonia Synod AIDS Programme
   (LISAP) 194
Livingstonia Theological College 195
Livulezi Mission 57
London Missionary Society (LMS)
   25, 32, 80, 127
Lord's Supper 7, 96
Loudon Mission 135
Loudon sub-station 53
Lovedale Mission 49
Lubwa station 88
Lundazi General Assembly 168
Lundazi Mission 217
Lundazi station 88

M

Madison Avenue Presbyterian Church
   (MAPC) 214
Madzimoyo station 75
Magwero Mission 75
Majiga Prayer House 145
Makololo 57
Malaria Control Programme 197
malaria, prevention 198

Malawi 1, 2, 5, 16, 17, 31, 37, 47,
   51, 74, 77, 88, 89, 92, 97,
   112, 114, 115, 117, 132, 141,
   144, 153, 215, 216, 229, 230,
   245
   aid 178
Malawians 56, 58
Malawi Broadcasting Corporation
   (MBC) 184
Malawi, Central Region 2, 97, 133,
   237
Malawi Children's Feeding
   Programme 213
Malawi Congress Party (MCP) 115,
   122
Malawi Council of Churches (MCC)
   102, 117, 119
Malawi Government 212
Malawi Mission Partnership
   Committee of Pittsburgh
   Presbytery 203
Malawi, Northern Region 2, 97, 152
Malawi Presbytery 80
Malawi Republican Constitution 180
Malawi synods 93
Malembo Mission 57
Malingunde Women's Centre 213
Manyamula Congregation of
   Engalaweni Presbytery 199
marriage, Christian 128
marriage, regulations 163
Matiki congregation 136
Matope 72
Mbwabwa 133
men's guilds 108, 109
Meyers Park Presbyterian Church
   198
Milenje River 135, 136, 145
Ministers' Missionary Union 41
missionaries
   DRCM 113, 133, 134
   Dutch Reformed Church (DRC)
      19
   early cooperation 250

European 79
Livingstonia 60, 127, 133
LMS 127
Nkhoma 127
PCUSA 216
rivalry 84
Scottish 60, 113
to Malawi 40
women 106
Xhosa 55, 56, 64
Missionary Conference, 1904 79
Missionary Conference, 1910 79
Missionary Conference, General 78
missionary paternalism 223
missions
   Church of Scotland 25, 29, 30
   in Central Africa 189
   Malawi 24, 25, 37, 41, 68, 86
   New England 29
   Presbyterian 128
   Zambia 88
Mkhalapakati 109
M'mbelwa Ngoni 54
Moderates 15, 30, 35, 36, 37
monks, Columbanus 25
Montfortians 85
Moody and Sankey, mission to
   Scotland 36
mother churches 190, 226
Mountain View Presbyterian Church
   198, 199
Mozambique 232
Mozambique Presbytery 80
Mpale 133
Mpasa 133
Mpasadzi River 135, 141
Mulanje 69
Mulanje Mission Hospital 201, 207
Mulanje Mission Hospital Orphan
   Care Programme 204
Mvera 56, 74–76
Mvera Mission 57, 79
Mvera Presbytery 233
Mvera school 98

Mwanjezi 133
Mwenzo station 88
Myers Park Presbyterian Church 191,
   199, 226
Mzimba 143
Mzuzu City 58, 143, 237

N
Nadere Reformatie 38, 39
nationalism, African 114
Ndirande Orphanage 206
Nederduitse Gereformeerde Kerk
   (NGK) 43
Neno Girls Mission School 202
Neno Girls Secondary School 204
Netherlands Reformed Church 18
New Covenant 7
New Testament 8
   Chinyanja translation 85
Ngerenge-Mbeya Presbytery 232
Ngoni 52–54, 63
Ngoni of Mzimba 34
Ngoni people 135
Njuyu 74
Njuyu Mission 73
Njuyu sub-station 53
Nkhoma Institute for Continued
   Theological Training
   (NIFCOTT) 100
Nkhoma Mission 1, 22, 23, 25, 37,
   38, 40, 41, 47, 80, 85, 87, 99,
   100, 126, 127, 133, 134, 207,
   232
Nkhoma Mission Hospital 212
Nkhoma Mountain 75
Nkhoma Presbytery 81, 86, 91, 126,
   129
   withdrawal from CCAP 126, 128
Nkhoma Synod 1, 2, 17, 19, 43, 47,
   51, 71, 87, 94, 95, 97–100,
   102, 107–109, 111–113,
   115–117, 119–122, 125,
   130–132, 134–143, 145,
   147, 150–152, 160, 161, 167,

172, 174, 175, 177, 182–184,
186, 208, 209, 211–214, 222,
229–238, 243–245
  border dispute 173
  general secretary 177
  Malawian leadership 208
Nkhoma University 100, 103, 222
Nkhotakota 85
Nkhotakota District 135, 136
"No Border Policy" 145
Nsadzu station 75
Ntcheu 69
Ntcheu District 133
Nyabira School (primary school) 102
Nyanje station 75
Nyasa Industrial Mission 23
Nyasaland 41, 59, 113, 114
Nyasa Mission 85

O
Old Covenant 7
Open Terms Debate 118
Orange Free State Synod 127
Orbus Centre for the Care of Orphans and Vulnerable Children 202
ordination
  Malawian pastors 71
  of women 94, 105–108
Overtoun Institution 58, 59, 76, 98

P
Partnership Agreement of 2003 208
pastors
  African 60
  indigenous 60, 61, 82
  living standards CCAP 224
Patronage Act 14
PCI Board of Mission Overseas (BMO) 194
Pentecostal 110
Pentecostal denominations 95
Pentecostal Revival 22, 23

"Perseverance of the Saints" 11
Phoka-Tumbuka 58
Pietism 22
  in Germany 38
Pitlochry Parish, Scotland 194
Poland 5
politicians, Malawian 150
politics, multiparty 116
pornography 121
Presbyterian Aid (PresAid) 215, 216
Presbyterian Church in Australia 216
Presbyterian Church in Canada 191, 197, 204, 205
Presbyterian Church in Ireland (PCI) 191, 194, 195, 216, 217
Presbyterian Church in Taiwan (PCT) 212
Presbyterian Church of Australia 214, 215, 216
Presbyterian Church of East Africa (PCEA) 83
Presbyterian Church of Malawi (PCM) 241
Presbyterian Church of the USA (PCUSA) 198, 202, 203, 216
Presbyterian Church of Victoria (Australia) 201
Presbyterian Mission Agency 216
Presbyterian polity 8, 12, 13, 18–20, 93
Presbyterian World Service and Development (PWS&D) 197, 204
presbyteries, Malawian 233
presidents, Malawi 122
Propagation of the Gospel at Home 29
prostitution 121
Protestant Reformation 38
Public Affairs Committee (PAC) 119, 204
Puritanism 22
  in England 38

Q
Queen's Cross Church, Scotland 201

R
race relations 114
Raven Trust 196
Reform Act of 1832 15
Reformation 8, 17, 22, 26
  doctrines of 38
  Dutch 19
  Scottish 12, 13, 14, 25
Reformed Churches in the Netherlands 18
Reformed Church in America (RCA) 213
Reformed Mission League of the Netherlands 167, 200
Reformed Theology 5, 6, 7, 12, 17, 20, 21, 28, 44, 120, 246
revivalism, Scotland 35, 36
Roman Catholic Church 7, 8, 26, 117
Roman Catholicism 13
Romans 1:11 Trust 216, 217
Rusa River 133

S
sacraments
  baptism 7
  Lord's Supper 7
scholarships 198, 204
schools, medical 103
Scotland 5, 9, 16, 25, 29, 185
Scotland Malawi Partnership 206
Scots Confession 20
Scottish Confession of Faith 13
Scottish Covenanters 38
Scottish Society for the Propagation of Christian Knowledge (SSPCK) 29
Scripture Union 23
Second Helvetic Confession 20
secular humanism 121
services
  charismatic 96
  contemporary 96, 110, 111
  English 98
Shepherd of the Hills Presbyterian Church 198, 199
Shire Highlands 63, 68
Shorter Catechism 27
single-party era 115
societal evils, condemnation 121
society, Malawian 119
socio-economic ills, Malawian 119
South Africa 2, 5, 9, 17, 19, 38, 41, 49, 77, 89, 113, 126, 132, 210, 230–233, 235, 244, 245
South African General Mission 85
South African Revival of 1860 43
spirituality, charismatic 110, 111
State of Emergency of 1959 114
Stellenbosch Kweekschool 43
St Michael's and All Angels Church 68, 96, 201, 206
Student Christian Organisation of Malawi (SCOM) 24, 110, 111
Switzerland 5
synodical borders 135
  dispute 131, 132, 134–142, 144, 147, 184
synodical boundaries
  abolishment 245
  abolition of 239
  dispute 184, 240, 243, 245
synodical property, transfer of 139
Synod of Dort 10, 11
Synod of Fife 29
Synod of Harare 112
Synod of Livingstonia 1, 2, 9, 17, 19, 21, 43, 47, 51, 54, 87, 88, 94–97, 99–102, 107–109, 112, 113, 116, 117, 121, 125, 132, 134–143, 145, 147, 150–153, 160, 161, 167, 172, 174–176, 180, 182–184, 186, 192–200, 207, 214, 217, 222,

226, 229–234, 236–238,
242–246
  border dispute 173
Synod of Moray 29
Synod of the Church of Central
  Africa Presbyterian 93
Synod of Zambia 1, 16, 19, 21, 47,
  86, 88, 93, 94, 99, 103, 107,
  108, 112, 125, 160, 161, 175,
  184, 216–218, 222, 230,
  232–234, 238, 244
  Education Committee 103
synods
  oneness 240
  unity of 93

T
Taiwanese Government 212
Tamanda Mission 134
Tamanda station 88
Tanfield Hall 16
Tanganyika 54
tensions, unity of CCAP 125
theologians, feminist 109
Theological Education by Extension
  in Malawi (TEEM) 206
theological students, African 60
Third Term Debate 118
Thirty-Nine Articles of the Church of
  England 20
Tidzalerana Shelter 207
Titukule Ana Programme 204
Tonga 52, 53, 97
"Total Depravity" 10
training, theological 98, 107
TULIP 10
twinning
  congregational 194, 199, 201
  partners 200
  presbyteries 191

U
Uganda 217
Umanyano wa Madodana 108

Umanyano wa Ŵanakazi 104
"Unconditional Election" 10
United Church of Central Africa in
  Rhodesia (UCCAR) 83
United Church of Zambia (UCZ) 83
United Democratic Front (UDF)
  179, 180
United Free Church of Scotland
  (UFC) 1, 16, 17, 79, 82, 192,
  242
United Presbyterian Church of
  Scotland (UP) 16, 82, 192,
  242
Uniting Reformed Church in
  Southern Africa (URCSA)
  208
unity, racial 70
universities, church-related 104
Universities Mission to Central Africa
  (UMCA) 23, 62, 83–85
University of Livingstonia 101, 103,
  198
  Lusangazi 222
University of Malawi 99
Uyombe station 88

V
Veto Act 15
Village of Chinkwiri 133
violence, political 120

W
Water and Sanitation Programme
  198
Westminster Calvinism 28
Westminster Confession of Faith 12,
  13, 20, 27
White Fathers 85
women
  indigenous 106
  position in CCAP 91
Women Missionary Union 40
women's guilds 104, 105, 108, 109
Worcester 43

Word and Deed Ministries 214
World War I 80, 84
worship
  charismatic 111
  contemporary 95

Y
Yao (language) 64
youth
  ministry 109
  organizations 110
  urban 111

Z
Zambezi Evangelical Church 23
Zambezi Industrial Mission 23, 84, 85
Zambia 2, 82, 88, 153, 176, 215, 217, 232
  CCAP synod 250
  eastern province 75
Zambia Presbytery 80
Zimbabwe 1, 2, 86, 131, 153, 232
  CCAP synod 250
Zomba 55, 69
Zomba at Chinamwali 173
Zomba City 142
Zomba Theological College 99, 100, 101, 167, 205–207, 215

Index of Names

A
Arminius, James 10

B
Bain, J. H. 57
Baker, William 51
Baloyi, Clifford 180
Banda, Hastings Kamuzu 115
Banda, Joyce 119, 180
Banda, Mezuwa 194
Barth, Karl 21
Berkouwer, G. C. 21
Beza, Theodore 21
Blake, Robert 75
Bokwito, Tom 63
Booth, Joseph 23, 84
Brainerd, David 29
Bryce, James 30
Bucer, Martin 20
Buchanan, John 63, 65
Bullinger, Heinrich 20
Burns, William 42
Bush, Luis 221

C
Calvin, John 5–8, 10, 12–14, 17, 19–21, 230, 238, 249
Carey, William 31, 33
Caseby, Alexander 61
Chalmers, Thomas 16, 32, 33, 42
Charles V, King (of Spain) 17
Chavura, Violet 206
Chiang, Samuel 221
Chibambo, W. P. 166

Chifungo, Davidson 183
Chikuse, Chief 53, 57
Chilapula, Mercy 107
Chingota, Felix 118, 135, 173, 174
Chirnside, Andrew 48, 65
Chirwa, Jonathan 60
Chitsulo, Takuze 182
Chiyenda, Y. A. 119
Cowan, John 50
Cridland, J. S. 75
Cross, Kerr 59

D
Domingo, Charles 61
Duff, Alexander 49
Duncan, Jonathan 63
Du Toit, Koos 75

E
Edwards, Jonathan 31
Elmslie, Dr and Mrs 73
Erskine, Ebenezer 14

F
Fenwick, George 63, 65
Fraser, Donald 34, 79
Fuller, L. K. 27

G
Gillespie, Thomas 15
Gonin, Henri 40
Goold, William Henry 50
Gützlaff, Karl 31

H

Hammond, Peter 31
Henderson, Henry 51, 52, 55, 63, 64, 66
Henderson, M. H. 134
Hetherwick, Alexander 71, 78, 79
Hine, John Edward 84
Hofmeyr, A. L. 79
Hofmeyr, Nicolaas 39, 43
Hofmeyr, Servaas 40
Hope, John 15
Howie, Robert 50

I

Inglis, Glenn 205

J

Jack, James William 50
Jackson, J. 87
Jele, Wyson Moses Kauzobafa 88
Jesus Christ 6, 7, 8, 11, 15, 26, 247
Johnston, George 50
Jumbe, Master 150

K

Kadawati, MacDonald 180
Kamwana, Kenani 61
Kaonga, Victor 241, 242
Kapeni, Chief 63, 65
Kasakula, George 151
Kawale, Winston R. 169, 178, 212
Kevan, Sue 196
Knox, John 12
Koyi, William 54–56, 64
Kulupando, Grace 206
Kumwenda, S. M. 105
Kundecha, Stephen 71

L

Latourette, Kenneth Scott 34
Laws, Robert 16, 35, 51, 53, 55, 57, 59, 64, 67, 73, 74, 78, 80, 82, 192, 242
Liebenberg, A. J. 134

Livingstone, David 23, 31, 32, 34, 35, 37, 44, 48, 49, 62, 206
Luther, Martin 7, 8, 20

M

MacDonald, Duff 64–67
MacFadyen, John 50
Macklin, T. Thornton 63
Macrae, John 37, 50
Mangisa, Reynold 180
Marrs, Uel 195
Martin, Jack 106
Maseko, G. J. 175
Matecheta, Harry Kambwiri 71
Maulana, Alex 183
M'bawa, Collin 176
Mburu, Thuo 39
McCracken, John 59, 76
McIntosh, Hamish 60, 192
McKidd, Alexander 40
McKinnon, William 49
Mentz, J. F. 126
Mgawi, K. J. 175, 177
Milne, William 63
Mngunana, Shadrack 54
Moffat, Robert 25, 32
Moir, John 50
Mpezeni, Chief 75
Mponda, Chief 63
Msiska, Stephen Kauta 114
Muluzi, Bakili 118, 179
Munthali, Maurice C. E. 140
Munyimbili, Greyson 198
Murray, A. C. 40, 56, 71–75, 78, 87
Murray, A. G. 79
Murray, Andrew, Jr. 40, 42, 43
Murray, Andrew, Sr. 41
Murray, Emma 40
Murray, John 42
Murray, Louis 57
Murray, Martha 75
Murray, W. H. 75, 134
Murray, William 85
Mutharika, Bingu wa 181
Mvula, H. K. 141

Index of Names

Mwale, Stonham Sande 212
Mwasi, Yesaya Zerenji 60, 61
Mzembe, Patrick Chaŵeya 193

N
Namalambe, Albert 56, 57
Ncozana, Silas 175
Ndiwo, Amoni Phiri 57
Neethling, Johan 43
Neil, Stephen 68, 230
Njewa, Kafumbi 168
Nkhoma, Kondwani 217
Nkhonjera, Lapani 169
Nkomazana, Fidelis 32
Nkunika, M. A. 105
Ntintili, Mapassa 54, 55, 64
Nyasulu, T. P. K. 162, 175–177
Nyirenda, S. S. 175
Nyondo, Levi 121, 182, 194

P
Paas, Steven 207
Patrick, Mary 106
Pauw, Christoff Martin 76, 80
Phiri, Kanyama 182
Phiri, Kings 182
Prentice, George 134
Pretorius, J. L. 41, 135
Pringle, Alexander 65

R
Ramakukani, Chief 57
Rankin, D. J. 65
Reid, Isobel 106
Retief, J. A. 134
Riddell, Alexander 51
Ritchie, Bruce 27–30
Ross, Andrew 66–68
Ross, Kenneth 114, 139

S
Sazuze, Kagaso 55
Schaafsma, Lieuwe 206
Schoffeleers, Matthew 117
Scott, Archibald 66

Scott, David Clement 66–70, 73, 78
Sheldrick, Caroline 196
Simpson, Allan 50
Smythies, Charles Alan 84
Sneddon, Sandy 178
Stephen, John 50
Stevenson, James 49
Stewart, James (civil engineer) 55, 64
Stewart, James (of Lovedale) 34, 54, 55, 64, 72
Sturrock, John 138, 139

T
Tembo, Susan 217
Thompson, T. Jack 56
Tomani 56, 57, 74
Tweya, Hezekia 60

V
van de Riet, W. F. 134
van der Lingen, Gottlieb 40
van Rheenen, Gailyn 220, 221
van Riebeeck, Jan 19, 39
van Wyk, Jurgens Johannes 14
Vermigli, Peter Martyr 21
Vlok, Mrs 75
Vlok, T. C. B. 40, 56, 74, 87

W
Walker, John 63
Walls, Andrew 24, 27, 36, 41
Wauchope, Isaac Williams 54
White, James 49
William I, King (of the Netherlands) 18
William the Silent 18

Y
Young, Edward 51
Young, James 49

Z
Zeze, W. S. 115
Zwingli, Ulrich 8, 20

Langham Literature, with its publishing work, is a ministry of Langham Partnership.

Langham Partnership is a global fellowship working in pursuit of the vision God entrusted to its founder John Stott –

> *to facilitate the growth of the church in maturity and Christ-likeness through raising the standards of biblical preaching and teaching.*

Our vision is to see churches in the majority world equipped for mission and growing to maturity in Christ through the ministry of pastors and leaders who believe, teach and live by the Word of God.

Our mission is to strengthen the ministry of the Word of God through:
- nurturing national movements for biblical preaching
- fostering the creation and distribution of evangelical literature
- enhancing evangelical theological education

especially in countries where churches are under-resourced.

Our ministry

Langham Preaching partners with national leaders to nurture indigenous biblical preaching movements for pastors and lay preachers all around the world. With the support of a team of trainers from many countries, a multi-level programme of seminars provides practical training, and is followed by a programme for training local facilitators. Local preachers' groups and national and regional networks ensure continuity and ongoing development, seeking to build vigorous movements committed to Bible exposition.

Langham Literature provides majority world preachers, scholars and seminary libraries with evangelical books and electronic resources through publishing and distribution, grants and discounts. The programme also fosters the creation of indigenous evangelical books in many languages, through writer's grants, strengthening local evangelical publishing houses, and investment in major regional literature projects, such as one volume Bible commentaries like the *Africa Bible Commentary* and the *South Asia Bible Commentary*.

Langham Scholars provides financial support for evangelical doctoral students from the majority world so that, when they return home, they may train pastors and other Christian leaders with sound, biblical and theological teaching. This programme equips those who equip others. Langham Scholars also works in partnership with majority world seminaries in strengthening evangelical theological education. A growing number of Langham Scholars study in high quality doctoral programmes in the majority world itself. As well as teaching the next generation of pastors, graduated Langham Scholars exercise significant influence through their writing and leadership.

To learn more about Langham Partnership and the work we do visit **langham.org**

www.ingramcontent.com/pod-product-compliance
Lightning Source LLC
Chambersburg PA
CBHW070234240426
43673CB00044B/1787

This study of the shepherd metaphor in Ezekiel 34 constitutes a stimulating challenge to everyone who reflects on one of the most important problems facing believing communities across Africa: the theological-ethical agenda of leadership.

Ezekiel 34 is investigated against the traumatic backdrop of the Babylonian exile, a socio-economical and cultic understanding of shepherding in the context of animal husbandry in the Ancient Near East, the emphasis on the covenant in Deuteronomic theology and the strong indictment of Israelite leadership as shepherds. The challenging conclusion is that Ezekiel 34 juxtaposes the failed Israelite leadership with a theological and eschatological use of the shepherd metaphor that points towards Yahweh as the Shepherd of his people – despite the fact that they are in exile!

Prof. Hendrik L Bosman
Old and New Testament, Stellenbosch University, South Africa

Biwul's theological examination of symbolism in Ezekiel is a thought provoking work. The writer is keenly aware that what is lacking within his immediate and wider contexts is the near absence of transparent and accountable leadership. The author clearly points out in his treatment of the shepherd motif the fact that both the Shepherd and the flock have divine responsibilities, which if not addressed would lead to the structural dislocation of society.

Therefore, in a subtle way, the author sets out to address the preponderance of leadership failures and other challenges emanating from both the leaders of the people as well as the non-responsiveness of the led to responsible followership. Using appropriate stylistic and literary devices of investigative research, the author superbly assesses Ezekiel's symbolism using the motif of the shepherd and his flock. He opined and rightly too that the bane of the present day society is the ever growing cases of leadership failures, as a result of the absence of the fear of God. This work is a piece of literature, which possess both the power and capacity to catch the attention of its reader, no matter how well placed or grossly disadvantaged.

Rev. Jotham Maza Kangdim
Associate Professor of Old Testament
Department of Religious Studies, University of Jos, Nigeria